T0328638

CONSTITUTIONAL CONTAGION

Constitutional law has helped make Americans unhealthy. Drawing from law, history, political theory, and public health research, *Constitutional Contagion* explores the history of public health laws, the nature of liberty and individual rights, and the forces that make a nation more or less vulnerable to contagion. In this groundbreaking work, Wendy Parmet documents how the Supreme Court departed from past practice to stymie efforts to mitigate the COVID-19 pandemic and demonstrates how pre-pandemic court decisions helped to shatter the social contract, weaken democracy, and perpetuate the inequities that made the United States especially vulnerable when COVID-19 struck. Looking at judicial decisions from an earlier era, Parmet argues that the Constitution does not compel the stark individualism and disregard of public health that is evident in contemporary constitutional law decisions. Parmet shows us why, if we are to be a healthy nation, constitutional law must change.

Wendy E. Parmet is George J. and Kathleen Waters Matthews University Distinguished Professor of Law at Northeastern University. Her books include *The Health of Newcomers: Immigration, Health Policy and the Case for Global Solidarity* with Patricia Illingworth.

Constitutional Contagion

COVID, THE COURTS, AND PUBLIC HEALTH

Wendy E. Parmet

Northeastern University

CAMBRIDGE
UNIVERSITY PRESS

CAMBRIDGE
UNIVERSITY PRESS

Shaftesbury Road, Cambridge CB2 8EA, United Kingdom

One Liberty Plaza, 20th Floor, New York, NY 10006, USA

477 Williamstown Road, Port Melbourne, VIC 3207, Australia

314–321, 3rd Floor, Plot 3, Splendor Forum, Jasola District Centre, New Delhi – 110025, India

103 Penang Road, #05–06/07, Visioncrest Commercial, Singapore 238467

Cambridge University Press is part of Cambridge University Press & Assessment, a department of the University of Cambridge.

We share the University's mission to contribute to society through the pursuit of education, learning and research at the highest international levels of excellence.

www.cambridge.org
Information on this title: www.cambridge.org/9781009098335

DOI: 10.1017/9781009093835

First published 2023

A catalogue record for this publication is available from the British Library.

Library of Congress Cataloging-in-Publication Data
Names: Parmet, Wendy E., author.
Title: Constitutional contagion : COVID, the courts and public health / Wendy E. Parmet, Northeastern University, Boston.
Description: Cambridge, United Kingdom ; New York, NY : Cambridge University Press, 2023. | Includes bibliographical references and index.
Identifiers: LCCN 2022038654 | ISBN 9781009098335 (hardback) | ISBN 9781009096157 (paperback) | ISBN 9781009093835 (ebook)
Subjects: LCSH: COVID-19 (Disease) – Law and legislation – United States.
Classification: LCC KF3803.C68 P37 2023 |
DDC 344.7304/3624144–dc23/eng/20220930
LC record available at https://lccn.loc.gov/2022038654

ISBN 978-1-009-09833-5 Hardback
ISBN 978-1-009-09615-7 Paperback

For Anna, Dan, and Ron

Real liberty for all could not exist under the operation of a principle which recognizes the right of each individual person to use his own, whether in respect of his person or his property, regardless of the injury that may be done to others.

Jacobson v. Massachusetts (1905)

CONTENTS

Acknowledgments . . . . *page* ix

List of Abbreviations. xi

    Introduction: Disaster Awaits 1

1   A New Approach 9

2   *Salus Populi Suprema Lex* 27

3   The End of *Salus Populi* 50

4   COVID Comes to Court 71

5   The Mandate Wars 91

6   An Asymmetry of Rights 116

7   An Unequal Pandemic 140

8   The Infodemic 161

9   An Unhealthy Polity 183

    Conclusion: "A Republic, if You Can Keep It" 211

Index 225

ACKNOWLEDGMENTS

In a time of social isolation, I was fortunate to collaborate with many wonderful colleagues at Northeastern University and across the country. Jeremy Paul offered unparalleled encouragement as well as astute edits and comments on the entire manuscript. Many other brilliant scholars, including Judith Olans Brown, David Frankford, Gregg Gonsalves, Claudia E. Haupt, Peter D. Jacobson, Richard Kay, Dorit Rubinstein Reiss, Dan Urman, Lindsay F. Wiley, and John Fabian Witt, provided thoughtful comments on one or more chapters. The book is much improved by their efforts. Many Northeastern University School of Law students provided research support as well as fact and cite checking: Niloufar Asgari, Alexandra Baskfield, Julia Brown, Hui Chen, Lindsey Gill, Andrea Goodman, Brianna Heller, Maya Hill, Kathleen Moore, Katherine Reynolds, Connor Scholes, and Julia Winett. Special thanks to Emily Kaiser, who continued to work on this project even after graduation; to Faith Khalik, who provided outstanding cite checking; and Scott Akehurst-Moore from the Northeastern Law Library. Stephanie Sykes was an outstanding proofreader and editor, and Matt Gallaway at Cambridge University Press has consistently offered support and wise counsel. Finally, many thanks to my husband, Ron Lanoue, who put up with the hours I spent locked away working on this project. Without his support, I could not have written this book.

ABBREVIATIONS

ACA	Affordable Care Act of 2010
AIAN	American Indian and Alaska Native
ARPA	American Rescue Plan Act of 2021
BCRA	Bipartisan Campaign Reform Act of 2002
BIPOC	Black, Indigenous, and people of color
CDC	Centers for Disease Control and Prevention
CDOH	Commercial determinants of health
CMS	Centers for Medicare and Medicaid Services
CPC	Crisis pregnancy center
DHS	Department of Homeland Security
EPA	Environmental Protection Agency
ETS	Emergency temporary standard
EUA	Emergency use authorization
FDA	Food and Drug Administration
FEC	Federal Election Commission
FECA	Federal Election Campaign Act of 1971
INA	Immigration and Nationality Act of 1952
MMR	Measles, mumps, and rubella (vaccine)
NFIB	*National Federation of Independent Businesses v. Department of Labor* (2022)
NIH	National Institutes of Health
OECD	Organisation for Economic Co-operation and Development
OSH	Occupational Safety and Health Act of 1970
OSHA	Occupational Safety and Health Administration
PAC	Political action committee

PPE	Personal protective equipment
PREP	Public Readiness and Emergency Preparedness Act of 2005
PRWORA	Personal Responsibility and Work Opportunity Reconciliation Act of 1996
RCD	*Roman Catholic Diocese of Brooklyn v. Cuomo* (2020)
RFRA	Religious Freedom Restoration Act of 1993
SARS-CoV-2	Severe acute respiratory syndrome coronavirus 2
SDOH	Social determinants of health
SNAP	Supplemental Nutrition Assistance Program
VRA	Voting Rights Act of 1965
WHO	World Health Organization

INTRODUCTION
Disaster Awaits

February 28, 2020. The scene that day felt surreal as crowds enjoyed fresh fish, listened to music, and danced in the warm breeze of a Barbados evening. Were they oblivious to the impending disaster? Could they have imagined that within two years, almost six million people would die from a virus that had already begun its deadly march across the globe? Or, aware of the danger, were they just trying to enjoy a few joyous moments before the siege began?

I wanted to feel their mirth. All through my vacation – the last requiring an airplane that my husband and I would take for almost two years – the rumble of impending doom grew louder, the headlines grimmer. More and more cases of a deadly new coronavirus infection were reported. South Korea was facing an epidemic; northern Italy, a catastrophe. On February 25, Dr. Nancy Messonnier, director of the National Center for Immunization and Respiratory Diseases at the Centers for Disease Control and Prevention (CDC), warned Americans that "disruption to everyday life might be severe."[1]

With the inevitable storm approaching, I began spending more time away from the beach, working with brilliant colleagues in public health and law on a letter, eventually signed by more than eight hundred public health experts, to Vice President Mike Pence and other policymakers with recommendations on how the United States should respond to the

---

[1] Nathaniel Weixel, *Top Health Official Warns Coronavirus Spread Appears Inevitable in US*, HILL (Feb. 25, 2020), https://thehill.com/policy/healthcare/484530-top-health-official-warns-coronavirus-spread-in-us-inevitable-its-not-a.

coming catastrophe.[2] The letter shared our thoughts about what should and should not be done. It was propelled by our recognition that the United States was more vulnerable than many realized. Despite decades of pandemic preparedness planning, our public health system was underfunded. Millions of Americans lacked access to affordable health care. Millions more lacked paid sick leave. Our population had higher rates of chronic disease than people in other wealthy countries. Our letter explained that an effective response to the pandemic would "protect the health and human rights of everyone in the US" and "provide adequate funding and support" to help those who are "most vulnerable because of their economic, social or health status."[3]

We wrote the letter knowing that the prospects for an effective response were not propitious. We knew that the United States was led by a president who eschewed facts and embraced misinformation while stirring white racial resentment and xenophobia. The nation was also deeply divided, and entering an election year.

There were also things I did not fully appreciate in February 2020. After years writing about how societies respond to public health crises, I worried that vulnerable populations would be scapegoated. I also feared that Donald Trump would use the crisis to enhance his own powers, perhaps even by calling off the November election.

Much (but not all) of this happened. There was a marked rise in hate crimes during the pandemic, especially against Asian Americans,[4] and Trump did issue emergency orders targeting immigrants.[5] Yet his primary mode throughout 2020 was to downplay rather than exaggerate the risks posed by the novel coronavirus. The pattern that he set of COVID-19 denialism and the embrace of misinformation continued

---

[2] Gregg S. Gonsalves et al., *Achieving a Fair and Effective COVID-19 Response: An Open Letter to Vice-President Mike Pence, and Other Federal, State and Local Leaders from Public Health and Legal Experts in the United States* (Mar. 2, 2020), https://law.yale.edu/sites/default/files/area/center/ghjp/documents/final_covid-19_letter_from_public_health_and_legal_experts.pdf.

[3] *Id.*

[4] Associated Press, *More than 9,000 Anti-Asian Incidents Have Been Reported since the Pandemic Began*, NPR (Aug. 12, 2021), www.npr.org/2021/08/12/1027236499/anti-asian-hate-crimes-assaults-pandemic-incidents-aapi.

[5] Wendy E. Parmet, *Immigration Law's Adverse Impact on COVID-19*, in Assessing Legal Responses to COVID-19, 240, 241 (Scott Burris et al. eds., 2020), https://static1.squarespace.com/static/5956e16e6b8f5b8c45f1c216/t/5f4d6578225705285562d0f0/1598908033901/COVID19PolicyPlaybook_Aug2020+Full.pdf.

throughout the pandemic, helping to explain why counties that voted for Trump in 2020 ended up with higher death rates than those that voted for his opponent.[6]

Even more troubling was the inability or unwillingness of many Americans to recognize the social nature of a pandemic. American individualism has many virtues, but it can mislead when epidemics strike. In order to reduce contagion, we need to understand the risks we pose to others and the risks they pose to us. We also need to accept a type of social compact in which we all take some steps to protect others knowing that they will do the same for us. For a short time in the spring of 2020, it seemed as if most Americans agreed, as people from across the partisan divide reduced social contacts and supported pandemic-mitigation measures.[7]

But the price that individuals and families paid for public health measures was high, the economic and social supports to weather them were inadequate, and the public health messaging was terrible. Although the federal government provided significant financial support, many people lost jobs and businesses. Children lost the opportunity to learn along with the social supports that schools provide. Social isolation took its toll on Americans' mental health and well-being. Meanwhile, some politicians and media personalities were happy to spread misinformation and blame public health measures or those with opposing political beliefs rather than the virus for the calamity. By February 2022, Americans' willingness to accept almost any public health measures had declined.[8] Many had come to view the public health system rather than COVID-19 as the enemy.

Increasingly, the courts accepted that conclusion. As the pandemic progressed, courts – led by an energized conservative majority on the Supreme Court – began giving more weight to the costs that public health measures imposed on freedom than to the lives the measures were designed to save. Many courts also cabined executive authority, making

[6] David Leonhardt, *U.S. Covid Deaths Get Even Redder*, N.Y. TIMES (Nov. 24, 2021), www.nytimes.com/2021/11/08/briefing/covid-death-toll-red-america.html.

[7] David Lazer et al., *Report #1, COVID-19 National and State Data*, COVID STATES PROJECT (Apr. 20, 2020), www.covidstates.org/reports/covd-19-national-and-state-data.

[8] Nate Cohn, *Americans Are Frustrated with the Pandemic. These Polls Show How Much*, N.Y. TIMES (Feb. 8, 2022), www.nytimes.com/2022/02/08/us/politics/covid-restrictions-americans.html.

it harder for health officials at all levels of government to implement measures that were grounded on the best available science. Indeed, in some cases it appeared that the courts cared neither about what the science said nor about the cost of their decisions on the public's health.

Early in the pandemic, my hope was that the courts would prevent overreaches, even as they accepted reasonable public health measures that were needed to save lives. But as I watched the pattern of judicial decisions unfold over the next two years, I was struck by the fact that in many instances, courts were impeding our ability to save lives, while deepening the distrust and division that undermined our pandemic response. Looking deeper, I realized that courts had also helped create the conditions that had left us so vulnerable to the pandemic.

These developments should not have been surprising. Commentators have long noted that courts, especially the Supreme Court, play an outsized role in shaping public policy. Think about the role of the courts in debates over segregation, abortion, gun policy, and the Affordable Care Act (ACA). In all these cases (and many more), judicial decisions – particularly those relying on constitutional law – helped to determine the policies that affect our lives. It shouldn't be shocking, therefore, to suggest that courts might bear some responsibility for the fact that the US response to COVID-19 was bumbling at best, and that more Americans died from the coronavirus in the first two years of the pandemic than residents of any other high-income nation.[9]

This book explores the courts' role in that disaster. More specifically, it examines how judicial decisions – especially constitutional law decisions – that privileged a particularly thin and one-sided conception of liberty helped to undermine our response to the pandemic and amplify the forces that tear at our social fabric. The book also discusses how courts in an earlier era, when epidemics were more common, understood the relationship between public health and liberty. Although deeply flawed in many ways, this older view, represented by the ancient legal maxim *salus populi suprema lex* – the health (or welfare) of the people is the highest law – serves as a reminder that our Constitution does not condemn us to accepting uncontrolled

---

[9] Benjamin Mueller & Eleanor Lutz, *U.S. Has Far Higher Covid Death Rate than Other Wealthy Countries*, N.Y. TIMES (Feb. 1, 2022), www.nytimes.com/interactive/2022/02/01/science/covid-deaths-united-states.html.

contagion. Nor does it deny the possibility of a social compact.[10] The protection of the public's health is one part of that compact. If we are to be a healthy people, we need to reclaim it.

The story that follows begins in November 2020, as Amy Coney Barrett joins the Supreme Court and a strengthened conservative majority – in the midst of the worst pandemic in over a century – upends long-settled understandings of how courts should review public health measures. Chapter 2 then explores the era of *salus populi*, showing how courts attempted to reconcile individual liberty with public health protection prior to the New Deal. Chapter 3 reviews the rejection of that jurisprudence during the New Deal and the development in the mid-twentieth century of an approach that grants greater protection to some, but not all, individual rights.

The next chapters look at how the courts applied and remade those protections during the COVID-19 pandemic. Chapter 4 focuses on decisions relating to laws mandating social distancing. Chapter 5 considers the courts' response to vaccine and mask mandates. In both chapters, we see how far the courts traveled from the jurisprudence of *salus populi* and the many ways in which they tied public health's hands. We also observe how some judges became players in the increasingly strident culture war that erupted over COVID-19 policies. If the courts did not sow the discord in the United States, they did not temper it either.

Chapters 6 through 9 widen the lens, looking beyond the COVID cases to the role that constitutional law has played in generating the vulnerabilities that the pandemic exploited. Chapter 6 discusses how American law rejected the right to health, as well as constitutional rights for any of the many social benefits – from education to housing – that could have buffered people during the pandemic. Chapter 7 looks at how the courts' narrow conception of equal protection permitted structural racism, xenophobia, and other deep-seated social infirmities to generate inequities that disproportionately killed people of color early in the pandemic.

Chapter 8 considers the impact of misinformation during the pandemic, and how the Supreme Court's increasingly strong protections

---

[10] Adrian Vermeule, *Supreme Court Justices Have Forgotten What the Law Is For*, N.Y. Times (Feb. 3, 2022), www.nytimes.com/2022/02/03/opinion/us-supreme-court-nomination.html.

for freedom of speech – especially commercial speech – helped to unleash a toxic informational environment. As a result, deaths continued to climb even after lifesaving vaccines became widely available. Chapter 9 explores the relationship between health and democracy, suggesting that in a very deep and fundamental way, our health is imperiled because our democracy is impaired. Here, too, the courts have played a deleterious role, privileging the rights of campaign donors over those of voters while reducing the public's influence over health policy.

The conclusion notes the dangers ahead but reminds us that the worst-case scenario is not inevitable. The pandemic could not have been stopped, but much of its toll was preventable. So, too, we can remedy the diseases that plague our democracy. While our constitutional system will always make public health prevention messy and imperfect, it does not condemn us to the level of disease and despair we have experienced. That required judicial interpretation, along with a legal mindset that had lost sight of liberty's fuller meaning.

Along the way, the book explores what makes a population healthy or ill. It also considers the tension between the need to protect individuals from government overreach and the need to provide them with protections that only governments can offer. The problem is less that the Court has protected some rights than that it has protected a few too fully while neglecting others altogether. More so, it has forgotten *salus populi* and the public's right to have their elected officials take scientifically grounded steps to protect their health. It has also lost sight of contagion's most compelling lesson: Our own health depends on the health of others.

Before turning to the story, two caveats are in order. First, this is not a book about methods of constitutional interpretation. Indeed, the book purposefully eschews long-standing debates about originalism versus living constitutionalism. Many brilliant scholars have entered that fray. My aim is different: to explore how judicial decisions relying on very different modes of interpretation have shaped our capacity to be healthy – biologically and politically – and to remind us that the Constitution has and can be understood differently.

Second, I offer no endorsement of any particular public health policy, either during or before the pandemic. Indeed, I recognize that many of the policies that public health officials and experts recommended during the pandemic were, in hindsight, problematic. In part that is because the science changes quickly during a pandemic. Advice given based on Monday's data may no longer be valid by Tuesday. It is also because public health, like any field, is imperfect. The people who practice it have varied strengths and perspectives. Throughout the pandemic, they disagreed with one another. Some may have underestimated and others likely overestimated the economic, social, and political costs of mitigation measures. Others mangled their messaging. Many were challenged by political interference and misinformation spread by their political bosses.[11]

Yet if the book does not take a position on any particular public health policy intervention, it does accept the perhaps contestable view that the public's health (*salus populi*) is part of the common good – and, as such, an important legal and political goal.[12] That does not mean that any particular policy put forth in the name of public health is well conceived or worth the costs (in terms of liberty, social pain, or dollars). It does mean that health should *matter*, and that because it does, we need to recognize the interdependence that contagion creates and accept that our health is not only in our hands. We also need a legal system that allows people, acting through their elected representatives and appointed officials, to take reasonable, scientifically grounded steps to safeguard health. As the preamble to the Constitution states, our nation was founded to "provide for the common defense, promote the general Welfare, and secure the Blessings of Liberty." The Constitution was not designed to and does not demand that we disregard the general welfare. Nor does it command the courts to do so.

More than two years into the pandemic, there are many reasons to worry. While deaths from COVID-19 have fallen significantly from their peak, many Americans are still dying from the disease. In addition, new variants keep emerging. We may be on the road to endemicity or just experiencing the downside of one of many waves. We also remain a deeply fractured nation, one in which the threat of authoritarianism and political violence feels palpable. The future of our democracy seems as imperiled as the future of our health.

---

[11] Claudia E. Haupt & Wendy E. Parmet, *Lethal Lies: Government Speech, Distorted Science, and the First Amendment*, 2022 U. ILL. L. REV. 1809, 1813–1814. 1809.

[12] WENDY E. PARMET, POPULATIONS, PUBLIC HEALTH, AND THE LAW 62–68(2009).

The two are inextricably related, and our constitutional law has played a dramatic role in magnifying the precarity of both.

One could be forgiven for wanting to act as if the pandemic was over and carry on as if it were February 2020, but the dangers to our collective health and our democracy are too grave. We need to understand and engage. We need also to remember that our Constitution has not always demanded acquiescence to contagion. We should not permit it to do so now.

1   A NEW APPROACH

On Thanksgiving Eve 2020, as millions of Americans prepared to spend the holiday apart from family and friends because of the COVID-19 pandemic, the Supreme Court by a 5–4 vote blocked New York governor Andrew Cuomo's order limiting attendance at religious services in areas where the virus was spreading profusely.[1] Issued from its so-called shadow docket, the term that legal scholar William Baude coined to describe emergency orders issued without the benefit of oral argument,[2] *Roman Catholic Diocese of Brooklyn v. Cuomo* (hereinafter referred to as *RCD*) heralded a dramatic departure from the Court's traditional approach to public health laws: No longer would the Court offer any deference to health officials – not even during a pandemic.

Although *RCD* marked a momentous change in the Court's jurisprudence, its roots were wide and deep. Most proximally, it emerged from the chaos, tragedy, and tumult that marked 2020: the nation's failure to control a raging pandemic, a steep recession that followed years of widening inequality, a president who ignored democratic norms and sowed social discord, a bitterly contested election, a long-delayed racial reckoning, and the proliferation of misinformation and conspiracy theories. All these elements helped set the stage for *RCD* and the Supreme Court decisions that followed it.

RCD also emerged from a jurisprudential path that courts and legal scholars began to pave decades earlier. That path, which turned away from long-established understandings of the relationship between

---

[1] Roman Cath. Diocese of Brooklyn v. Cuomo, 141 S. Ct. 63 (2020) (per curiam).
[2] William Baude, *Foreword: The Supreme Court's Shadow Docket,* 9 N.Y.U. J. L. & Liberty 1, 4–5 (2015).

public health powers and individual rights, helped to erode the social compact. It also facilitated the United States' catastrophic response to COVID-19, and it continues to threaten the nation's ability to confront myriad other challenges, from climate change to the enduring health inequities created by racial injustice. Thanks in part to law, the United States is not a healthy country. Nor is it well situated to confront future challenges.

A NATION DIVIDED

The stark division among the justices in *RCD* was not the only schism apparent in November 2020. That plague-ridden month saw a nation deeply divided. For a brief time in March and early April 2020, most Americans were united in their attitudes toward pandemic mitigation measures. As cases and deaths from COVID-19 climbed exponentially that spring, the mood was predominantly one of fear and solidarity. In New York, the pandemic's early epicenter within the United States, many residents opened their windows and stood on their balconies banging pots and pans in a show of thanks to health care and other essential workers.[3] In Washington, DC, Congress quickly approved three relief bills that offered extended and enhanced unemployment compensation, provided payroll protection loans for businesses, and supported COVID testing and treatment.[4]

Despite that swift congressional action, President Donald Trump largely left the task of controlling the pandemic to the states.[5] In the absence of a coordinated federal response or effective vaccines or therapies, public health experts urged state leaders to implement a range of non-pharmaceutical interventions such as closing schools and businesses to reduce social interaction and "flatten the curve."

[3] Adam Jeffrey, *New Yorkers Stop and Give Daily Thanks and Gratitude for Coronavirus Frontline Workers*, CNBC (Apr. 5, 2020), www.cnbc.com/2020/04/05/new-yorkers-stop-and-give-daily-thanks-and-gratitude-for-coronavirus-frontline-workers.html.
[4] Kellie Moss et al., *The Coronavirus Aid, Relief, and Economic Security Act: Summary of Key Health Provisions*, KAISER FAMILY FOUND. (Apr. 9, 2020), www.kff.org/coronavirus-covid-19/issue-brief/the-coronavirus-aid-relief-and-economic-security-act-summary-of-key-health-provisions.
[5] ANDY SLAVITT, PREVENTABLE: THE INSIDE STORY OF HOW LEADERSHIP FAILURES, POLITICS, AND SELFISHNESS DOOMED THE U.S. CORONAVIRUS RESPONSE 112–17 (2021).

The goal was to slow the virus's exponential spread to prevent the health care system from crashing. Already, strict quarantines and lockdown orders had been imposed in China, South Korea, and Italy, where the virus first hit hard.

In March 2020, state governors followed the advice of health experts and used their general emergency powers, which are usually used in response to hurricanes, wildfires, and other natural disasters, to impose an unprecedented series of mitigation measures. They closed schools and nonessential businesses, prohibited nonurgent medical care, and, in some places, required people to stay at home except when engaging in a limited number of "essential activities."[6] Some governors barred in-person worship; others mandated mask-wearing. Life as Americans knew it came to an abrupt and eerie halt.[7]

At first, polls showed widespread approval for such measures. Even as businesses closed and the economy buckled, governors were applauded for taking decisive action to keep people safe. With his daily press briefings outlining the scope of the crisis and the measures he was taking, New York's Cuomo became a "rock star."[8] The unity, however, did not last long.

Many factors led to the divisions over COVID-19 that roiled the United States over the course of the pandemic and helped to exacerbate its toll. Among them was the rampant proliferation of misinformation about the dangerousness of COVID-19 and the efficacy of putative cures (such as taking the anti-malaria drug hydroxychloroquine, and at one point even ingesting household cleaners) that spread across the Internet and social media – much of it pushed by Trump and his allies – and helped erode public trust and solidarity.[9] Later, after vaccines became available, political polarization and the continued proliferation

---

[6] Lindsay F. Wiley, *Democratizing the Law of Social Distancing*, 19 YALE J. HEALTH POL'Y L. & ETHICS 50, 7276 (2020).

[7] Katie Zezima et al., *Coronavirus Is Shutting Down American Life as States Try to Battle Outbreak*, WASH. POST (Mar. 13, 2020), www.washingtonpost.com/national/coronavirus-outbreak-shutdown-america/2020/03/13/d8589434-6550-11ea-acca-80c22bbee96f_story.html.

[8] Geoff Herbert, *Rock Star? Gov. Cuomo Appears on a Cover of Rolling Stone Issue about Coronavirus*, SYRACUSE.COM (Apr. 13, 2020), www.syracuse.com/news/2020/04/rock-star-gov-cuomo-appears-on-cover-of-rolling-stone-issue-about-coronavirus.html.

[9] Wendy E. Parmet & Jeremy Paul, *Post-Truth Won't Set US Free: Health Law, Patient Autonomy, and the Rise of the Infodemic*, in COVID-19 AND THE LAW: DISRUPTION, IMPACT, AND LEGACY (I. Glenn Cohen et al. eds., forthcoming 2023).

of misinformation undermined efforts to vaccinate the population, leaving Americans vulnerable as new variants surged.[10]

Conspiracy theories about the causes and cures of epidemics were not new. Societies have always responded to pandemics by seeking scapegoats and buying snake oil. Nevertheless, dangerous and divisive misinformation about the novel coronavirus – what the World Health Organization (WHO) termed an "infodemic"[11] – spread with special ferocity and toxicity during the COVID-19 pandemic. Conspiracy theorists and quacks were not, however, the only ones muddying the message. Public health officials bore some of the responsibility. For example, in early March 2020, Dr. Anthony Fauci, director of the US National Institute of Allergy and Infectious Disease at the National Institutes of Health (NIH), stated that there was "no reason" for people to wear masks, and that mask-wearing might even make matters worse.[12] A few weeks later, the Centers for Disease Control and Prevention (CDC) advised people to indeed wear masks,[13] at which point Fauci and other health officials changed course and urged everyone to do so. He later explained that his earlier comments were motivated by the concern that the general public might hoard masks when health care workers were struggling to find adequate supplies of personal protective equipment (PPE).[14] Whatever the reason, the about-face did not bolster confidence in public health officials.

The inconsistency among state orders almost certainly added to the confusion. Unlike the federal government, the states have so-called

---

[10] Emily Anthes & Alexandra E. Petri, *C.D.C. Director Warns of a "Pandemic of the Unvaccinated,"* N.Y. Times (July 22, 2021), www.nytimes.com/2021/07/16/health/covid-delta-cdc-walensky.html; Alyssa Lukpat & Alexandra E. Petri, *U.S. Vaccination Rates Have Stalled with Another Potential Uptick Coming,* N.Y. Times (Mar. 21, 2022), www.nytimes.com/2022/03/21/us/vaccination-rates-covid-cases.html.

[11] *See Infodemic,* World Health Org. (last visited Apr. 15, 2022), www.who.int/health-topics/infodemic#tab=tab_1; *see infra* Chapter 8.

[12] *Fact Check: Outdated Video of Fauci Saying "There's No Reason to Be Walking Around in a Mask,* Reuters (Oct. 8, 2020), www.reuters.com/article/uk-factcheck-fauci-outdated-video-masks/fact-checkoutdated-video-of-fauci-saying-theres-no-reason-to-be-walking-around-with-a-mask-idUSKBN26T2TR.

[13] *Id.*

[14] *See* Grace Panetta, *Fauci Says He Doesn't Regret Telling Americans Not to Wear Masks at the Beginning of the Pandemic,* Bus. Insider (July 16, 2020), www.businessinsider.com/fauci-doesnt-regret-advising-against-masks-early-in-pandemic-2020-7.

police powers, which enable them to act to protect the public's health or welfare. The federal government lacks such powers. Yet it has long used the authority granted to it by Article I of the Constitution, including the powers to regulate interstate commerce and tax and spend for the general welfare, to undertake measures to protect the public's health. Think, for example, of the Food and Drug Administration (FDA), which oversees the supply of drugs and vaccines, or the Environmental Protection Agency (EPA), whose mission is to protect the public from unclean air and water. Or consider the federal government's funding of biomedical research and health care through Medicare, Medicaid, and Obamacare. Still, the states have usually taken the lead when it comes to containing communicable diseases within their borders.[15] And with Trump's blessing, they took it during the pandemic.[16]

There are advantages to this approach, not least of which is that states can tailor their responses to disparate conditions – and in the spring of 2020, conditions varied widely across the country. New York faced a horrifying surge, while many rural states had few cases. Further, the reliance on state decision-making allows states to learn from one another, as happened when states copied orders first imposed in New York and California.

There are also dangers to relying on the states to control a pandemic. For one thing, viruses don't respect state borders. One state's tolerance of contagion inevitably leads to more cases in neighboring states. For another, states can face competitive pressure to loosen public health measures as businesses see customers flee to states that have fewer restrictions. Policy variations among states can also send the misleading signal that a pandemic is only a problem for some states, or some people.

In spring 2020, COVID-19 did seem, in large measure, to be confined to coastal states. For a time, much of the heartland was spared. Initially, New York, New Jersey, and Connecticut were especially hard-hit. So, too, were Massachusetts, Illinois, and the states on the

---

[15] *See* Lindsay F. Wiley, *Federalism in Pandemic Prevention and Response*, in COVID-19 POLICY PLAYBOOK II: LEGAL RECOMMENDATIONS FOR A SAFER, MORE EQUITABLE FUTURE 64 (Scott Burris et al. eds., 2021), https://static1.squarespace.com/static/5956e16e6b8f5b8c45f1c216/t/6064ad386b6e756cabb56f96/1617210684660/COVIDPolicyPlaybook-March2021.pdf.

[16] SLAVITT, *supra* note 5, at 112–17.

West Coast.[17] Many residents in red states could and did feel immune to the pandemic's impacts (if not to the virus itself), and their political leaders began to unwind and then question the need for mitigation measures. Perhaps as a result, by 2022, many such states ended up with higher death tolls than blue states.[18]

There were other epidemiological and social divides.[19] As early as March 2020, it was apparent that COVID was far more lethal to seniors, especially those who lived in nursing homes and other congregate settings, than to the young and healthy. This disparity led some to question whether the entire population should be subject to pandemic restrictions simply to protect high-risk elders. Texas lieutenant governor Dan Patrick told Fox News host Tucker Carlson that "as a senior citizen," he was willing to risk his own survival "in exchange for keeping the America that all America loves for your children and grandchildren."[20] Echoing that sentiment, in October, a group of influential scientists with support from a conservative think tank issued the Great Barrington Declaration, which argued that the "most compassionate approach" would be to revoke all mitigation measures for the population as a whole, while putting in place "focused protection" for those at highest risk from COVID-19 due to age or health status.[21]

Other divides were based on race, class, and immigration status. Early on, public health experts recognized that communities of color were hit especially hard by COVID.[22] We will return to these dramatic disparities

[17] William H. Frey, *Mapping COVID-19's Spread from Blue to Red America*, Brookings Inst. (June 3, 2020), www.brookings.edu/blog/the-avenue/2020/05/29/mapping-covid-19s-spread-from-blue-to-red-america.

[18] Steven H. Woolf, *The Growing Influence of State Governments on Population Health in the United States*, JAMA (Mar. 11, 2022), https://jamanetwork.com/journals/jama/fullarticle/2790238.

[19] Slavitt, *supra* note 5, at 149–71.

[20] Adrianna Rodriguez, *Texas' Lieutenant Governor Suggests Grandparents Are Willing to Die for US Economy*, USA Today (Mar. 24, 2020), www.usatoday.com/story/news/nation/2020/03/24/covid-19-texas-official-suggests-elderly-willing-die-economy/2905990001.

[21] Peter J. Hotez, *America's Deadly Flirtation with Antiscience and the Medical Freedom Movement*, 131 J. Clinical Investigation 1, 2 (2021); Martin Kulldorff, Sunetra Gupta, & Jay Bhattacharya, *The Great Barrington Declaration* (Oct. 4, 2020), https://gbdeclaration.org. www.washingtonpost.com/us-policy/2020/01/31/trump-weighs-tighter-china-travel-restrictions-response-coronavirus.

[22] *See, e.g.*, Samantha Artiga, Bradley Corallo, & Olivia Pham, *Racial Disparities in COVID-19: Key Findings from Available Data and Analysis*, Kaiser Family Found. (Aug. 17, 2020), www.kff.org/racial-equity-and-health-policy/issue-brief/racial-disparities-covid-19-key-findings-available-data-analysis.

in later chapters. For now, suffice it to say that a conglomeration of social factors, including systemic racism, disproportionate employment in essential occupations, overcrowded housing, lack of sick pay, fear of immigration authorities, and lack of access to health care made those who were the most socially vulnerable before the pandemic the most vulnerable to COVID.[23] Conversely, those who could work from home and had good health insurance and quality housing felt less vulnerable. Disproportionately, the less vulnerable were white Americans. Thus, both the risk of COVID-19 and concern about it cleaved like so many other issues along America's racial divide.

Even apart from the pandemic, the structural racism that has long shaped American life seemed especially evident and contentious in 2020. On May 25, 2020, while much of the country was still subject to significant COVID-related restrictions, Minneapolis police officer Derek Chauvin murdered George Floyd by kneeling on his neck for nine minutes. A videotape of the slow, agonizing death soon went viral, spurring an unprecedented wave of Black Lives Matter protests around the country and eventually the globe.[24] As with the COVID orders, support for the protests initially transcended racial and political lines. Soon, however, support for the movement splintered[25] after a few protests turned violent – overwhelmingly, they were not – and Trump turned his Twitter feed against the protesters.

The divisions over both COVID policies and Black Lives Matter protests aligned with partisan polarization. As political scientists have noted, partisanship, coalescing along racial lines, had been rising in the United States for decades before the pandemic.[26] American political parties had once consisted of broad demographic and ideological

---

[23] Sandro Galea, *Introduction: Politics, Policies, Law, and Health in a Time of COVID-19*, in COVID-19 POLICY PLAYBOOK II: LEGAL RECOMMENDATIONS FOR A SAFER, MORE EQUITABLE FUTURE 12–13 (Scott Burris et al. eds., 2021); Carol L. Galletly et al., *Assessment of COVID-19-Related Immigration Concerns among Latinx Immigrants in the US*, 4 JAMA NETWORK OPEN 1, 1 (2021).

[24] Audra D. S. Burch et al., *The Death of George Floyd Reignited a Movement. What Happens Now?* N.Y. TIMES (Oct. 5, 2021), www.nytimes.com/2021/04/20/us/george-floyd-protests-police-reform.html.

[25] *See* Deja Thomas & Juliana Menasce Horwitz, *Support for Black Lives Matter Has Decreased Since June but Remains Strong among Black Americans*, PEW RSCH. CTR. (Sept. 16, 2020), www.pewresearch.org/fact-tank/2020/09/16/support-for-black-lives-matter-has-decreased-since-june-but-remains-strong-among-black-americans.

[26] James A. Monroe, *Partisanship, Dysfunction, and Racial Fears: The New Normal in Health Care Policy*, 41 J. HEALTH POL., POL'Y & L. 827, 832–36 (2016).

coalitions, but a "great sorting" had occurred since the civil rights movement.[27] Political parties had become closely identified with geography, educational status, race, and religiosity. Increasingly, rural, working-class whites voted Republican, while college-educated, urban whites and people of color voted Democratic.[28] As more Americans lived in like-minded communities, gathering their news from their own media bubbles, the sense that there were two Americas experiencing two different sets of truth hardened.

All these schisms predated Trump's presidency and the onset of COVID. As Trump himself tweeted, "It wasn't Donald Trump that divided this country, this country has been divided for a long time!"[29] Still, with his highly charged rhetoric, proclivity for lying and spreading misinformation, and passion for dividing the world between his people and everyone else, Trump compounded the divisions and weakened the nation's capacity to respond to a public health crisis.

From the start, Trump consistently downplayed the threat. On January 22, 2020, he assured the nation, "We have it totally under control. It's one person coming in from China. We have it under control."[30] A few days later, his secretary of health and human services Alex Azar declared a public health emergency, and Trump barred travel from China by non-US nationals on January 31.[31] Still, his administration claimed that the public faced no significant threat.[32] As Trump explained to Bob Woodward in February 2020, "I wanted to always play it down. I still like playing it down."[33]

---

[27] *See* David Beckworth, *David French on Political Polarization in America and Its Impact on the 2020 Elections*, MERCATUS CTR. (Nov. 2, 2020), www.mercatus.org/bridge/podcasts/ 11022020/david-french-political-polarization-america-and-its-impact-2020-elections.

[28] *Trends in Party Affiliation among Demographic Groups*, PEW RSCH. CTR. (Mar. 20, 2018), www .pewresearch.org/politics/2018/03/20/1-trends-in-party-affiliation-among-demographic-groups.

[29] Dan Balz, *Trump Is Right. He Didn't Create the Country's Divisions. But Will He Heal Them?* WASH. POST (Jan. 19, 2017), www.washingtonpost.com/politics/trump-is-right-he-didnt-create-the-countrys-divisions-but-will-he-heal-them/2017/01/19/896f4374-de56-11e6-ad42-f3375f271c9c_story.html.

[30] Matthew J. Belvedere, *Trump Says He Trusts China's Xi on Coronavirus and the US Has It "Totally Under Control,"* CNBC (Jan. 22, 2020), www.cnbc.com/2020/01/22/trump-on-coronavirus-from-china-we-have-it-totally-under-control.html.

[31] Erica Werner et al., *Trump Administration Announces Mandatory Quarantines in Response to Coronavirus*, WASH. POST (Jan. 31, 2020), www.washingtonpost.com/us-policy/2020/01/31/ trump-weighs-tighter-china-travel-restrictions-response-coronavirus/.

[32] *Id.*

[33] BOB WOODWARD, RAGE 12 (2020).

The virus, of course, did not comply. On January 21, 2020, the CDC announced the first confirmed novel coronavirus case in the United States in Washington State.[34] By February, severe acute respiratory syndrome coronavirus 2 (SARS-CoV-2), the virus that causes COVID-19, was spreading rapidly in coastal cities, but we didn't know it because we didn't test for it. In early February 2020, the CDC distributed flawed testing kits to state health departments. Even after the kits were fixed, supplies remained limited and the CDC blocked laboratories from using their own tests.[35] As a result, physicians and health departments were in the dark as cases multiplied.[36] So was the public.

But pandemics can't be hidden for long. By late February 2020, COVID's presence was hard to deny. On February 25, Nancy Messonnier, director of the CDC's National Center for Immunization and Respiratory Diseases, warned Americans that "disruption to everyday life might be severe."[37] The stock market crashed. Trump was "reportedly furious."[38] Messonnier, however, was prescient. On February 28, Washington State confirmed the first US fatality, associated with an outbreak in a nursing home in Kirkland.[39] A few days later, another outbreak flared in New Rochelle, New York. On March 10, Cuomo announced the creation of a "containment area" around parts of that city.[40]

Life for Americans rapidly began to change. On March 11, 2020, the National Basketball Association suspended its season.

[34] AJCM Staff, *A Timeline of COVID-19 Developments in 2020*, Am. J. Managed Care (Jan. 1, 2021), www.ajmc.com/view/a-timeline-of-covid19-developments-in-2020.

[35] *See* Bob Ortega et al., *How the Government Delayed Coronavirus Testing*, CNN (Apr. 9, 2020), www.cnn.com/2020/04/09/politics/coronavirus-testing-cdc-fda-red-tape-invs/index.html.

[36] *See* Dina Temple-Raston, *CDC Report: Official Knew Coronavirus Test Was Flawed but Released It Anyway*, NPR (Nov. 6, 2020), www.npr.org/2020/11/06/929078678/cdc-report-officials-knew-coronavirus-test-was-flawed-but-released-it-anyway.

[37] *Transcript for the CDC Telebriefing Update on COVID-19*, CDC (Feb. 26, 2020), www.cdc.gov/media/releases/2020/t0225-cdc-telebriefing-covid-19.html.

[38] Pippa Stevens, *Trump Is Reportedly Furious That the Stock Market Is Plunging on Coronavirus Fears*, CNBC (Feb. 25, 2020), www.cnbc.com/2020/02/25/trump-is-reportedly-furious-with-the-plunging-stock-market-due-to-coronavirus-fears.html.

[39] Eric Boodman & Helen Branswell, *First Covid-19 Outbreak in a U.S. Nursing Home Raises Concerns*, STAT (Feb. 29, 2020), www.statnews.com/2020/02/29/new-covid-19-death-raises-concerns-about-virus-spread-in-nursing-homes.

[40] Bill Chappell, *Coronavirus: New York Creates "Containment Area" around Cluster in New Rochelle*, NPR (Mar. 10, 2020), www.npr.org/sections/health-shots/2020/03/10/814099444/new-york-creates-containment-area-around-cluster-in-new-rochelle.

That same day, Trump addressed the nation from the Oval Office. Although somber in tone, he continued to reassure, emphasizing that the risk to the young and healthy was "very, very low."[41] He also created confusion by incorrectly stating that he was halting "all travel from Europe to the United States for the next 30 days."[42] Immediately, Americans rushed home from Europe, creating long lines at airports that only accelerated the spread of the virus within the United States.[43]

Throughout March 2020, Trump's message vacillated. At times, he stressed the seriousness of the threat. Other times, he seemed to suggest that there was no cause for alarm. On March 16, he advised the elderly to stay home and asked all Americans to avoid gatherings of more than ten people. A few days later, he urged states to "reopen" by Easter Sunday, April 12.[44] In mid-April, as protesters demanded that Michigan "reopen," he tweeted "Liberate Michigan!" along with "Liberate Minnesota," focusing his wrath on Democratic governors and their public health orders, even though the metrics offered by his own task force suggested that stringent public health measures should remain in place.[45]

By then, political polarization had taken hold, and red and blue states began to diverge in their responses. On April 29, Florida governor Ron DeSantis announced that he was ending public health restrictions in early May, and on April 30, Georgia governor Brian Kemp lifted most restrictions in his state.[46] By then, many Republicans were denouncing COVID orders as violations of liberty. Many Democrats, in contrast,

---

[41] *Read President Trump's Speech on Coronavirus Pandemic: Full Transcript*, N.Y. TIMES (Mar. 11, 2020), www.nytimes.com/2020/03/11/us/politics/trump-coronavirus-speech.html.

[42] *Id.*

[43] Greg Miller et al., *One Final Virus Infusion: Trump's Move to Block Travel from Europe Triggered Chaos and a Surge of Passengers from the Outbreak's Center*, WASH. POST (May 23, 2020), www.washingtonpost.com/world/national-security/one-final-viral-infusion-trumps-move-to-block-travel-from-europe-triggered-chaos-and-a-surge-of-passengers-from-the-outbreaks-center/2020/05/23/64836a00-962b-11ea-82b4-c8db161ff6e5_story.html.

[44] Kevin Liptak et al., *Trump Says He Wants the Country "Opened Up and Just Raring to Go by Easter," Despite Health Experts' Warnings*, CNN (Mar. 24, 2020), www.cnn.com/2020/03/24/politics/trump-easter-economy-coronavirus/index.html.

[45] Wendy E. Parmet, *The COVID Cases: A Preliminary Assessment of Judicial Review of Public Health Powers during a Partisan and Polarizing Pandemic*, 57 SAN DIEGO L. REV. 999, 1009 (2020).

[46] *Id.*

focused their attention and concern on the virus. A once-in-a-century public health crisis had become yet another battle in the deepening US cultural-political-racial conflicts.

The 2020 election only exacerbated the discord. Throughout the campaign, Trump's challenger, Democrat Joe Biden, emphasized the president's failure to take the virus seriously, promising that controlling the pandemic would be his top priority. Trump, on the other hand, downplayed the threat, holding large rallies of unmasked supporters and mocking Biden for wearing a mask.[47]

The November 3d election did not quell the political rancor. Although large majorities of Americans continued to support most public health measures, including stay-at-home orders, travel restrictions, caps on sporting events and restaurant dining, and limits on in-person K–12 schools (which garnered somewhat less support), public opinion was split along partisan lines.[48] Republicans and Trump voters were far less approving of most COVID restrictions than Democrats and Biden voters.[49] That partisan alignment over public health measures would continue into 2022.

The partisan divide was also evident in reactions to the November 2020 election. Throughout the campaign, Trump questioned the election's integrity and continually declined to say whether he would respect the results.[50] Yet despite the challenges of holding an election in the midst of a major pandemic, record numbers of Americans turned out to vote, electing Biden by a healthy margin in the popular vote. Still, Trump refused to concede defeat. Instead, he and his allies ramped up their attacks, amplifying the "big lie" – the stubborn insistence that the election had been stolen.

By Thanksgiving week, a POLITICO/Morning Consult poll found that 70 percent of Republicans did not believe that the

[47] Ashley Collmann, *Two Days Before His Coronavirus Diagnosis, Trump Mocked Biden for Wearing a Face Mask*, BUS. INSIDER (Oct. 2, 2020), www.businessinsider.com/trump-coronavirus-mocked-biden-face-mask-presidential-debate-2020-10.

[48] Matthew Baum et al., *The COVID States Project #25: Public Support for Measures Aimed at Curbing COVID-19*, OSF PREPRINTS (Feb. 20. 2021), https://osf.io/8pcyn.

[49] *Id.*

[50] Sanya Mansoor, *"I Have to See." President Trump Refused to Say if He Will Accept the 2020 Election Results*, TIME (July 19, 2020), https://time.com/5868739/trump-election-results-chris-wallace.

election was free or fair.[51] After losing numerous legal challenges to the election, including at the Supreme Court,[52] Trump egged on his supporters to storm the Capitol as Congress certified the results of the Electoral College. The January 6 insurrection was ultimately put down, but not before several hours of mayhem that shocked the nation and the world. On January 20, 2021, Biden was inaugurated as the forty-sixth president. By then, more than 400,000 Americans had died from a pandemic that was far from over.[53]

A TRADITION OF DEFERENCE

In 2020, the Supreme Court could not escape political or viral turmoil. As will be discussed more fully in Chapters 2 and 3, long before the pandemic, courts and scholars debated how to reconcile constitutional rights with public health laws. Although there was no consensus on some issues, most jurists and scholars accepted several principles: First, the protection of public health is a core component of the states' police power, the sovereign authority that states retained when they joined the union. Second, safeguarding public health is an important, even compelling, state function. Hence, even fundamental individual rights – those rights such as free speech that receive the strongest judicial protection – can be abridged when the means of doing so are narrowly tailored to protect public health. Third, courts should give significant weight or deference to the expertise and decisions of public health officials, not only in but especially during a pandemic.[54]

That doesn't mean that courts should or did affirm all state actions taken in the name of public health. At least since the late nineteenth

---

[51] Catherine Kim, *Poll: 70 Percent of Republicans Don't Think the Election Was Free and Fair*, POLITICO (Nov. 9, 2020), www.politico.com/news/2020/11/09/republicans-free-fair-elections-435488.

[52] *See* Chapter 9.

[53] Cecelia Smith-Schoenwalder, *U.S. Coronavirus Death Toll Tops 400,000 Day before Biden's Inauguration*, U.S. NEWS (Jan. 19, 2021), www.usnews.com/news/national-news/articles/2021-01-19/us-coronavirus-death-toll-tops-400-000-day-before-bidens-inauguration.

[54] *See, e.g.,* LAWRENCE O. GOSTIN & LINDSAY F. WILEY, PUBLIC HEALTH LAW: POWER, DUTY, RESTRAINT (3d ed. 2016).

century, courts have accepted that the Constitution places important restraints on public health powers, and that courts should intervene when an exercise of those powers "has no real or substantial relation to [public health protection], or is, beyond all question, a plain, palpable invasion of the rights secured by fundamental law."[55] In support of that proposition, lawyers looked to the Supreme Court's 1905 decision in *Jacobson v. Massachusetts*, which upheld a law requiring residents to be vaccinated against smallpox or pay a $5 fine.[56]

Jacobson, however, was from an era that was both constitutionally and epidemiologically different than our own. It predated the jurisprudential revolutions of the New Deal and the civil rights era, as well as the conservative counter-revolution that began in the 1970s. *Jacobson* also came before the discovery of antibiotics and the epidemiological transition in which noncommunicable diseases such as cancer or heart disease replaced (pre-COVID) infectious diseases as the most common causes of death. In 1905, the fear of contagion was still commonplace, and a jurisprudence that prioritized public health protection, albeit while setting some important but inexact limits, seemed unremarkable. In the post-antibiotic world, when individual behaviors rather than contagion were viewed as the greatest health threat, the prioritization of public health over individual rights seemed less compelling.

As Chapter 3 more fully discusses, *Jacobson*'s understanding of the relationship between the police power, individual rights, and judicial review was challenged in the mid-twentieth century, as fear of epidemics declined and earlier understandings of the police power faded. At the same time, public health experts began to question whether the restriction of individual rights was necessary for or even conducive to public health protection. For example, during the AIDS epidemic in the 1980s and 1990s, many health experts argued that restrictive and punitive approaches would backfire by causing stigma and discrimination that could deter people from testing and safer practices.[57] Jonathan Mann, then the head of the WHO's global AIDS program,

---

[55] Jacobson v. Massachusetts, 197 U.S. 11, 31 (1905).
[56] *Id.*
[57] *See, e.g.,* LAWRENCE O. GOSTIN & ZITA LAZZARINI, HUMAN RIGHTS AND PUBLIC HEALTH IN THE AIDS PANDEMIC (1997).

explained that the protection of human rights should not be seen as a threat to public health, but rather as a critical foundation for it.[58]

Changes in constitutional law and legal theory also challenged *Jacobson*'s preeminence. In the last forty years, the Supreme Court has expanded – or, in the words of Justice Elena Kagan, "turn[ed] the First Amendment into a sword" to be used "against workaday economic and regulatory policy."[59] This enhanced scrutiny for First Amendment claims, especially those brought by commercial interests, aligned with an increasing distrust by conservative scholars and jurists of the regulatory state.[60] It also put First Amendment doctrine on a collision course with public health laws that regulated the marketing of products, such as tobacco, sugary sodas, or even firearms that were associated with noncommunicable diseases and injuries.[61] To some legal scholars, this enhanced judicial review of public health laws that aimed at noncommunicable diseases in particular was justified, at least on ethical and policy grounds, because such laws were paternalistic.[62] In an influential 2003 paper, legal scholar Richard Epstein argued that regulations that sought to protect people from noncommunicable diseases are paternalistic and therefore problematic.[63] Nevertheless, he accepted that states should protect people from communicable diseases. Doing so, he claimed, stayed within the proper bounds of the "old public health."[64]

In the early days of the COVID-19 pandemic, most courts seemed to agree that whatever the legal status of laws relating to noncommunicable diseases, orders issued to stem an infectious pandemic should continue to receive substantial (but not unlimited) deference.[65] In the spring of 2020, as states issued emergency orders, litigants across

---

[58] Jonathan M. Mann, *Medicine and Public Health, Ethics and Human Rights*, 27 HASTINGS CTR. RPT. 6, 9–11 (1997).

[59] Janus v. Am. Fed'n, 138 S. Ct. 2448, 2501 (2018) (Kagan, J., dissenting).

[60] Robert Post & Amanda Shanor, *Adam Smith's First Amendment*, 128 HARV. L. REV. F. 165 (2015).

[61] Claudia E. Haupt & Wendy E. Parmet, *Public Health Originalism and the First Amendment*, 78 WASH. & L. L. REV. 231, 233 n.2 (2021).

[62] See Wendy E. Parmet, *Paternalism, Self-Governance, and Public Health: The Case of E-Cigarettes*, 70 U. MIAMI L. REV. 879, 887–95 (2016) (reviewing the paternalism critique).

[63] Richard A. Epstein, *Let the Shoemaker Stick to His Last: A Defense of the "Old" Public Health*, 46 PERSP. IN BIOLOGY & MED. S138, S138–59 (2003).

[64] *Id.* at S139.

[65] Parmet, *supra* note 45, at 1013–17.

the country ran to court, raising every conceivable constitutional and statutory claim. The vast majority of courts rejected those claims, applying the deference traditionally accorded public health orders.[66]

A few courts, however, blocked COVID-related orders. In one early and telling case that echoed the partisan divide to come, Judge Justin Walker, whom Trump had appointed to the Western District of Kentucky (and would later place on the Court of Appeals for the D.C. Circuit), enjoined an order by Louisville mayor Greg Fischer barring drive-through religious services on Easter Sunday.[67] Likening the mayor's order to something one might see on the "pages of a dystopian novel, or perhaps the pages of the *Onion*," Walker expounded on the long history of Christians' persecution, dating back to the Gospels.[68] To Walker, the mayor's order was not simply an overreaction to the pandemic, it was an attack on the plaintiffs' belief in the Passion of Christ.

Then, in May 2020, as some (mostly red) states began to "reopen," the US Court of Appeals for the Sixth Circuit issued two decisions blocking restrictions on worship imposed by Kentucky governor Andy Beshear. The first, *Marysville Baptist Church v. Beshear*, blocked an order restricting drive-through worship services, asking "why can someone safely interact with a brave deliverywoman but not a stoic minister?"[69] Rejecting the notion that deference was due, the court asserted, "While the law may take periodic naps during a pandemic, we will not let it sleep through one."[70] The following week, the same court enjoined the governor's order restricting in-person religious services.[71]

On May 29, the Supreme Court entered the fray. In *South Bay United Pentecostal Church v. Newsom*, another case from the shadow docket, the Court rejected an emergency petition asking it to enjoin California's restrictions on in-person worship by a 5–4 vote.[72] As is customary when the Court rejects emergency petitions, the majority did not publish an opinion. However, Chief Justice John Roberts, who voted with the majority, wrote a powerful concurring opinion.

---

[66] *See infra* Chapter 4.
[67] On Fire Christian Ctr. v. Fischer, 453 F. Supp. 3d 901 (W.D. Ky. 2020).
[68] *Id.* at 905.
[69] Maryville Baptist Church, Inc. v. Beshear, 957 F. 3d 610, 615 (6th Cir. 2020).
[70] *Id.* at 615.
[71] Roberts v. Neace, 958 F. 3d 409 (6th Cir. 2020).
[72] S. Bay United Pentecostal Church v. Newsom, 140 S. Ct. 1613 (2020) (per curiam).

In it, he stressed the case's procedural posture (an emergency petition seeking to overturn a lower court decision) as a reason for the Court to deny the petition. He also cited *Jacobson* in support of the Court's long-standing tradition of offering deference to politically accountable officials in matters relating to public health.[73]

Although Roberts's opinion was relatively unremarkable, given the case's posture and the prevailing precedent, the more conservative justices did not agree. Justice Brett Kavanaugh, joined by Justices Clarence Thomas and Neil Gorsuch, wrote a strong dissent.[74] In it, they argued that the state's decision to restrict worship while leaving some secular activities open discriminated against religion in violation of the First Amendment's free exercise clause. To the dissenters, no deference was due to the state because the orders limited religious worship. Instead, they wrote, the Court should have applied strict scrutiny, the most stringent form of judicial review, which few state laws can survive.

Less than two months later, in *Calvary Chapel Dayton Valley v. Sisolak*, the Court once again from its shadow docket, and once again by a 5–4 vote, rejected a petition to enjoin a Nevada order imposing a 50 percent capacity limit on gatherings for religious worship.[75] This time, multiple heated dissents emphasized that the state had placed less stringent standards on casinos, a fact that no doubt pointed to the tension between economic interests and public health that continued throughout the pandemic. In his dissent, Justice Samuel Alito added that *Jacobson* had no relevance to a First Amendment case since it was not decided under that amendment.[76] In his own dissent, Kavanaugh warned, "This Court's history is littered with unfortunate examples of overly broad judicial deference to the government when the government has invoked emergency powers."[77] Though powerful, these were only dissents. For four more months, as the election roiled the nation and the pandemic and the pandemic's death toll mounted, deference remained the prevailing legal standard.

---

[73] *Id.* at 1613 (Roberts, C. J., concurring).
[74] *Id.* at 1614 (Kavanaugh, J., dissenting).
[75] Calvary Chapel Dayton Valley v. Sisolak, 140 S. Ct. 2603 (2020).
[76] *Id.* at 2608 (Alito, J., dissenting).
[77] *Id.* at 2615 (Kavanaugh, J., dissenting).

A NEW MAJORITY

On September 18, 2020, less than seven weeks before the presidential election, liberal icon Ruth Bader Ginsburg died, leaving a vacancy on the Supreme Court. Trump and Republican Senate majority Leader Mitch McConnell rushed to fill it before the presidential election.

A little over four years earlier, in the last year of the Obama administration, McConnell had refused to allow either hearings or a vote on Merrick Garland, Barack Obama's nominee for the Court following Antonin Scalia's death. At the time, McConnell stated, "The American people are perfectly capable of having their say on this issue, so let's give them a voice. ... The Senate will appropriately revisit the matter when it considers the qualifications of the nominee the next president nominates, whoever that might be."[78] When McConnell offered that statement, the presidential election was almost eight months away. When Ginsburg died, it was less than seven weeks away, and many voters had already cast their ballots. Yet this time, there would be a quick hearing and confirmation.

On September 26, 2020, in a Rose Garden ceremony, Trump introduced his nominee, Amy Coney Barrett. The forty-eight-year-old Barrett, who sat on the US Court of Appeals for the Seventh Circuit, had clerked for Scalia and was a strong favorite of anti-abortion advocates and conservatives.[79] In the ceremony introducing her to the nation, Trump called her a "woman of unparalleled achievement, towering intellect, sterling credentials and unyielding loyalty to the Constitution."[80] Given the Republicans' control of the Senate, her confirmation was all but assured. On October 26, less than two weeks before the election, the Senate confirmed her nomination by a 52–48 vote.[81]

---

[78] Amita Kelly, *McConnell: Blocking Supreme Court Nomination "About a Principle, Not a Person,"* NPR (Mar. 16, 2016) www.npr.org/2016/03/16/470664561/mcconnell-blocking-supreme-court-nomination-about-a-principle-not-a-person.

[79] Peter Baker & Maggie Haberman, *Trump Selects Amy Coney Barrett to Fill Ginsburg's Seat on the Supreme Court,* N.Y. Times (Oct. 15, 2020) www.nytimes.com/2020/09/25/us/politics/amy-coney-barrett-supreme-court.html.

[80] Tessa Berenson, *Donald Trump Nominates Amy Coney Barrett to the Supreme Court,* Time (Sept. 26, 2020), https://time.com/5893561/donald-trump-amy-coney-barrett-supreme-court.

[81] Barbara Sprunt, *Amy Coney Barrett Confirmed to Supreme Court, Takes Constitutional Oath,* NPR (Oct. 26, 2020), www.npr.org/2020/10/26/927640619/senate-confirms-amy-coney-barrett-to-the-supreme-court.

Barrett's nomination did not, however, go quite as smoothly as Trump might have wished. A few days after the Rose Garden ceremony, in which unmasked guests sat close to one another and later mingled in celebration, both Trump and the first lady contracted COVID-19,[82] as did at least a dozen other people who attended the ceremony.[83] Even so, less than three weeks later, Clarence Thomas administered the oath of office to the new Justice Barrett.[84] A few days later, Biden was elected president.

Three weeks after that, with three Trump appointees seated on the bench, the Supreme Court rewrote public health law with *RCD*. In the months and years that followed, as the pandemic ebbed and resurged, the new majority built upon and expanded *RCD*, striking public health measures imposed by Democratic governors and the Biden administration. In the process, the Court tossed aside long-settled understandings of the separation of powers and governments' ability to protect public health. It also handcuffed the nation's response to a still-deadly pandemic that would go on to kill more than one million Americans.

Elections have consequences. So, too, do Supreme Court decisions.

---

[82] Ann Gerhart & Lucio Villa, *Rose Garden Ceremony Attendees Who Tested Positive for Coronavirus*, WASH. POST (Oct. 7, 2020), www.washingtonpost.com/graphics/2020/politics/coronavirus-attendees-barrett-nomination-ceremony/.

[83] LAWRENCE WRIGHT, THE PLAGUE YEAR: AMERICA IN THE TIME OF COVID 210 (2021).

[84] Morgan Chalfant, *Barrett Sworn in as Supreme Court Justice by Thomas*, HILL (Oct. 26, 2020), https://thehill.com/homenews/administration/522889-barrett-sworn-in-as-supreme-court-justice-by-thomas.

2 *SALUS POPULI SUPREMA LEX*

The legal tradition that the Supreme Court tossed aside in *Roman Catholic Diocese v. Cuomo* predates the Constitution.[1] Although it had long been fraying, that tradition reflected a very different understanding of the relationship between liberty and public health laws than that imagined by many contemporary Americans.

Today, we often think of individual liberty as the lack of governmental restraint – what political theorist and philosopher Sir Isaiah Berlin called "negative liberty."[2] This is the freedom of the apocryphal state of nature, the freedom that the philosopher John Locke described when he spoke of the liberty "for every one to do what he lists, to live as he pleases, and not to be tyed by any Laws."[3] It might include the freedom to decline to wear a mask, reject vaccination, or generally do whatever one pleases.

So understood, all laws that restrict individual choice limit liberty. But as Locke recognized, because we do not live alone in a state of nature, not all of our liberties can be respected. Nor does the Constitution protect all of our negative liberties. It does, however, safeguard those that are commonly termed "fundamental rights." Yet even these are not absolute. As the old adage goes, the "right to swing [one's] arms ends just where the other man's nose begins."[4] The key question thus becomes: Where does the other person's nose begin? If we view our actions as

---

[1] Roman Cath. Diocese of Brooklyn v. Cuomo (hereinafter cited as *RCD*), 141 S. Ct. 63 (2020) (per curiam).

[2] Isaiah Berlin, *Two Concepts of Liberty, in* Four Essays on Liberty 121–22 (1990).

[3] John Locke, Two Treatises of Government 264 (Peter Laslett ed., 1960) (1690).

[4] *See* Zechariah Chafee, Jr., *Freedom of Speech in War Time*, 32 Harv. L. Rev. 932, 957 (1919).

primarily affecting only ourselves – what English philosopher John Stuart Mill called "self-regarding" actions – then we are likely to view the scope of negative liberty as relatively large, because, by definition, the interests of others cannot justify restrictions on most of our actions. Alternatively, if we perceive many of our actions as affecting others – what Mill termed "other-regarding" actions – then we will accept a larger space for regulation and a narrower role for individual rights.[5]

In the years leading up to the COVID-19 pandemic, many Americans viewed health as resulting primarily from self-regarding actions. Despite the government's increasing role in subsidizing health care, and reams of research showing that health is largely determined by myriad social factors,[6] many Americans believed that their health was in their own hands, and equally, that the choices they made affected only them (or their families).[7] As a result, public health laws, from restrictions on smoking to taxes to laws mandating insurance, were frequently derided as liberty-limiting impositions of the nanny state.

For many years, this libertarian critique was aimed primarily at laws that targeted noncommunicable diseases, such as diabetes.[8] Contagious diseases – especially those that were airborne – were viewed differently precisely because an individual's infection can affect others. Further, with a communicable disease, the rate of disease in a population – its prevalence – impacts the risks to individuals. The more people who have the disease, the great the risk everyone faces. As a result, it can be difficult if not impossible for people to protect themselves as long as many others are engaging in activities that perpetuate contagion.

Most Americans seemed to understand this in the spring of 2020, as tens of millions of people stayed home in an effort to "flatten the curve."

[5] JOHN STUART MILL, *On Liberty*, in JOHN STUART MILL: A SELECTION OF HIS WORKS 96–119 (John M. Robson ed., 1966) (1859).

[6] Paula Braveman & Laura Gottlieb, *The Social Determinants of Health: It's Time to Consider the Causes of the Causes*, 129 PUB. HEALTH REPS. 19, 19 (2014); *see generally* U.S. Dep't of Health & Hum. Servs., Off. of Disease Prevention and Health Promotion, *Social Determinants of Health Literature Summaries*, HEALTHY PEOPLE 2030, https://health.gov/healthypeople/priority-areas/social-determinants-health/literature-summaries (last visited Apr. 15, 2022).

[7] Aziza Ahmed & Jason Jackson, *Race, Risk, and Personal Responsibility in the Response to COVID-19*, 121 COL. L. REV. F. 47, 52–59 (2021).

[8] *See, e.g.*, Richard A. Epstein, *Let the Shoemaker Stick to His Last: A Defense of the "Old" Public Health*, 46 PERSP. IN BIOLOGY & MED. 138, 143 (2003); Mark A. Hall, *The Scope and Limits of Public Health Law*, 46 PERSP. IN BIOLOGY & MED. 199, 206 (2003).

Early in the pandemic, most Americans seemed to grasp that their actions could impact the community's level of viral transmission, not to mention the strain on the health care system. Even as late as December 2020, a strong majority of Americans believed that it was everyone's responsibility to wear a mask.[9]

Yet not everyone agreed. As the pandemic progressed, many Americans, especially those identifying as Republicans, came to view COVID-19 infection through an individualistic lens.[10] After Joe Biden took office and vaccines became widely available, his administration also adopted that individualistic framing. In May 2021, CDC director Dr. Rochelle Walensky explained, "We really want to empower people to take this responsibility into their own hands."[11] Biden's administration continued to follow that approach in many of its policies through the delta and omicron surges in 2021 and 2022.

Once health risks are viewed in this manner, pandemic mitigation measures appear as intrusions on individual liberty. And when those laws touch upon fundamental rights, such as freedom of speech or freedom of religion, Americans turn to the courts. In *RCD*, the Supreme Court signaled support for such claims.[12]

Health, however, has not always been seen as a matter of individual responsibility. Earlier generations, which were more accustomed to epidemics, were more inclined to accept that their own health and liberty affected – and often depended on – the actions of others.[13] They also recognized that only concerted actions, usually through law, could control contagion. In this bygone world, the liberty that enabled people to stay healthy was recognized as one of the reasons we have governments. Rights and liberty, likewise, were viewed as

[9] Lunna Lopes et al., *KFF Health Tracking Poll – December 2020: COVID-19 and Biden's Health Care Agenda*, KAISER FAM. FOUND. (Dec. 18, 2020), www.kff.org/coronavirus-covid-19/report/kff-health-tracking-poll-december-2020.

[10] *Id.*; German Lopez, *America Still Needs to Learn from Its Biggest Pandemic Failure*, VOX (June 4, 2021), www.vox.com/22458461/covid-19-collectivism-individualism-vaccine-failure-america.

[11] Ed Yong, *The Fundamental Question of the Pandemic Is Shifting: We Understand How This Will End. But Who Bears the Risk That Remains?*, ATLANTIC (June 9, 2021), www.theatlantic.com/health/archive/2021/06/individualism-still-spoiling-pandemic-response/619133.

[12] *RCD*, 141 S. Ct. at 63.

[13] JOHN FABIAN WITT, AMERICAN CONTAGIONS: EPIDEMICS AND THE LAW FROM SMALLPOX TO COVID-19, 13 (2020).

inherently limited by the common good.[14] This was reflected in the jurisprudence of the preantibiotic era.

THE HISTORY OF PUBLIC HEALTH LAWS

Far from being innovations of the nanny state, public health laws date back to antiquity. The Old Testament commanded the separation of lepers.[15] When bubonic plague ravaged Eurasia, many governments required individuals who were ill, as well as members of their households, to stay home.[16] By 1348, Venice had established regulations for dealing with ships carrying infected travelers; in 1377, the Republic of Ragusa (today Dubrovnik, in Croatia) required ships to stay in the harbor for thirty (and later forty) days before coming to port.[17] This practice gave rise to the term "quarantine," from the Italian for "forty" – *quarantena*.[18]

Numerous early English laws likewise aimed to prevent the spread of communicable diseases. As early as the fourteenth century, English ordinances required the abatement of nuisances, such as rats, that were thought to harbor disease.[19] A 1518 royal proclamation required that houses with contagion be marked with straw for forty days.[20] In 1578, the Privy Council issued its first book of plague orders.[21] Among other things, these edicts levied a tax assessment for the provision of care of plague victims and ordered the quarantining of victims and their families for up to six weeks.[22] In 1603, Parliament codified

---

[14] ADRIAN VERMEULE, COMMON GOOD CONSTITUTIONALISM 24 (2022); Scott Burris, *Individual Liberty, Public Health, and the Battle for the Nation's Soul*, REGUL. REV. (June 7, 2021), www .theregreview.org/2021/06/07/burris-individual-liberty-public-health-battle-for-nations-soul.

[15] *Leviticus* 13:46 (King James).

[16] Wendy E. Parmet, *AIDS and Quarantine: The Revival of an Archaic Doctrine*, 14 HOFSTRA L. REV. 53, 55 (1985).

[17] GEOFF MANAUGH & NICOLA TWILLEY, UNTIL PROVEN SAFE: THE HISTORY AND FUTURE OF QUARANTINE 17 (2021).

[18] *Id.* at 15.

[19] Wendy E. Parmet, *Health Care and the Constitution: Public Health and the Role of the State in the Framing Era*, 20 HASTINGS CONST. L. Q. 268, 282–83 (1993).

[20] *Id.* at 283.

[21] *Id.*

[22] *Id.* at 283–84.

the isolation of plague victims.[23] Sir William Blackstone considered this law of the "highest importance."[24]

Public health laws followed the English to the North American colonies. In 1622, East Hampton, Long Island, issued what might have been the first quarantine order in the British colonies of North America.[25] In the years that followed, quarantine orders were relatively common,[26] but they were hardly the only public health laws in the colonial period. For example, starting in the early eighteenth century, Boston heavily regulated variolation, the predecessor to vaccination in which the pus of smallpox patients was injected under the skin of healthy individuals to prevent them from having a severe case of smallpox.[27] The American colonies also regulated the practice of medicine, sanitation, and trades and practices that were perceived as posing a threat to the public's health. Drawing from the tradition of the English poor laws, state and local laws usually provided for the care of the indigent who were ill.[28]

To be sure, before the middle of the nineteenth century, public health laws relied on an incomplete and often erroneous understanding of the causes of epidemics and the steps that can help to mitigate them. As legal historian John Fabian Witt explains, public health laws reflected divergent and often inconsistent ideas about the etiology of epidemics.[29] So-called quarantinists focused on the dangers of contagion. Although they did not understand the role of pathogens, they recognized that some diseases spread among people, and they tried to stem transmission by isolating the sick and quarantining ships and newcomers. Sanitarians, in contrast, believed that epidemics arose from miasmas emanating from the filth that was commonplace in cities and towns.[30] In their view, public health laws should focus on sanitation and the regulation of trades and practices, such as slaughterhouses, that generated filth. Yet while sanitarians and quarantinists

---

[23] 1 Jac. 1, c. 31 (1603).
[24] 4 WILLIAM BLACKSTONE, COMMENTARIES *161.
[25] Parmet, *supra* note 16, at 56.
[26] Parmet, *supra* note 19, at 288.
[27] *Id.* at 288–89.
[28] POLLY J. PRICE, PLAGUES IN THE NATION: HOW EPIDEMICS SHAPED AMERICA 9 (2022).
[29] WITT, *supra* note 13, at 13–60.
[30] *Id.* at 28.

disagreed about the specific measures that governments should employ
to reduce contagion, few argued that governments should do *nothing*.
Laissez-faire was not a viable option. Nor was it considered essential
to safeguarding the liberty secured by the Constitution.

Rather, in the early days of the American republic, the risk of inac-
tion was all too clear. In 1793, for example, a yellow fever outbreak in
Philadelphia, then the nation's capital, killed 10 to 15 percent of the
city's residents in a little over three months.[31] Foreshadowing 2020,
the debates over the response to that epidemic became entangled with
partisan wrangling over other domestic and international issues, particularly the stance the United States should take in regard to the war
that engulfed Europe following the French Revolution.[32] Philadelphia's
response to yellow fever also followed a pattern that continued until
the middle of the nineteenth century: When the outbreak struck, the
mayor established "an extralegal committee of citizen volunteers" to
take charge and do what had to be done – cleaning the city, establishing
a hospital, caring for the sick and orphaned, and burying the dead.[33]

Although the responses were often ad hoc, too late, and ineffec-
tual, most Americans agreed that governments *ought* to act, and sometimes take measures that would today seem extreme to mitigate deadly
outbreaks.[34] As legal historian William Novak explains, "[P]ublic
regulatory power remained an omnipresent factor in early nineteenth-
century economic, political, and social life."[35] While these regulations
covered a wide range of activities, those related to the public health
received special reverence. Supreme Court justice Robert Cooper
Grier expressed the common sentiment in 1847, stating that laws
that seek to protect public health, peace, and morals "are from their
very nature of primary importance; they lie at the foundation of social
existence; they are for the protection of life and liberty, and necessarily compel all laws on subjects of secondary importance, which relate
only to property, convenience, or luxury, to recede when they come in

[31] Martin S. Pernick, *Politics, Parties, and Pestilence: Epidemic Yellow Fever in Philadelphia and the Rise of the First Party System*, 29 Wm. & Mary Q. 559, 559 (1972).

[32] *Id.* at 560–62.

[33] *Id.* at 559–60.

[34] Price, *supra* note 28, at 5.

[35] William J. Novak, *Common Regulation, Legal Origins of State Power in America*, 45 Hastings L. J. 1061, 1076 (1994).

collision, '*salus populi suprema lex*'"[36] – the well-being and health of the public is the highest law.

The Latin maxim that Grier quoted is an ancient one, sometimes attributed to the Roman statesman and legal philosopher Cicero.[37] Frequently invoked by common-law judges, it expressed the widely held belief that protecting the public's health is foundational to law and governance,[38] and is indeed one of the reasons why we have governments.[39] From this aphorism, early jurists concluded that laws that aimed to protest the public's health, safety, and morals warranted special regard by the courts. Some went further, suggesting, as the Vermont Supreme Court did in 1830, that when there is a danger of infection, "it becomes the duty of the selectman to take the most prudent measures to prevent the spreading of the disease."[40]

A DIFFERENT VIEW OF RIGHTS

Today, *salus populi* seems like an alien concept that invites courts to acquiesce to the subordination of individual liberty. There is some merit to this critique. The judiciary's support of slavery and later Jim Crow laws, as well as the appropriation of Native American lands, attests to the atrocities that coexisted with the courts' embrace of *salus populi*. In a viciously unequal society, those with power and privilege decide what *salus populi* commands. Often, their decisions perpetuate inequities. We will return to these salient critiques in subsequent chapters. For now, what is critical is the fact that eighteenth- and nineteenth-century courts did not view *salus populi* as sanctioning restrictions on liberty. Rather, they believed that liberty was interdependent with protections for the public's health.

To appreciate this earlier view, it is necessary to recall that the Framers established the federal government as one of limited, enumerated powers. As Chapter 1 notes, the power to protect the public's health, safety, and morals – known as the police power – resided with the states. In 1824,

[36] Thurlow v. Massachusetts, 46 U.S. 504, 632 (1847).
[37] WITT, *supra* note 13, at 19; PRICE, *supra* note 28, at 4.
[38] BURRIS, *supra* note 14.
[39] *Id.*; Parmet, *supra* note 19, at 316–19.
[40] Hazen v. Strong, 2 Vt. 427, 433 (1830).

Chief Justice John Marshall explained in *Gibbons v. Ogden* that "inspection laws, quarantine laws," and "health laws of every description" fell within the mass of powers that the states retained when they joined the Constitution.[41] These powers "flow[ed] from the acknowledged power of a State, to provide for the health of its citizens."[42]

Although the antebellum Supreme Court was clear that the full scope of the police power could not be enumerated, the police power, as shown by *Gibbons*, was always closely associated with laws that sought to prevent the spread of disease. At times, the Supreme Court even treated the determination of whether a law sought to protect health, safety, or morals as dispositive of whether it fell within the state's police power or the federal government's authority over interstate commerce.[43] To oversimplify, if a law appeared to be a health regulation, then the Court in the 1800s would usually accept that it was an exercise of the police power and hence within the state's prerogative. On the other hand, if the law did not seem to be about health, safety, or morals, the Court might conclude that it was an unconstitutional regulation of interstate commerce. Although the Court altered its approach as the nineteenth century progressed to one that sought to reconcile state and federal interests,[44] its decisions continued to associate police power with state regulation of health, safety, and morals.

Critically, before Reconstruction, individuals had very few federal constitutional "rights" with which to challenge the states' police power. The rights they had were mostly based on state law. Yet even under state law, individual rights were seldom treated as trumps that limited the reach of the police power.[45] As Novak explains, legal discourse in the nineteenth century "refused to separate public powers and private rights in favor of an over-arching notion of a 'well-ordered' and 'well-regulated' community, in which liberties and powers, rights and duties

---

[41] Gibbons v. Ogden, 22 U.S. 1, 203 (1824).

[42] *Id.* at 205.

[43] *E.g.*, Mayor of New York v. Miln, 36 U.S. (11 Pet.) 102 (1837); Wilson v. Blackbird Creek Marsh Co., 27 U.S. 245, 251 (1829); *contra* Smith v. Turner (Passenger Cases), 48 U.S. 283, 393–400 (1849).

[44] *See, e.g.*, Cooley v. Bd. of Wardens, 53 U.S. 299, 313–15 (1851).

[45] Jud Campbell, *Natural Rights and the First Amendment*, 127 YALE L. J. 246, 253–59 (2017).

were mutually interwoven."[46] In effect, individual "rights" existed only in relation to the police power and the common good. Because individuals had no "right" to endanger public health or safety, laws that aimed to protect those interests could not violate individual rights.

That syllogism was deeply embedded in early American law. In private law, it was reflected in the law of nuisance, where courts employed another common law maxim, *sic utere tuo ut alienum non laeda*s (do not use your property so as to injure others) to rule that property owners had no right to use their property in ways that were injurious to the property rights of others.[47] Public law cases challenging state and local laws and regulations echoed a similar refrain.

The 1828 case *In re Vandine* offers an illustration.[48] The plaintiff challenged a Boston sanitary ordinance that required individuals who collected "house dirt" (i.e., bodily waste) and offal to be licensed. Writing for the Massachusetts Supreme Judicial Court, Justice Samuel Putnam acknowledged that the law restrained trade. Nevertheless, he ruled that there could be no right to disregard a law that was designed to protect public health.[49]

Less than twenty-five years later, in *Commonwealth v. Alger* (1851), Justice Lemuel Shaw explained for that same court that

> rights of property, like all other social and conventional rights, are subject to such reasonable limitations in their enjoyment, as shall prevent them from being injurious, and to such reasonable restraints and regulations established by law, as the legislature, under the governing and controlling power vested in them by the constitution, may think necessary and expedient.[50]

Shaw added that though it is "much easier to perceive and realize the existence and sources of this power, than to mark its boundaries, or prescribe limits to its exercises," the police power surely extended to laws prohibiting "buildings from being used for hospitals for contagious diseases," or the erection of dams when doing so

---

[46] Novak, *supra* note 35, at 1070.
[47] Jeff L. Lewin, Boomer *and the American Law of Nuisance: Past, Present, and Future*, 54 ALB. L. REV. 189, 196–97 (1990).
[48] *See In re* Vandine, 23 Mass. 187 (1828).
[49] *Id.* at 192–93.
[50] Commonwealth v. Alger, 61 Mass. 53, 85 (1851).

would raise "noxious exhalations, injurious to health and dangerous to life."[51] In support, Shaw quoted *"sic utere tuo, ut alienum non laedas."*[52]

Antebellum courts applied the same logic when other interests – including those we might call "fundamental rights" – were at stake. As Witt discusses, a New York court upheld a regulation barring the internment of bodies in lower New York, even though the law seemed to infringe on a church's vested rights.[53] To contemporary eyes, the law might appear to violate religious liberty, but to early nineteenth-century lawyers, no such problem appeared and no such claim was made. Instead, the church argued that the law violated a lease between the church and the city. The court rejected that claim, explaining that the lease offered no right against a later legislative action aimed at preventing a practice that was injurious to health.[54]

None of this is to say that public health powers were unlimited in the early nineteenth century. Despite *salus populi*, courts overturned police power laws when they found that the public entity lacked the requisite legal authority under a specific state statute.[55] In addition, courts frequently employed the concept of necessity to cabin public health actions. As Justice Shaw explained in *Taylor v. Plymouth* (1844), a case brought by property owners who sought compensation after their building was razed to slow a fire, "if there be no necessity, then the individuals who do the act shall be responsible."[56] To Shaw, necessity seemed relatively easy to ascertain in the case of a fire: "It is obvious that the mode in which the pulling down of a house tends to stop a fire is, that it makes a gap; it breaks the continuity of combustible materials, which would otherwise feed and extend the flames."[57] As the century advanced, the requirement of necessity would open the door to new ways of cabining the police power.

[51] *Id.* at 85–86.
[52] *Id.* at 86.
[53] WITT, *supra* note 13, at 24–25 (discussing Brick Presbyterian Church v. Mayor of N.Y., 5 Cow. 538, 1826 WL 2038 (N.Y. Sup. Ct. 1826)).
[54] Brick Presbyterian Church, 5 Cow. at 538.
[55] WITT, *supra* note 13, at 67–69 (citing People v. Roff, 3 Park. Crim. 215, 233 (N.Y. 1856)).
[56] Taylor v. Inhabitants of Plymouth, 49 Mass. (8 Met.) 462, 465 (1844).
[57] *Id.*

CONSTITUTIONAL LIMITATIONS

As industrialization and laissez-faire economics took off following the Civil War, legal theorists and litigants began to challenge earlier conceptions of the police power. Rather than seeing it as plenary and unbounded, they viewed it as constrained, limited to discrete categories. They also began to see individual rights as imposing limits on the police power. Nevertheless, throughout the nineteenth century and into the early twentieth, courts continued to recite *salus populi* and insist that it applied to public health regulations, especially those relating to communicable diseases.[58] They did so even as states established professional public health boards that were granted broad authority to do whatever they deemed necessary to protect the public's health.[59] Likewise, public health laws that touched on speech and or other activities that today are treated as fundamental constitutional rights continued to be found – if not simply presumed – to be constitutional.[60]

The Fourteenth Amendment served as the chief legal vehicle for the changes to the police power jurisprudence in the late nineteenth and early twentieth centuries. Ratified in 1868, it reversed the denial of citizenship to African Americans rendered by the Supreme Court in the infamous *Dred Scott v. Sandford* that was decided in 1856.[61] It also required states to respect the "privileges or immunities of citizens of the United States," to provide all persons with "equal protection of the laws," and not to deprive them of "life, liberty, or property, without due process of law."[62] It was those provisions that opened the door to reconsidering the relationship between the police power and individual liberty.

The new approach developed gradually as courts began to articulate a more confined understanding of the police power, seeing it as

---

[58] Richard Epstein, *In Defense of the Old Public Health: The Legal Framework for the Regulation of Public Health*, 69 BROOK. L. REV. 1421, 1427, 1430–33 (2004).

[59] Metro. Bd. of Health v. Heister, 37 N.Y. 661 (1868); *see* John Fabian Witt, *The Law of Salus Populi: Epidemics and the Law*, YALE REV. (Mar. 30, 2020), https://yalereview.org/article/law-salus-populi.

[60] *See* Claudia E. Haupt & Wendy E. Parmet, *Public Health Originalism and the First Amendment*, 78 WASH. & LEE L. REV. 231, 276–79 (2021).

[61] Dred Scott v. Sandford, 60 U.S. 393, 454 (1856); *see, e.g.*, Gregory E. Maggs, *A Critical Guide to Using the Legislative History of the Fourteenth Amendment to Determine the Amendment's Original Meaning*, 49 CONN. L. REV. 1069, 1083–84 (2017).

[62] U.S. CONST. amend. XIV.

limited to instead of identified with laws that pertained to public health, safety, and morals. Eventually, courts came to hold that even public health laws were only within the police power if they were reasonable or necessary to achieve their public health goal.[63] Yet even then, courts did not argue that individual rights could limit reasonable public health laws. *Salus populi* was diminished, but it was not rejected outright.

The transformation was evident in the Supreme Court's first foray into the Fourteenth Amendment, the so-called *Slaughter-House Cases* of 1873.[64] At issue was a Louisiana law that prohibited slaughtering within New Orleans and required all slaughtering in a district outside the city to be conducted in the facilities of a newly formed company, the Crescent City Live-Stock Landing and Slaughter-House Company. The law, which was modeled on sanitary regulations in other cities, was designed to address the notoriously filthy industry and protect a city that was repeatedly ravaged by yellow fever and cholera.[65]

A group of butchers challenged the law, arguing that it violated the Fourteenth Amendment by violating their privileges and immunities as US citizens, denied them equal protection of the law, and violated their rights to due process.[66] The Court, in an opinion by Justice Samuel Miller, denied all their claims. Most famously, Miller construed the amendment's privileges or immunities clause as protecting only the privileges of federal citizenship, thereby consigning that clause to constitutional oblivion for more than a hundred years.[67]

Moving beyond the privileges or immunities clause, Miller wrote that the regulation of slaughtering easily fell within the police power.[68] Miller, a physician who had long been interested in public health and sanitation,[69] explained that "the security of social order, the life and health of the citizen, the comfort of an existence in a thickly populated

[63] Viemeister v. White, 179 N.Y. 235, 238 (1904).
[64] Slaughter-House Cases, 83 U.S. 36, 59 (1873).
[65] Michael A. Ross, *Justice Miller's Reconstruction: The Slaughter-House Cases, Health Codes, and Civil Rights in New Orleans, 1861–73*, 64 J. S. Hist. 649, 653–54 (1998).
[66] *Slaughter-House*, 83 U.S. at 66.
[67] Michael K. Curtis, *Resurrecting the Privileges or Immunities Clause and Revising the Slaughter-House Cases without Exhuming Lochner: Individual Rights and the Fourteenth Amendment*, 38 B.C. L. Rev. 1, 73–75 (1996).
[68] *Slaughter-House*, 83 U.S. at 62 (quoting James Kent, Commentaries on American Law, Vol. II 340 (5th ed. 1884)).
[69] Ross, *supra* note 65, at 668–69.

community, the enjoyment of private and social life, and the beneficial use of property" all depend on the police power.[70] The Fourteenth Amendment, he argued, did not crimp that power, nor did it upend earlier police power jurisprudence. Thus, to Miller, as legal scholar Michael A. Ross has shown, the amendment did not prevent the then-multiracial Louisiana legislature from addressing public health threats.[71]

In their dissents, Justices Stephen Field and Joseph Bradley offered a very different perspective. In his opinion, Field did not question that the police power "undoubtedly extends to all regulations affecting the health, good order, morals, peace, and safety of society."[72] But, he explained, "under the pretense of prescribing a police regulation the State cannot be permitted to encroach upon any of the just rights of the citizen."[73] He went on to conclude that only some of the provisions of the Louisianan law were actually necessary to protect sanitation. Thus, like the majority in *RCD*, he refused to accept the state's word as to what was and was not necessary to protect the public's health.

In his dissent, Bradley agreed, finding that the legislature, "under pretence [*sic*] of making a police regulation for the promotion of the public health," had violated the plaintiffs' liberty to pursue their own lawful employment.[74] Bradley thus saw individual liberty as including a far more expansive category of natural rights than did Miller or earlier jurists. He also seemed to accept that it was the courts' job to examine state regulations to ensure that laws that the state claimed protected public health actually did so, lest the police power serve as a pretext for the evisceration of liberty. Still, he did not question that the state could enact public health laws, nor did he assert that individual rights could limit legitimate uses of the police power. He just did not accept that Louisiana's law was a legitimate exercise of the police power.

In the years that followed *Slaughter-House*, the Court confronted ever more challenges to state regulations. Initially, it adhered to its earlier understanding of the relationship between liberty and the police power.

[70] *Slaughter-House*, 83 U.S. at 62.
[71] Ross, *supra* note 65, at 661.
[72] *Slaughter-House*, 83 U.S. at 87 (Field, J., dissenting).
[73] *Id.*
[74] *Id.* at 111 (Bradley, J., dissenting).

For example, in upholding a law regulating the price of grain storage in *Munn v. Illinois* (1876), the Court stated:

> When one becomes a member of society, he necessarily parts with some rights or privileges which, as an individual not affected by his relations to others, he might retain. "A body politic," as aptly defined in the preamble of the Constitution of Massachusetts, "is a social compact by which the whole people covenants with each citizen, and each citizen with the whole people, that all shall be governed by certain laws for the common good."[75]

Over time, the Court began to move closer to the *Slaughter-House* dissents, imagining a very different relationship between the police power and constitutional rights, as well as a far more robust role for the federal courts. For example, in *Mugler v. Kansas* (1887), the Court in an opinion by Justice John Marshall Harlan asserted that the Court would not accede to every purported application of the police power.[76] While upholding a state law barring the manufacture and sale of liquor, Harlan explained that "it does not at all follow that every statute enacted ostensibly for the promotion of [public morals, the public health or public safety] is to be accepted as a legitimate exertion of the police power of the state. There are, of necessity, limits beyond which legislation cannot rightfully go."[77] He added, if a "statute purporting to have been enacted to protect the public health, the public morals, or the public safety, has no real or substantial relation to those objects, or is a palpable invasion of rights secured by fundamental law, it is the duty of the courts to so adjudge, and thereby give effect to the Constitution."[78]

Ten years later, in *Allgeyer v. Louisiana* (1897), the Court found that a state law regulating insurance contracts crossed those lines:

> The "liberty" mentioned in the [Fourteenth Amendment] means not only the right of the citizen to be free from the mere physical restraint of his person, as by incarceration, but the term is deemed to embrace the right of the citizen to be free in the enjoyment of all his faculties, to be free to use them in all lawful ways; to live and work where he will; to earn his livelihood by any lawful calling; to pursue any livelihood or

[75] Munn v. Illinois, 94 U.S. 113, 124 (1876) (quoting MASS. CONST. pmbl.).
[76] Mugler v. Kansas, 123 U.S. 623, 661 (1887).
[77] *Id.*
[78] *Id.*

avocation, and for that purpose to enter into all contracts which may be proper, necessary and essential to his carrying out a successful conclusion the purposes above mentioned.[79]

Despite this shift toward what would become known as economic substantive due process – because the Court seemed to rely on the Fourteenth Amendment's due process clause to protect economic rights – the Court continued to accept that traditional public health regulations (as it understood them) fell within the police power and did not invade liberty.[80] This preferential treatment for public health laws was apparent in the 1889 opinion by Justice Field, one of the *Slaughter-House* dissenters, in *Dent v. West Virginia*.[81] *Dent* challenged a West Virginia law requiring a license to practice medicine. Field accepted that it "is undoubtedly the right of every citizen of the United States to follow any lawful calling, business, or profession he may choose, subject only to such restrictions as are imposed upon all persons of like age, sex and condition."[82] Nevertheless, he explained that "few professions require more careful preparation by one who seeks to enter it than that of medicine," and "due consideration, therefore, for the protection of society may well induce the State to exclude from practice those who have not such a license."[83]

Compagnie Francaise de Navigation a Vapeur v. Louisiana State Board of Health (1902)[84] offers another important – if troubling – example of the Court's acceptance of traditional public health laws during the era of economic substantive due process. In *Compagnie*, the Louisiana Board of Health banned the arrival of immigrants, including healthy immigrants, into areas of the state experiencing outbreaks of infectious disease on the theory that immigrants provided fuel to the contagious fire. In an opinion by Justice Edward Douglass White, Jr., the Court first found that the state had not stepped on Congress's power to regulate commerce because the states' power to "enact and enforce quarantine

---

[79] Allgeyer v. Louisiana, 165 U.S. 578, 589 (1897).

[80] Wendy E. Parmet, *From Slaughter-House to Lochner: The Rise and Fall of the Constitutionalization of Public Health*, 40 AM. J. LEGAL HIST. 476, 495 (1996).

[81] Dent v. West Virginia, 129 U.S. 114 (1889).

[82] *Id.* at 121.

[83] *Id.* at 122–23.

[84] Compagnie Francaise de Navigation a Vapeur v. La. State Bd. of Health, 186 U.S. 380 (1902).

laws for the safety and the protection of the health of their inhabitants" had been recognized by Congress and was "beyond question."[85] White then disposed quickly of the Fourteenth Amendment claim, stating that "in the last analysis it reduces itself to the proposition that the effect of the Fourteenth Amendment was to strip the government, whether state or national, of all power to enact regulations protecting the health and safety of the people."[86] This, White believed, was an absurdity.

State courts and treatise writers agreed. In 1876, the Supreme Judicial Court of Maine explained that "the maxim *salus populi suprema lex* is the law of all courts and countries. The individual right sinks in the necessity to provide for the public good."[87] Likewise, even as treatise writers expounded on the limits to the police power, they insisted that public health laws fell within the police power and were therefore constitutional. Even Thomas Cooley, perhaps the leading advocate of the theory of "constitutional limitations" – which holds that the Constitution limits the police power – conceded that "lives, limbs, health, comfort, and quiet" fell within that power.[88] In 1890, Leroy Parker and Robert H. Worthington went further, arguing in their treatise that the protection of health was both "legitimate and [one of the] most important functions of civil government."[89]

JACOBSON AND *LOCHNER*

In 1905, the Supreme Court decided two cases that came to epitomize its revised approach to the police power. The first, *Jacobson v. Massachusetts*, upheld a Cambridge, Massachusetts, vaccination mandate.[90] In the century-plus that followed, *Jacobson* remained the Court's leading public health law course, which it cited approvingly in

---

[85] *Id.* at 387.
[86] *Id.* at 393.
[87] Haverty v. Bass, 66 Me. 71, 74 (1876).
[88] THOMAS M. COOLEY, A TREATISE ON THE CONSTITUTIONAL LIMITATIONS WHICH REST UPON THE LEGISLATIVE POWER OF THE STATES OF THE AMERICAN UNION 573 (2d ed. 1871).
[89] LEROY PARKER & ROBERT H. WORTHINGTON, THE LAW OF PUBLIC HEALTH AND SAFETY, AND THE POWERS AND DUTIES OF BOARDS OF HEALTH 1 (1892).
[90] Jacobson v. Massachusetts, 197 U.S. 11 (1905).

a wide range of cases.[91] The second case, *Lochner v. New York*, struck a law setting maximum hours for bakery workers.[92] Over time, *Lochner* became synonymous with the dangers of judicial overreach. The distinctions between the Court's treatment of the two cases and their divergent fates are critical to understanding how American courts came to view the courts' role in adjudicating challenges to the police power.

Jacobson arose from a smallpox outbreak that hit the East Coast in the early years of the twentieth century.[93] In response, the Massachusetts legislature empowered local boards of health to require that all residents be vaccinated or pay a $5 fine. Vaccine mandates were not new in 1900. Vaccination had been controversial ever since British physician Edward Jenner had observed in 1796 that when injected under the skin, cowpox serum conferred immunity against smallpox.[94] Many thought that vaccination, as Jenner's technique was called, was unnatural, even ungodly.[95] Critics also claimed that vaccination could be dangerous. At the time, that was true, as the serum used was not sterile and could spread other diseases.[96] Efforts to control smallpox through vaccination also faced another problem: As the practice spread, the risk of contagion declined. As it did so, fear of the ancient scourge diminished, and vaccination began to be viewed as a greater threat than the disease it was designed to prevent.[97]

To ensure widespread vaccination and reduce outbreaks, states employed a variety of techniques that would be familiar to contemporary eyes. In 1810, Massachusetts passed a law requiring every town to appoint a committee to provide low-cost vaccinations.[98] A few years later, Boston became the first city to require that schoolchildren be vaccinated in order to attend public school.[99] In 1855, Massachusetts

---

[91] Daniel Farber, *The Long Shadow of Jacobson v. Massachusetts: Public Health, Fundamental Rights, and the Courts*, 57 SAN DIEGO L. REV. 833, 842 (2020).

[92] Lochner v. New York, 198 U.S. 45 (1905).

[93] MICHAEL WILLRICH, POX: AN AMERICAN HISTORY 2 (2011).

[94] *See* KAREN L. WALLOCH, THE ANTIVACCINE HERESY: JACOBSON V. MASSACHUSETTS AND THE TROUBLED HISTORY OF COMPULSORY VACCINATION IN THE UNITED STATES 13–17 (2015).

[95] WILLRICH, *supra* note 93, at 12–14.

[96] WALLOCH, *supra* note 94, 27–58.

[97] Wendy E. Parmet, *Rediscovering* Jacobson *in the Era of COVID-19*, 100 B.U. L. REV. ONLINE 117, 119 (2020).

[98] WALLOCH, *supra* note 94, at 19.

[99] Parmet, *supra* note 97, at 119.

required that all residents be vaccinated.[100] In the decades that
followed, many other states passed some type of vaccine mandate.[101]

In both the United States and Europe, opposition to such policies was
fierce. With the danger of smallpox diminished, opponents began to view
vaccine mandates as threats to individual liberty. They also began to seek
individual exemptions, envisioning that individuals should be able to opt
out of public health laws.[102] They brought those claims to court, arguing
that liberty extends to control over one's person. That idea was not wholly
new. As the Court explained in *Union Pacific Railway Co. v. Botsford*
(1891), the common law had long protected "the right of every individual
to the possession and control of his own person, free from all restraint
or interference of others, unless by clear and unquestionable authority
of law."[103] But the notion that the Constitution limited the state's ability
to impose laws, like vaccine mandates, that aimed to stem the spread of
contagion was rejected by most courts in the pre–New Deal period.[104]

There were, however, some notable exceptions. Perhaps the most
interesting one arose from San Francisco's efforts to combat plague,
which struck the city's Chinatown in 1900. Health officials, as was
common at the time, viewed the risk through a racialized lens, believing that residents of Chinese descent were especially vulnerable to
the disease and especially likely to spread it. To prevent that, officials
required residents of Chinese origin to be inoculated with an experi-
mental vaccine, known as Kaffkine's prophylactic, prior to leaving the
city. A federal district court enjoined the order, finding that the vaccine was dangerous and that the order was racially based and ill suited
to protect the public's health.[105] The city then established a quarantine around Chinatown that was enforced only against the Chinese
American community. The same court enjoined that order too, ruling
that although the police power was broad, it was the duty of the court
to strike health laws that were unreasonable and discriminatory.[106]

[100] WALLOCH, *supra* note 94, at 6.
[101] *Id.*
[102] STEVEN JOHNSON, EXTRA LIFE: A SHORT HISTORY OF LIVING LONGER 55–57 (2021).
[103] Union Pac. Ry. Co. v. Botsford, 141 U.S. 250, 251 (1891).
[104] *See, e.g.*, Blue v. Beach, 56 N.E. 89 (Ind. 1900); *see also, e.g.*, Viemeister v. White, 72 N.E. 97, 97 (N.Y. 1904); Abeel v. Clark, 24 P. 383 (Cal. 1890).
[105] Wong Wai v. Williamson, 103 F. 1, 8 (N.D. Cal. 1900).
[106] Jew Ho v. Williamson, 103 F. 10, 26 (N.D. Cal. 1900).

Although few courts blocked vaccines laws for being discriminatory, other turn-of-the-century courts emphasized the limits of the police power, even as they upheld vaccine mandates. For example, in 1900 in *Blue v. Beach*, the Indiana Supreme Court upheld a law requiring schoolchildren to be vaccinated "in view of the great public interest."[107] Nevertheless, the court cautioned that such "measures or means must have some relation to the end in view, for, under the guise of the police power, personal rights and those pertaining to private property will not be permitted to be arbitrarily invaded by the legislative department."[108] The court added that judges have the duty "to review such legislation and determine whether it in reality relates to, and is appropriate to secure, the object in view."[109]

In 1904, the New York Court of Appeals applied comparable reasoning in upholding a state law requiring that children be vaccinated in order to attend school. The court stated, "a statute entitled [*sic*] a health law must be a health law in fact as well as in name."[110] Still, the court accepted that "when the sole object and general tendency of the legislation is to promote the public health, there is no invasion of the Constitution, even if the enforcement of the law interferes to some extent with liberty or property."[111]

In *Jacobson*, the Supreme Court adopted a similar stance, extolling the reach and importance of the police power and the state's right to protect the public from disease, but also stressing the limitations on that power. The defendant, Henning Jacobson, was a minister who had emigrated from Sweden. He rejected vaccination as dangerous to his health (he and his son had had adverse experiences with prior vaccinations) and as incompatible with his religious beliefs.[112] With the support of organized antivaccinationists, he and several codefendants resisted when the Cambridge Board of Health demanded that he be vaccinated or pay the $5 fine. To Henning and his codefendants, the mandate violated the rights bestowed by the preamble to

---

[107] Blue v. Beach, 56 N.E. at 92.
[108] *Id.* at 93.
[109] *Id.*
[110] *Viemeister*, 72 N.E. at 97.
[111] *Id.*
[112] Parmet, *supra* note 97, at 121.

the Constitution as well as the Fourteenth Amendment.[113] Despite the religious roots of his objections, he did not raise a First Amendment free exercise claim; in 1905, the Court had yet to rule that the free exercise clause applied to the states. That did not happen until 1940.[114]

By a 7–2 vote, the Court rejected Jacobson's defenses. Harlan's opinion for the Court reflected older conceptions of the police power as well as the newer theory of constitutional limitations. The result was an opinion that both extolled the role of public health laws within the social compact and hinted at the limits of such laws. The opinion also added some critical observations about the role of public health authorities, as well as the importance of judicial deference to expertise.

The Court's decision began with Harlan quickly dismissing Jacobson's claim that the Constitution's preamble gave him any rights – a proposition that courts continue to reject. Harlan then turned to a discussion of the police power, quoting from *Gibbons* that it includes "health laws of every description."[115] He then went on to offer an eloquent testament to the principle of *salus populi*, without ever citing the maxim:

> There are manifold restraints to which every person is necessarily subject for the common good. On any other basis organized society could not exist with safety to its members. … Real liberty for all could not exist under the operation of a principle which recognizes the right of each individual person to use his own, whether in respect of his person or his property, regardless of the injury that may be done to others.[116]

Harking back to the antebellum conception of liberty, Harlan added, "even liberty itself, the greatest of all rights, is not unrestricted license to act according to one's own will. It is only freedom from restraint under conditions essential to the equal enjoyment of the same right by others. It is, then, liberty regulated by law."[117] This, he explained, was the "fundamental principle of the social compact" enshrined in the Massachusetts constitution.[118] Though he did not use the term, he in

[113] *Id.*
[114] *See* Cantwell v. Connecticut, 310 U.S. 296, 303 (1940).
[115] *Jacobson*, 197 U.S. at 25 (quoting Gibbons v. Ogden, 22 U.S. at 203).
[116] *Id.* at 26.
[117] *Id.* at 26–27 (quoting Crowley v. Christensen, 137 U.S. 86, 89–90 (1890)).
[118] *Id.* at 27.

effect claimed that public health laws could enhance what Isaiah Berlin called positive freedom – the liberty that provides individuals with the means to achieve their own goals.[119]

Yet if Harlan understood that laws can enable "real liberty," he also accepted that the Fourteenth Amendment protected a realm of negative liberty that included bodily integrity. He explained, "there is, of course, a sphere within which the individual may assert the supremacy of his own will, and rightfully dispute the authority of any human government, – especially of any free government existing under a written constitution, to interfere with the exercise of that will."[120] He also warned that courts might intervene when police power regulations were "unreasonable, arbitrary, and oppressive, and, therefore, hostile to the inherent right of every freeman to care for his own body and health in such a way as to him seems best."[121] Echoing his own words from *Mugler*, he added that the courts' power to review laws affecting the general welfare are limited to when "a statute purporting to have been enacted to protect the public health, the public morals, or the public safety has no real or substantial relation to those objects, or is, beyond all question, a plain, palpable invasion of rights secured by the fundamental law."[122] In such cases, it would be the Court's "duty" to strike the law and "give effect to the Constitution."[123] Later still, he added that vaccine mandates might be unconstitutional if they were "cruel and inhuman in the last degree" to a particular individual.[124]

By accepting that the Constitution provides some protection for bodily integrity, Harlan anticipated the Court's recognition in the mid-twentieth century of rights to privacy and autonomy.[125] He also foreshadowed the Court's later view that such rights should act as trumps against the police power. But to Harlan, that role remained relatively limited. For him, the question of whether a vaccine mandate was an appropriate response to a smallpox outbreak belonged in the first instance to the legislature, and in the second to the board of health

---

[119] BERLIN, *supra* note 2, at 131–34.
[120] Jacobson, 197 U.S. at 26.
[121] *Id.*
[122] *Id.* at 31 (quoting Mugler v. Kansas, 123 U.S. 623, 661 (1887)).
[123] *Id.*
[124] *Id.* at 38–39.
[125] *See* Chapter 3.

to which the legislature delegated the decision.[126] He explained that
the Court "would usurp the functions of another branch of government
if it adjudged, as a matter of law, that the mode adopted under the
sanction of the state, to protect the people at large was arbitrary, and
not justified by the necessities of the case."[127] Because the efficacy
of vaccination was common knowledge, and vaccine mandates were
commonly employed, he saw no reason to override that deference.[128]

   In a case that was argued the same week that *Jacobson* was decided,
the majority showed no such deference. *Lochner v. New York*[129] concerned a New York law that set maximum hours for bakeshop workers.
The state court found that the law was designed to protect the health
of the workers, who had high rates of respiratory diseases, as well as
the public that consumed the products the bakers prepared.[130] In his
dissent, Harlan found it "plain that this statute was enacted in order
to protect the physical well-being of those who work in bakery and
confectionary establishments."[131] To Harlan, the law easily survived
the framework laid out in *Jacobson*: It was a health law that had a "real
or substantial relation" to its object and was not "beyond all question,
a plain, palpable invasion of rights secured by fundamental law."[132]

   The majority saw matters quite differently. In an opinion by Justice
Rufus W. Peckham, who had dissented without writing an opinion
in *Jacobson*, the Court found that there was "no reasonable foundation" for finding the law "necessary or appropriate as a health law."[133]
Instead, Peckham concluded, the law was a labor regulation that
violated the bakers' liberty to contract to work more than the maximum
hours. In reaching this conclusion, Peckham argued that bakers were
not a unique class that faced special health risks. Nor was the law, in
his view, a public health law. As a result, the state could not violate
the bakers' liberty. Thus, Peckham accepted that the state could limit

[126] *Id.* at 27–28.
[127] *Jacobson*, 197 U.S. at 28.
[128] *Id.* at 30–33.
[129] *Lochner*, 198 U.S. 45 (1905).
[130] People v. Lochner, 177 N.Y. 145, 63 (1904), *rev'd*, 198 U.S. 45 (1905).
[131] *Lochner*, 198 U.S. at 69 (Harlan, J., dissenting).
[132] *Id.* at 68 (citing *Jacobson*, 197 U.S. at 31).
[133] *Id.* at 58.

liberty to protect public health, but he assumed that in order to protect liberty, the Court, rather than the state, should decide which laws were in fact public health laws.

As Justice Oliver Wendell Holmes pointed out in his famous *Lochner* dissent, the majority's belief that it had to keep the police power within tight bounds presupposed that the Constitution protected a particular form of social and economic policy.[134] It also seemed to privilege negative liberty to the detriment of positive liberty. The bakers had the "liberty" to work more than sixty hours per week; they did not have the liberty to work under healthier conditions. Nor did they have the liberty to use their political voice to convince the legislature to enact laws that would improve their working conditions.

The *Lochner* Court thus assumed that to safeguard negative liberty, the Court had to oversee the boundaries of the police power, deciding on its own what laws did and did not qualify as "public health" laws. As a result, a wide array of social and economic legislation became vulnerable to the Court's oversight. These are the attributes that won *Lochner* infamy and led to its rejection during the New Deal. Yet even as that happened, *Jacobson* – with its nod to the even earlier *salus populi* jurisprudence and its recognition that "real liberty" requires public health laws – endured. At least until 2020.

---

[134] *Id.* at 75 (Holmes, J., dissenting).

3 THE END OF *SALUS POPULI*

As many Americans protested against mask mandates and resisted vaccines during the COVID-19 pandemic, others lamented the intense individualism that seemed to overtake the nation.[1] Decisions that affected the health of others – whether to stay home, wear a mask, or be vaccinated – were often framed as matters of individual choice and personal responsibility. In turn, public health orders that constrained such choices were derided as violations of individual liberty. Republican member of Congress Marjorie Taylor Greene was among those who expressed this sentiment, tweeting that "vaccine mandates and passports violate individual freedoms."[2]

Following the Supreme Court's decision in *Roman Catholic Diocese v. Cuomo*, many courts appeared to share Greene's perspective. So, too, did many state legislatures, which rushed to limit the ability of governors and health officials to issue public health orders.[3] Florida governor Ron DeSantis, a prominent opponent of public health measures, issued an executive order "ensuring parents' freedom

---

[1] *E.g.*, Scott Burris, *Individual Liberty, Public Health, and the Battle for the Nation's Soul*, REGUL. REV. (June 7, 2021), www.theregreview.org/2021/06/07/burris-individual-liberty-public-health-battle-for-nations-soul; Paul Krugman, *The Cult of Selfishness Is Killing America*, N.Y. TIMES (July 27, 2020), www.nytimes.com/2020/07/27/opinion/us-republicans-coronavirus.html.

[2] Jessica Levinson, *What Marjorie Taylor Greene's Covid Tweet Gets Very, Very Wrong*, MSNBC (Aug. 10, 2021), www.msnbc.com/opinion/what-marjorie-taylor-greene-s-covid-tweet-gets-very-very-n1276424.

[3] NETWORK FOR PUB. HEALTH L. & NAT'L ASS'N OF CNTY. & CITY HEALTH OFF., PROPOSED LIMITS ON PUBLIC HEALTH AUTHORITY: DANGEROUS FOR PUBLIC HEALTH 5 (May 2021), www.naccho.org/uploads/downloadable-resources/Proposed-Limits-on-Public-Health-Authority-Dangerous-for-Public-Health-FINAL-5.24.21pm.pdf.

to choose" by barring mask mandates in public schools.[4] Even as the delta variant overwhelmed hospitals in the summer of 2021, DeSantis exclaimed: "We can either have a free society or we can have a bio-medical security state and I can tell you, Florida, we're a free state."[5]

In this environment, public health advocates often felt nostalgic for *Jacobson v. Massachusetts* and the constitutional law it represented.[6] Justice John Marshall Harlan's opinion stands for judicial deference to public health officials and the recognition that "real liberty" requires public health protection as well as individual choice. The rejection of that rich conception of liberty in favor of one that understands liberty as only encompassing an individual's unfettered right to exercise their own choices – regardless of the consequences to others – proved fatal during the pandemic. In the face of contagion, individuals cannot truly be free unless others consider the social impact of their actions.

THE MISUSE OF THE POLICE POWER

Despite its more nuanced conception of liberty, we should shed any rose-colored glasses before rushing to embrace *Jacobson* and the jurisprudence of its era. Although courts in the nineteenth and early twentieth centuries proclaimed respect for the common good[7] as well as the public's health, values that were often missing during the pandemic, the jurisprudence they employed condoned slavery and sanctioned Jim Crow.[8] It also affirmed laws and policies that oppressed Native Americans, immigrants, and women.[9] *Salus populi* may have been *suprema lex*, but many groups were excluded from the *populi*.

---

[4] Press Release, Office of the Governor, Governor DeSantis Issues and Executive Order Ensuring Parents' Freedom to Choose (July 30, 2021), www.flgov.com/2021/07/30/governor-desantis-issues-an-executive-order-ensuring-parents-freedom-to-choose.

[5] Fenit Nirappil et al., *DeSantis Criticizes Masks, Restrictions as Coronavirus Roars to Record Levels in Florida*, WASH. POST (Aug. 6, 2021), www.washingtonpost.com/health/2021/08/06/desantis-florida-coronavirus-surge.

[6] Jacobson v. Massachusetts, 197 U.S. 11 (1905); *see* Chapter 2.

[7] *See* ADRIAN VERMEULE, COMMON GOOD CONSTITUTIONALISM 52–90 (2022).

[8] *E.g.*, Plessy v. Ferguson, 163 U.S. 537, 544 (1896); Dred Scott v. Sandford, 60 U.S. 393, 406 (1857); *see* Johnathan Fabian Witt, *The Law of Salus Populi: Epidemics and the Law*, YALE REV. (Mar. 30, 2020), https://yalereview.org/article/law-salus-populi.

[9] *E.g.*, Lone Wolf v. Hitchcock, 187 U.S. 553, 564–68 (1903).

In addition, as *Lochner* illustrates,[10] by the early twentieth century, the Court applied a narrow conception of public health, accepting only some laws, such as vaccine mandates, as public health measures that fell within the police power, while holding that other laws, such as maximum hours laws, were outside of the police power and thus unconstitutional. The Court also assumed that courts had the job of ensuring that laws that states claimed were health laws really were health laws and not labor or economic laws.[11] Thus, even as courts continued to uphold traditional communicable disease laws, many other laws that addressed the social conditions that influence health – what today are termed the social determinants of health (SDOH)[12] – were held unconstitutional. As a result, even when courts accepted that *salus populi* was the highest law, they issued rulings that could undermine health.

Health officials likewise instituted many measures that harmed health and magnified health inequities. All too often, officials viewed racial minorities, immigrants, and other vulnerable populations as threats to the public's health rather than as part of the *populi* they were charged with serving. While some early public health researchers, such as Edwin Chadwick and Lemuel Shattuck, documented the role that poverty, overcrowding, and poor social conditions play in harming health, they viewed poverty as a sign of moral failing.[13] Other experts gave even less thought to social conditions; they simply treated poor and minority populations as vectors of contagion to be controlled.

Examples of oppressive and discriminatory applications of public health laws abound. In the late nineteenth century, health authorities in San Francisco repeatedly used public health protection to rationalize restricting the rights and opportunities of Asian immigrants, who were thought to carry disease.[14] In the early twentieth century, Los

[10] Lochner v. New York, 198 U.S. 45 (1905).
[11] *E.g.*, Adair v. United States, 208 U.S. 161, 174–79 (1908); Adkins v. Child. Hosp., 261 U.S. 525, 558–59 (1923).
[12] *See* Chapter 6.
[13] JOHN FABIAN WITT, AMERICAN CONTAGIONS: EPIDEMICS AND THE LAW FROM SMALLPOX TO COVID-19, 30–31 (2020).
[14] GEOFF MANAUGH & NICOLA TWILLEY, UNTIL PROVEN SAFE: THE HISTORY AND FUTURE OF QUARANTINE 131–32 (2021); NAYAN SHAH, CONTAGIOUS DIVIDES: EPIDEMICS AND RACE IN SAN FRANCISCO'S CHINATOWN 45–76, 120–57 (2001).

Angeles officials directed their efforts against plague at that city's so-called Mexican quarter.[15] In New York, officials targeted Russian Jewish immigrants to prevent the spread of typhus.[16] When the smallpox epidemic that prompted the mandate in *Jacobson* erupted in 1900, officials in Boston forcibly vaccinated African Americans, immigrants, and laborers.[17] Respect for the needs and health of such populations was rare.

This disregard for the health and interests of communities of color was especially evident in the infamous *Tuskegee Study of Untreated Syphilis in the Negro Male*,[18] which the US Public Health Service launched in 1932. The study followed the course of syphilis in Black men – without obtaining their informed consent or offering them effective treatments – even after antibiotics became available. While the Tuskegee study is the best known example, it is hardly the only public health or medical study that failed to respect the dignity or health of people of color.[19]

The unequal hammer of public health laws also fell heavily on poor women and sex workers. During and after World War I, under the unfortunately coined "American Plan," officials rounded up and detained women who were thought to be sex workers or who had failed to conform to traditional sexual mores, lest they spread sexually transmitted diseases.[20] Later, many jurisdictions enacted statutes that allowed police and health authorities to forcibly detain and treat women who were suspected of sex work.[21] Courts generally upheld these laws, ruling that if a woman was a sex worker, officials could reasonably conclude that she threatened the public's health.[22] Men were almost never subject to such laws.

[15] POLLY J. PRICE, PLAGUES IN THE NATION: HOW EPIDEMICS SHAPED AMERICA 52 (2022).
[16] HOWARD MARKEL, QUARANTINE! EAST EUROPEAN JEWISH IMMIGRANTS AND THE NEW YORK CITY EPIDEMICS OF 1892, 76–77 (1997).
[17] Wendy E. Parmet, Richard A. Goodman, & Amy Farber, *Individual Rights versus the Public's Health – 100 Years after Jacobson v. Massachusetts*, 352 N. ENG. J. MED. 652, 653 (2005).
[18] *The U.S. Public Health Service Syphilis Study at Tuskegee*, CTRS. FOR DISEASE CONTROL & PREVENTION (Apr. 22, 2021), www.cdc.gov/tuskegee/timeline.htm.
[19] *E.g.*, HARRIET A. WASHINGTON, MEDICAL APARTHEID: THE DARK HISTORY OF MEDICAL EXPERIMENTATION ON BLACK AMERICANS FROM COLONIAL TIMES TO THE PRESENT (2006).
[20] MANAUGH & TWILLEY, *supra* note 14, at 132–35; ALLAN M. BRANDT, NO MAGIC BULLET: A SOCIAL HISTORY OF VENEREAL DISEASE IN THE UNITED STATES SINCE 1880 84–92 (1985).
[21] Wendy E. Parmet, *AIDS and Quarantine: The Revival of an Archaic Doctrine*, 14 HOFSTRA L. REV. 53, 66–68 (1985).
[22] *Id.*

The Supreme Court's police power decisions also reflected the prejudices of their day. For example, in 1884 in *Barbier v. Connolly*,[23] the Court rejected a challenge to a San Francisco ordinance that was clearly aimed at the Chinese community and barred public laundries from washing or ironing clothes overnight. Rejecting the challenge, Justice Stephen Field, who had insisted in the 1873 *Slaughter-House Cases* that individuals had a constitutional right to pursue their vocation, saw no problem.[24] Two years later, however, in *Yick Wo v. Hopkins*, the Court showed the limit of its tolerance of San Francisco's anti-Chinese health legislation, ruling that the city violated the Constitution by applying another laundry ordinance "with an evil eye and unequal hand."[25]

The Court, however, rarely spotted that "evil eye" or "unequal hand." In 1896 in *Plessy v. Ferguson*, it upheld a Louisiana law requiring racial segregation in railroad cars.[26] Although that infamous opinion did not treat the Jim Crow law as a health law, the Court ruled that the maintenance of racial segregation and white supremacy fit squarely within the police power, granting that power a capaciousness it failed to see in *Lochner*.[27]

Jacobson itself served as authority for another of the Court's most disturbing cases, *Buck v. Bell* (1927).[28] That case affirmed the involuntary sterilization of Carrie Buck, a poor young woman who was committed to a state institution in Virginia for the "feeble-minded" after giving birth while unmarried. In a test case, the state sought to sterilize her using a statute that allowed for the involuntary sterilization of someone who was committed and was "insane, idiotic, feeble-minded, or epileptic, and by the laws of hereditary is the probably [*sic*] potential parent of socially inadequate offspring likewise afflicted."[29] In a brief, acerbic opinion by

[23] Barbier v. Connolly, 113 U.S. 27, 32 (1885).
[24] *Id.*
[25] Yick Wo v. Hopkins, 118 U.S. 356, 373–74 (1886). *See also* David E. Bernstein, Lochner, *Parity, and the Chinese Laundry Cases*, 41 Wm. & Mary L. Rev. 211, 249 (1999).
[26] *Plessy*, 163 U.S. at 540.
[27] *E.g.*, *Lochner*, 198 U.S. 45 (striking maximum hours for bakers); *Adkins*, 261 U.S. 525 (striking minimum wage for women); *but see* Muller v. Oregon, 208 U.S. 412 (1908) (upholding maximum hours law for women).
[28] Buck v. Bell, 274 U.S. 200 (1927).
[29] Paul A. Lombardo, Three Generations, No Imbeciles: Eugenics, the Supreme Court, and *Buck v. Bell* 99 (2010).

Justice Oliver Wendell Holmes, the Court permitted the sterilization. Citing only *Jacobson*, Holmes wrote, "The principle that sustains compulsory vaccination is broad enough to cover cutting the Fallopian tubes. ... Three generations of imbeciles are enough."[30]

As legal historian Paul Lombardo has recounted, the involuntary sterilization laws upheld in *Buck* helped inspire the Nazis' eugenics measures.[31] Revulsion against those policies, in turn, aroused opposition to involuntary sterilization and helped pave the way for the recognition of the rights of patients and human subjects in biomedical research.[32] The backlash also precipitated a new appreciation for the judicial protection for individual autonomy with respect to reproduction and health. Still, this appreciation often failed to protect vulnerable populations who continue to be scapegoated for diseases, as both Asian Americans and immigrants on the southern border were during the COVID-19 pandemic.[33]

THE REJECTION OF THE POLICE POWER JURISPRUDENCE

Even before 2020, the police power jurisprudence that had privileged public health protection during the first 150 years of the Constitution had eroded. As the twentieth century progressed, courts cited *salus populi* less and less frequently.[34] They also increasingly limited the police power by protecting certain individual rights, including rights to free speech, reproductive autonomy, religious liberty, and gun ownership. As courts did so, the recognition of *salus populi* and the interdependency of positive and negative rights that *Jacobson* propounded was lost, replaced by an approach that treated numerous negative rights as establishing strong "trumps" that can block governmental actions.

---

[30] 274 U.S. at 207 (citation omitted).

[31] LOMBARDO, *supra* note 29, at 199–218.

[32] *Id.* at 240–41.

[33] *See* Wendy E. Parmet, *Immigration Law's Adverse Impact on COVID-19*, in ASSESSING LEGAL RESPONSES TO COVID-19, 240–46 (Scott Burris et al. eds., 2020), https://static1.squarespace.com/static/5956e16e6b8f5b8c45f1c216/t/5f4d6578225705285562d0f0/1598908033901/COVID19PolicyPlaybook_Aug2020+Full.pdf.

[34] Based on search for "*salus populi*" in all cases in the LexisNexis database as of Aug. 8, 2021.

Initially, the Supreme Court's rejection of its police power jurisprudence stemmed less from a solicitude for individual rights than concern about the impact of that jurisprudence, as it had evolved in the decades since Reconstruction, on social and economic legislation.[35] As Holmes explained in his *Lochner* dissent, the Court had come to view the Constitution as demanding a particular "economic theory,"[36] one that precluded regulation of the market or the redistribution of wealth. As a result, legislatures and, by extension, voters had relatively little ability to redress many of the nation's most pressing problems, even though communicable disease laws were usually upheld.

By the Great Depression, the Court's approach to congressional authority and the police power became increasingly untenable. After the Court issued several decisions that threatened key parts of the New Deal agenda, including the National Industrial Recovery Act[37] and the Agricultural Adjustment Act,[38] President Franklin D. Roosevelt proposed a "court-packing plan" that would have permitted him to appoint six new justices.[39] Although the plan provoked outrage and was never enacted, it appeared to do the trick: Justice Owen Roberts changed his tune and began to join the more progressive members of the Court in upholding New Deal laws.[40] That "switch in time … saved nine," by reducing support for Roosevelt's Court-packing plan.[41] It also ended the long reign of the police power jurisprudence. In its place was a new approach in which a law's relationship to public health was less central.

Initially, the change posed little threat to traditional public health laws. To the contrary, the Court's new approach seemed to echo Harlan's insistence in *Jacobson* that liberty consisted not only in freedom from law but also in the health and safety that only law can provide.

---

[35] For a discussion of Progressive Era critiques of *Lochner*, see MORTON HORWITZ, THE TRANSFORMATION OF AMERICAN LAW, 1870–1960: THE CRISIS OF LEGAL ORTHODOXY 7–261 (1993).

[36] *Lochner*, 198 U.S. at 75 (Holmes, J., dissenting).

[37] A.L.A. Schechter Poultry Corp. v. United States, 295 U.S. 495, 549–51 (1935).

[38] United States v. Butler, 297 U.S. 1, 77–78 (1936).

[39] William E. Leuchtenburg, *The Origins of Franklin D. Roosevelt's "Court-Packing" Plan*, 1966 SUP. CT. REV. 347, 357–61, 365–67 (1966).

[40] John Q. Barrett, *Attribution Time: Cal Tinney's 1937 Quip, "A Switch in Time'll Save the Nine,"* 73 OKLA. L. REV. 229, 232–33 (2021).

[41] *Id.* at 230.

For example, in 1937, while rejecting a challenge to a minimum wage law for women, the Court explained, "In prohibiting [the deprivation of liberty] the Constitution does not recognize an absolute and uncontrollable liberty. Liberty in each of its phases has its history and connotation. But the liberty safeguarded is liberty in a social organization which requires the protection of law against the evils which menace the health, safety, morals, and welfare of the people."[42] Thus, the New Deal Court seemed to embrace *Jacobson*'s appreciation of positive liberty, even as it dispensed with the police power jurisprudence in which public health had played a privileged role.

Indeed, by giving the federal government and the states greater latitude to regulate the economy and redistribute wealth, the New Deal Court may have provided far more robust support for public health than did the earlier police power jurisprudence. Although the pre–New Deal Court gave special weight and importance to public health protection, upholding laws that aimed to protect public health even as it quashed other social and economic laws, the Court's narrow conception of public health impeded states' ability to tackle social and economic conditions that threaten health.[43] Thus, early twentieth-century courts permitted states to detain and forcibly treat people who were exposed to a communicable disease, but they made it hard for states to protect communities from the substandard housing or unsafe working conditions that can allow disease to spread. Clinging to a quarantinist conception of public health, the pre–New Deal Court was willing to accept limits on the liberty of individuals who were thought to be potentially contagious; it was far less tolerant of laws that sought to alter the social conditions in which contagion flourishes.

In contrast, by upholding a wide range of social and economic legislation, such as minimum wage laws, the New Deal Court allowed for a broader conception of liberty and more effective public health measures. Indeed, many laws that were accepted as constitutional only due to the New Deal Court's changed approach to the police power – including occupational safety laws, minimum wage laws, and tobacco regulations, to name just a few – have been credited by health

---

[42] W. Coast Hotel Co. v. Parrish, 300 U.S. 379, 391 (1937).
[43] *See* Chapter 6.

experts as contributing to the dramatic rise in life expectancy that took place during the twentieth century.[44]

The New Deal Court also valued the positive liberty of *self-governance*.[45] This is the freedom that inspired the American Revolution, the suffragettes, and the battle for voting rights for Black Americans – the liberty that comes from having a voice in how you are governed and, through that voice, the ability to influence the world in which you live. Importantly, some of our negative rights, including freedom of speech, are often said to merit protection precisely because of their relationship to self-governance.[46] Free speech allows people to learn about and express their views about public policies and political candidates.

But self-governance requires more than the ability to speak or even to vote. It demands that political action can be meaningful so that elected officials have the leeway to enact measures that redress voters' concerns and reflect their policy preferences. When courts, in the name of protecting negative liberties, limit the police power (or the scope of congressional power under Article I), they shrink self-governance, rendering voters' participation in democracy trivial. By granting the same wide deference to social and economic legislation that the Court previously accorded communicable disease laws, the New Deal Court helped safeguard self-governance, even as it offered less protection for some negative liberties, such as the liberty to run a business without regulation.

THE RETURN OF NEGATIVE RIGHTS

As the Court was changing its approach to reviewing public health laws, the nature of the health threats facing Americans also changed. Even before the New Deal, an epidemiological transition had

[44] *Ten Great Public Health Achievements – United States, 1900–1999*, CTRS. FOR DISEASE CONTROL & PREVENTION, www.cdc.gov/mmwr/preview/mmwrhtml/00056796.htm (last visited Apr. 15, 2022).

[45] Wendy E. Parmet, *Paternalism, Self-Governance, and Public Health: The Case of E-Cigarettes*, 70 U. MIA. L. REV. 879, 907–10 (2016); Robert Post, *Participatory Democracy and Free Speech*, 97 VA. L. REV. 477, 482 (2011).

[46] Post, *supra* note 45, at 482.

occurred in the United States and other industrialized nations.[47] With the great exception of the 1918 influenza pandemic, infectious diseases were killing fewer Americans, thanks to a range of public health measures – such as the provision of clean water and the pasteurization of milk – as well as the development of new vaccines and, ultimately, antibiotics. By the middle of the twentieth century, noncommunicable diseases replaced infectious diseases as the leading source of death in the United States, prompting Surgeon General William H. Stewart to boast in 1969 that it was time to "close the book on infectious diseases."[48]

As first HIV/AIDS and then COVID-19 would show, such triumphalism was misplaced. It nevertheless reflected an important empirical fact: Following the 1918 influenza pandemic, Americans no longer experienced the frequent deadly epidemics that had once been ubiquitous, and which had helped undergird their easy acceptance of communicable disease laws. In a world in which contagion is less common and antibiotics are available to cure many infections, the idea that one's own liberty depends on the health of others is less apparent.

So, too, as the toll inflicted by infectious diseases declined, noncommunicable diseases including heart disease, cancer, diabetes, and substance use disorders, along with motor vehicular accidents, became responsible for an increasing share of mortality in the United States. These new scourges demanded new legal tools, such as bans on cigarette advertising and seat-belt laws. Those new tools, in turn, raised new threats to negative liberty, even as the risks they addressed were more easily categorized as individual in nature.

The challenge the courts face in this changing environment is how to limit judicial decision-making so as to safeguard the positive liberties of health and self-governance without deferring so broadly as to unduly threaten negative liberty. Much constitutional theorizing has tried to solve that conundrum. For the last several decades,

---

[47] Robert E. McKeown, *The Epidemiological Transition: Changing Patterns of Mortality and Population Dynamics*, 3 AM. J. LIFESTYLE MED. 19S, 22S–25S (2009).
[48] FRANK M. SNOWDEN, EPIDEMICS AND SOCIETY: FROM THE BLACK DEATH TO THE PRESENT 451–52 (2020).

conservative proponents of originalism have claimed to resolve it by demanding that judges construe the Constitution in accordance with its original public meaning.[49] In contrast, some progressives seek to resolve it by promoting court reform or arguing that the Constitution should be interpreted as a "living" document whose meaning evolves over time.[50]

We will return to this challenge, which lies at the heart of American constitutionalism, in later chapters. For now, two points are critical. First, the Court never overruled *Jacobson* or, until 2020, backed away from its deferential stance toward traditional communicable disease laws. Indeed, even as the Court disowned most of the *Lochner* era's police power jurisprudence, it continued to cite *Jacobson* approvingly, signaling not only its acceptance of vaccine mandates but also the recognition that broad deference may be especially appropriate when the public's health is on the line.[51]

Second, through what is sometimes called "the New Deal settlement," the Court attempted to develop a doctrinal framework for constitutional decision-making that promised to constrain courts by demanding broad deference in most cases, while requiring stringent review in a limited subset of cases. In effect, the Court would respect positive liberty by acceding to the will of the elected branches and permitting legislation that promotes health and safety in the run-of-the-mill case, while providing robust judicial review in the service of a limited set of claims.

---

[49] *E.g.*, RANDY E. BARNETT, RESTORING THE LOST CONSTITUTION: THE PRESUMPTION OF LIBERTY 91 (2d ed. 2013); William Baude, *Originalism as a Constraint on Judges*, 84 U. CHI. L. REV. 2213, 2213–14 (2017); Lawrence B. Solon, *Originalist Methodology*, 84 UNIV. CHI. L. REV. 269, 270 (2017); Frank H. Easterbrook, *Textualism and the Dead Hand*, 66 GEO. WASH. L. REV. 1119, 1121–22 (1998).

[50] Daniel Epps & Ganesh Sitaraman, *The Future of Court Reform*, 134 HARV. L. REV. F. 398, 400–1 (2021); Charlie Savage, *Experts Debate Reducing the Supreme Court's Power to Strike Down Laws*, N.Y. TIMES (June 30, 2021), www.nytimes.com/2021/06/30/us/politics/supreme-court-commission.html (discussing the Presidential Commission on Court Reform); Calvin TerBeek, *The Search for an Anchor: Living Constitutionalism from the Progressives to Trump*, 46 L. SOC. INQ. 860, 861–63 (2021).

[51] *E.g.*, Prince v. Massachusetts, 321 U.S. 158, 166–67 (1944) ("The right to practice religion freely does not include liberty to expose the community or the child to communicable disease or the latter to ill health or death."). For a discussion of the Court's citations to *Jacobson*, see Daniel Farber, *The Long Shadow of* Jacobson v. Massachusetts*: Public Health, Fundamental Rights, and the Courts*, 57 SAN DIEGO L. REV. 833, 841–47 (2020).

The framework is often associated with footnote 4 in *United States v. Carolene Products* (1938).[52] That case concerned a federal law that banned the interstate shipment of "filled milk," a product that combined skim milk with other fats or oils. Under the Court's post–"switch-in-time" approach, this was an easy case. The question whether the law was "really" a public health law and thus not a regulation of commerce or a violation of due process was beside the point. All that mattered was that Congress, in its wisdom or folly, enacted the regulation. Self-governance, presenting as majoritarianism, should prevail.

In an opinion by Justice Harlan F. Stone, the Court analyzed the case in just that way. Stone began by citing *Gibbons v. Ogden* and noting that Congress's power over interstate commerce was "complete in itself."[53] He then dismissed the filled milk maker's due process claim, explaining that legislation should receive a presumption of constitutionality.[54] In a later case, *Williamson v. Lee Optical* (1955), the Court offered even greater deference, stating that "it is enough that there is an evil at hand for correction, and that it might be thought that the particular legislative measure was a rational way to correct it."[55] In other words, the state did not have to prove that the legislature actually relied on the justification that was offered to the court to establish the basis for the law; if the court could think of a legally permissible end that the law might serve, then the law would be found constitutional.

Despite granting such broad deference, the New Deal Court was careful not to relinquish its power of judicial review. In *Carolene Products*, for example, Stone stated that a statute would violate the due process clause if the legislature lacked a rational basis for enacting it.[56] By holding on to that power, the Court forced lawmakers (or at least the lawyers who defended the government's action in court)

---

[52] United States v. Carolene Prods. Co., 304 U.S. 144, 152 n.4 (1938); JOHN HART ELY, DEMOCRACY AND DISTRUST: A THEORY OF JUDICIAL REVIEW 75–104 (1980). For a different interpretation of the settlement, see Laura Weinrib, *Breaking the Cycle: Rot and Recrudescence in American Constitutional History*, 101 BOST. U. L. REV. 1857 (2021), www.bu.edu/bulawreview/files/2021/10/WEINRIB.pdf.

[53] *Carolene Prods.*, 304 U.S. at 147 (quoting Gibbons v. Ogden, 22 U.S. 1, 196 (1824)).

[54] *Id.*

[55] Williamson v. Lee Optical, Inc., 348 U.S. 483, 488 (1955).

[56] *Id.* at 153. Stone was discussing the due process clause of the Fifth Amendment but made clear that the same analysis would apply if the due process clause of the Fourteenth Amendment were at issue. *Id.* at 148.

to articulate the goal that the law was rationally designed to achieve. The common good remained relevant, even if much less central to the court's analysis.

More interesting, however, were Stone's musings in *Carolene Products* footnote 4 regarding the circumstances in which the Court might dispense with the presumption of constitutionality. According to Stone, the presumption might not apply when a law appears "on its face" to contravene "a specific prohibition of the Constitution, such as those of the first ten amendments," when it interferes with political processes, or when it aims at "discrete and insular minorities."[57]

With that, Stone proposed a solution to the question of how to defer to majoritarian decisions while protecting some negative rights and the interests of vulnerable populations. The Court would cast aside the presumption of constitutionality when laws violate the rights that are specifically enumerated in the Constitution (such as freedom of speech), discriminate against "discrete and insular minorities," or undermine the democratic process itself. As constitutional law scholar John Hart Ely explained in his influential book, *Democracy and Distrust,* this approach allowed the Court to respect the majority's will in most cases while also protecting the democratic process so that the laws that are enacted usually reflect that will.[58]

If the new framework was designed to solve the so-called counter-majoritarian dilemma that arises when an unelected court invalidates the actions of the political branches while protecting certain rights and vulnerable groups, it did not succeed. The most telling example is *Korematsu v. United States* (1944), which upheld the internment of Japanese Americans during World War II.[59] Decided just a few years after *Carolene Products*, *Korematsu* followed it in proclaiming that laws that "curtail the civil rights of a single racial group are immediately suspect" and should receive "the most rigid scrutiny"[60] – what we now call "strict scrutiny." The Court nevertheless relied on the flimsiest of evidence to uphold the racially based internment. In the face of war and racial animus, strict scrutiny proved to be anything but.

---

[57] 304 U.S. at 153 n.4.
[58] ELY, *supra* note 52, *passim.*
[59] Korematsu v. United States, 323 U.S. 214, 223–24 (1944).
[60] *Id.* at 216.

Despite its failure in *Korematsu* to apply exacting scrutiny even while insisting upon it, the Court continued to endorse and develop its new framework. Today, all law students learn about the three tiers of scrutiny. To greatly oversimplify, at the bottom tier, where judicial review is the most deferential, is the "rational basis test" that the Court applied in *Carolene Products* and *Williamson v. Lee Optical.* This test grants laws a presumption of constitutionality. It applies whenever the claimant fails to convince the court that a law has discriminated against a "suspect class," such as a racial or religious group, or has violated a right that the Supreme Court deems fundamental. When rational basis review is applied, the Court asks only whether the law is rationally related to a legitimate state interest. Health is such an interest, but so are many other state goals. Indeed, as *Williamson v. Lee Optical* showed, even hypothetical goals will usually suffice. In most cases, a court applying the rational basis test will find the law constitutional.

The middle tier is called "intermediate scrutiny." Here, the reviewing court is supposed to ask whether the contested law is substantially related to an important state interest.[61] For many years, the Court applied this standard to gender discrimination claims,[62] but it has also used the test in several other types of equal protection claims. In addition, as we'll see in Chapter 8, the Court has applied variants of the intermediate scrutiny test in First Amendment commercial speech cases. What is critical for now is that the test appears to grant a reviewing court far greater latitude than does the rational basis test. A court applying intermediate scrutiny can uphold or strike a challenged law depending on the facts. In that sense, intermediate scrutiny bears more than a passing resemblance to the pre–New Deal reasonableness analysis used in pre–New Deal police power cases such as *Jacobson*.

Finally, there is "strict scrutiny," the most exacting standard. Initially, it applied when laws discriminated against "suspect classes" (i.e., racial, ethnic, or religious groups) or infringed on rights that were enumerated in the Constitution. Over time, the Court also applied it or some lesser form of heightened scrutiny to some other rights, such as the right to privacy, which it deemed fundamental.

---

[61] *E.g.*, Craig v. Boren, 429 U.S. 190, 197 (1976).

[62] *Id.* Today, the Court requires an "exceedingly persuasive justification" to justify gender-based classifications. United States v. Va. Mil. Inst., 518 U.S. 515, 531 (1996).

When strict scrutiny is applied, the state generally has to show that the challenged law is the least restrictive means of achieving a compelling state interest. In theory, a state interest has to be more pressing to be "compelling" than to be "important," as used in intermediate scrutiny, or simply "legitimate," as applied under the rational basis test. However, the Court has failed to offer much insight as to what makes a law compelling. Traditionally, it has considered the protection of health and safety to qualify as such, but as we shall see, some of the justices have questioned whether mitigating a pandemic is always a compelling state interest.[63]

Although courts do not always strike laws that are subject to strict scrutiny,[64] few state or federal laws survive this standard of review, which led legal scholar Gerald Gunther to comment that strict scrutiny is "'strict' in theory and 'fatal' in fact."[65] Indeed, many constitutional controversies today center on whether the infringement of certain rights – such as same-sex marriage, gun ownership, or compelled commercial speech – trigger strict scrutiny.

Over time, the justices have offered different approaches and theories for answering those questions. They have also developed discrete subtests for different favored rights. Thus, despite the theoretical ubiquity of strict scrutiny, the analysis applied in free speech claims differs in important ways from that used in religious liberty cases. In addition, the Court has developed a rich (if not wholly coherent) framework for analyzing procedural due process rights that are implicated when states deprive individuals of their liberty interests or property.[66] In effect, each "right" against governmental action has its own complex (if not baroque) doctrine, which each jurist and scholar can defend or criticize according to their own preferred theory of interpretation.

These doctrinal particularities and interpretative debates need not detain us. What is important here is that regardless of the specific doctrine at issue and the interpretative approach applied, contemporary constitutional law relies on a critical shift from the approaches that the Court in the age of *salus populi* and during the New Deal.

---

[63] *E.g.*, Does 1–3 v. Mills, 142 S. Ct. 17, 20 (2021) (Gorsuch, J., dissenting).

[64] Adam Winkler, *Fatal in Theory and Strict in Fact: An Empirical Analysis of Strict Scrutiny in the Federal Courts*, 59 VAND. L. REV. 793, 8-8-09 (2006).

[65] Gerald Gunther, *Foreword: In Search of Evolving Doctrine on a Changing Court – A Model for a Newer Equal Protection*, 86 HARV. L. REV. 1, 8 (1972).

[66] *E.g.*, Mathews v. Eldridge, 424 U.S. 319 (1976).

Recall that under the pre–New Deal police power doctrine, the key issue was whether the state's purported goal was within the police power. When it was, *salus populi* was *suprema lex*. To be sure, as the doctrine of constitutional limitations took hold in the latter half of the nineteenth century, the Court insisted that a state law be reasonably related to an accepted (by the Court) police power goal. But that limitation was designed to ensure that the state's goals were not pretextual. The nature of the state's goal rather than the individual right remained critical.

In contrast, the New Deal Court dispensed with the notion that the police power included a limited set of goals. Returning to the earlier, antebellum approach, it viewed the states' police power as capacious. Likewise, allowing for a more activist federal government, the Court granted broad deference to Congress when it enacted regulations under the Constitution's commerce clause.[67] Thus, most federal and state laws were granted a presumption of constitutionality. At least initially, the exceptions to that presumption required by *Carolene Products* footnote 4 were few and far between.

Since then, the justices have enlarged the set of rights protected by strict scrutiny to the potential detriment of the positive liberties of self-governance and health. The shift began as liberal justices during the Warren and Burger Courts in the middle of the twentieth century developed and expanded on the right to privacy, an un-enumerated right that the Court initially claimed, while finding a right for married couples to use contraceptives, derived from "penumbras, formed by emanations from" the rights declared in the Bill of Rights.[68] Later, the Court held that the right to privacy (protected by the due process clauses of the Fifth and Fourteenth Amendments) extended to a woman's right to a previability abortion, as well as a competent individual's right to choose whether to end medical treatment.[69]

---

[67] United States v. Darby, 312 U.S. 100, 114–16 (1941); United States v. Carolene Prods. Co., 304 U.S. 144, 147–148 (1938).

[68] Griswold v. Connecticut, 381 U.S. 479, 484 (1965).

[69] Cruzan v. Dir., Mo. Dep't of Health, 497 U.S. 261, 287 (1989) (O'Connor, J., concurring) (right of competent individual to decline end-of-life care); Roe v. Wade, 410 U.S. 113 (1973) (right to abortion). As this book was in press, the Court overruled *Roe*, leaving the fate of constitutional protections for privacy uncertain. *See* Dobbs v. Jackson Women's Health Org., 142 S. Ct. 2228, 2301 (2022) (Thomas J., concurring); 142 S. Ct. 2229, 2319 (Breyer, J., Sotomayor, J., and Kagan, J., dissenting); chapter 10.

Notably, these cases limited the state's ability to override individual autonomy with respect to health, and helped to usher in a "patients' rights" revolution in which patients argued that they had a constitutional "right" to determine different aspects of their health care. Although courts have rejected some of these claims, these cases helped to undergird the notion, expressed frequently during the COVID-19 pandemic, that individuals have a "right" to choose what happens to their body.[70]

More recently, a far more conservative Court has emphasized a very different set of individual rights. In *District of Columbia v. Heller* (2008), for example, the Court declared that the Second Amendment established an individual right to own and carry firearms.[71] Further, as later chapters discuss, the Supreme Court has expanded the reach of the First Amendment's free speech clause in ways that make it increasingly difficult for governments to regulate campaign donations[72] or require health-related warnings.[73] Indeed, the Court's aggressive application of the free speech clause has led progressive scholars to claim that the Court's current First Amendment jurisprudence smacks of *Lochner*.[74] In making that analogy, they note that as in the *Lochner* era, the Court now appears to be imposing a deregulatory agenda.

There is a critical contrast, however, between the jurisprudence of the *Lochner* (and *Jacobson*) era and both the liberal Court's right to privacy cases and the more conservative Court's free speech cases. As noted above, before the New Deal, the nature of the state's goal, as the Court perceived it, was paramount. Since then, the nature of the individual's interest, rather than the state's goals, has become paramount. Although the left and right today might agree about very little when it comes to the Constitution, they both accept that negative rights, rather than *salus populi*, are *suprema lex*.[75]

---

[70] Wendy E. Parmet & Jeremy Paul, *Post-Truth Won't Set Us Free: Health Law, Patient Autonomy, and the Rise of the Infodemic*, in COVID-19 AND THE LAW: DISRUPTION, IMPACT, AND LEGACY (I. Glenn Cohen et al. eds., forthcoming 2023).

[71] District of Columbia v. Heller, 554 U.S. 570, 592 (2008).

[72] Citizens United v. FEC, 558 U.S. 310, 364–65 (2010).

[73] Nat'l Inst. of Fam. & Life Advocs. v. Becerra, 138 S. Ct. 2361, 2378 (2018).

[74] Genevieve Lasker, *The First Amendment's Real* Lochner *Problem*, 87 U. CHI. L. REV. 1241 (2020); Amanda Shanor, *The New* Lochner, 2016 WIS. L. REV. 133.

[75] For a contrasting view, see VERMEULE, *supra* note 7, at 1–15.

RIGHTS FOR HEALTH

During the COVID-19 pandemic, negative rights – such as the right not to wear a mask or not to be compelled to be vaccinated – often seemed in conflict with the positive liberty provided by public health measures. No doubt, many public health experts and advocates felt stymied by this emphasis on individual choice and negative liberty. They saw the demands for rights against COVID mitigation measures, and the charge that such measures denied freedom, as threatening the nation's capacity to lessen the pandemic's toll.

Negative rights, however, do not always undermine what Justice Harlan called "real liberty." At times, the vindication of such rights has little or no impact on the health of individuals and communities. After all, some liberty-limiting public health measures may be ineffective. For example, early in the pandemic, California and some other states closed beaches and parks. The aim was to reduce social interaction and slow the virus's spread, but because outdoor transmission turned out to be rare,[76] liberty (although no fundamental right) was limited for little or no public health benefit. Critically, such errors are especially likely to happen early in an outbreak. When information is sparse, officials may in good faith impose restrictions on liberty that turn out, in hindsight, to have been unnecessary.

Yet even restrictions on liberty that are supported by the science can backfire. As Geoff Manaugh and Nicola Twilley note, "when faced with an imminent quarantine order, large portions of a targeted population are almost guaranteed to flee, sometimes carrying the disease with them, seemingly invalidating the purpose of the intended lockdown in the process."[77] This may have happened early in the COVID-19 pandemic in Wuhan, China.[78] Likewise, President Trump's announcement of a travel ban from Europe prompted thousands of Americans to hastily repatriate, creating not only chaos in the airports but also conditions ripe to spread the virus that the ban was supposed to

---

[76] Tommaso Celeste Bulfone et al., *Outdoor Transmission of SARS-CoV-2 and Other Respiratory Viruses: A Systematic Review*, 223 J. INFECTIOUS DISEASES 550, 558 (2021).
[77] MANAUGH & TWILLEY, *supra* note 14, at 8.
[78] *Id.*

keep out.[79] Quarantines – or the fear of them – may also cause people to try to evade authorities, "driv[ing] a disease underground, making its spread harder to track, let alone to control."[80] In some cases, strict quarantines can even lead to riots and the breakdown of civil authority.[81] In any of these scenarios, whatever health benefits that quarantines were aimed at achieving may be undermined.

Restrictions on negative rights can undermine health in many other circumstances, too. Police violence, in which the state violates an individual's bodily integrity and liberty to act, offers a powerful example. As public health scholars Hannah L. F. Cooper and Mindy Fullilove explain, studies show that "living in conditions of excessive police violence adversely affects health."[82] Sometimes the limitations on negative liberty that harm health even come from the measures imposed by health officials. *Wong Wai v. Williamson* and *Jew Ho v. Williamson*, which were discussed in Chapter 2, provide stark illustrations. The bubonic plague outbreak that health officials sought to control in San Francisco in 1900 posed a very real threat to the health and liberty of Chinatown's residents. Yet as the court found, the racially based measures that officials imposed reflected racial prejudice more than a careful attempt to protect public health.[83] In such cases, judicial intervention can push officials to go back to the drawing board and develop a more effective response. Indeed, after *Wong Wai* and *Jew Ho* were decided, San Francisco's officials chose to work with rather than against the Chinatown community, implementing measures that were less restrictive of individual rights, less discriminatory, and more effective.[84]

More subtly, public health measures that trample too hard on negative liberty can foster stigma and discrimination, magnifying the health

---

[79] *Id.* at 9.

[80] *Id.*

[81] Yanzhong Huang, *The SARS Epidemic and Its Aftermath in China: A Political Perspective*, in LEARNING FROM SARS: PREPARING FOR THE NEXT DISEASE OUTBREAK (Stacey Knobler et al., eds. 2004).

[82] Hannah L. F. Cooper & Mindy Fullilove, *Editorial: Excessive Police Violence as a Public Health Issue*, 93 J. URBAN HEALTH 1, 2 (2016).

[83] Wong Wai v. Williamson, 103 F. 1, 9 (N.D. Ca. 1900); Jew Ho v. Williamson, 103 F. 10, 23 (N.D. Ca. 1900).

[84] SHAH, *supra* note 14, at 225–50.

problem they seek to mitigate. That is one of the lessons from HIV/
AIDS epidemic, but it applies to many other health problems, including
substance use disorders, mental illness, sexually transmitted infections,
and numerous other stigmatized conditions. As legal scholars Sharifah
Sekalala and John Harrington explain, "the early HIV/AIDS response
raised serious questions about the public health efficacy" of the traditional
approach, which limited liberty for the public good.[85] People "whose
rights were violated experienced stigma and discrimination, leaving them
marginalized and," paradoxically, "more vulnerable to HIV."[86]

This recognition has led many scholars and activists to call for a
more robust role for judicial review to promote health. For example,
in the 1980s, many school boards responded to public hysteria over
AIDS by barring HIV-positive children, including Ryan White, an
HIV-positive thirteen-year-old boy with hemophilia who became the
public face of victims of HIV-based discrimination.[87] Because HIV,
unlike COVID-19, is not airborne, these policies made little sense
from a public health perspective. Instead, they hardened the stigma
surrounding the disease. In such cases, court decisions vindicating the
rights of people who are HIV-positive could assist rather than undermine public health.

Negative rights can also be crucial for creating the political conditions that permit nations to be healthy – what public health expert
Daniel E. Dawes has called the political determinants of health.[88]
Dawes identifies voting and advocacy as important influences on a
society's health. Public health policy expert Jennifer Ruger adds that
"violations in individual rights to freedom of assembly, association,
and expression" may have undermined China's response to the SARS
outbreak in 2003.[89] We will come back to these points later. For now,
what is critical is that the negative rights, including protections for

---

[85] Sharifah Sekalala & John Harrington, *Communicable Diseases, Health Security, and Human Rights: From AIDS to Ebola*, in FOUNDATIONS OF GLOBAL HEALTH AND HUMAN RIGHTS 221 (Lawrence O. Gostin & Benjamin Mason Meier eds., 2020), at 221.

[86] *Id.*

[87] *See Who Was Ryan White?*, HEALTH RES. & SERVS. ADMIN., https://hab.hrsa.gov/about-ryan-white-hivaids-program/who-was-ryan-white (last visited Apr. 15, 2022). For a discussion of these cases, *see* Wendy E. Parmet & Daniel J. Jackson, *No Longer Disabled: The Legal Impact of the New Social Construction of HIV*, 23 AM. J. L. MED. 7, 9, 16–20 (1997).

[88] DANIEL E. DAWES, THE POLITICAL DETERMINANTS OF HEALTH 7 (2020).

[89] J. P. Ruger, *Democracy and Health*, 98 Q. J. MED. 299, 302 (2005).

decisional autonomy and freedom of speech, can sometimes provide the conditions necessary for safeguarding health and reducing health inequities. Further, as legal scholar Michael McCann has explained, the prospect of judicial relief can catalyze movements that seek to push policy.[90] In this way, the potential for judicial protection for negative rights can lead groups to exercise self-governance and promote policy changes that promote health.

In short, the relationship between health, liberty, and judicial review is complex. Judicial review on behalf of negative rights can limit self-governance and health, but it can also nourish both. Likewise, positive rights can provide the "real liberty" that people need to be healthy enough to enjoy their negative liberties. But government actions in the name of health can also diminish health, embed inequity, and diminish human dignity.

Getting the balance right is not easy. Since the AIDS crisis, the public health community has largely advocated that courts should give more weight to negative rights as well as to equal protection. The nation's failed response to COVID-19, however, suggests that the pendulum might have swung too far in that direction.

---

[90] Michael McCann, *Law and Social Movements: Contemporary Perspectives*, 2 ANN. REV. L. & SOC. SCI. 17, 27 (2006).

4 COVID COMES TO COURT

March 2020 was a unique moment in American history. In the course of a few days, life in the United States (and much of the world) changed dramatically. Governors in all fifty states issued emergency declarations and imposed a range of orders in an effort to "flatten the curve" to prevent an exponential rise in COVID-19 cases that could crash their health care systems. These "social distancing laws," as public health law expert Lindsay F. Wiley has termed them, banned gatherings, restricted travel, closed "nonessential" businesses and schools, and required people to wear masks in public.[1] In contrast to individual isolation and quarantine orders, these orders reached broadly and did not depend on individualized assessments of risk. Instead, they worked at a population level to reduce the virus's prevalence in communities as a whole. This approach benefits everyone, yet, as sociologist and physician Nicholas A. Christakis explains, because they "impose burdens on citizens who remain (or at least appear) uninfected, these efforts can provoke resentment and even resistance."[2] And so they did.

The use of social distancing laws to slow a pandemic was not novel. During the 1918 influenza pandemic, cities banned public gatherings,

---

[1] Lindsay F. Wiley, *Democratizing the Law of Social Distancing*, 19 YALE J. HEALTH POL'Y, L. & ETHICS 50, 55 (2020); *see Sources of State Emergency Power Authority, 2020*, BALLOTPEDIA (2021), https://ballotpedia.org/Sources_of_state_emergency_power_authority,_2020 (last visited Apr. 18, 2022) (listing state orders).

[2] NICHOLAS A. CHRISTAKIS, APOLLO'S ARROW: THE PROFOUND AND ENDURING IMPACT OF CORONAVIRUS ON THE WAY WE LIVE 89 (2020).

closed schools and business, and in some cases mandated masks.[3] As in the twenty-first century, some Americans believed that these measures violated their freedom. Nevertheless, legal challenges "were largely rejected by the courts," which generally saw social distancing laws as reasonable restrictions designed to slow the pandemic.[4]

In the decades that followed the 1918 pandemic, antibiotics and vaccines became more central to the fight against contagion. As they did, social distancing measures fell out of favor, leaving the "law of social distancing" undeveloped.[5] It remained that way even as fears of another potential flu pandemic or bioterrorism grew after 9/11 and the anthrax attacks on the US mail that followed a few weeks later. For example, in the fall of 2001, the CDC asked public health law specialist Lawrence O. Gostin and his colleagues to draft a Model State Emergency Health Powers Act (MSEHPA).[6] The act they wrote sought to align state public health powers that target discrete individuals, such as isolation and quarantine, with contemporary notions of constitutional rights, especially procedural due process.[7] But even though the MSEHPA granted broad powers to state officials, it said relatively little about social distancing measures.

After the MSEHPA was drafted, researchers who studied the 1918 pandemic reported on the positive impact of "early, sustained, and layered" social distancing measures.[8] The federal government then began to incorporate such measures into its preparedness plans.[9] Nevertheless, the quarantine regulations that the CDC promulgated in 2017 – just a few short years before COVID-19 emerged – remained largely silent about community-wide approaches.[10]

[3] J. Alexander Navarro & Howard Markel, *Politics, Pushback, and Pandemics: Challenges to Public Health Orders in the 1918 Influenza Pandemic*, 111 AM. J. PUB. HEALTH 416, 416–17 (2021).

[4] Wiley, *supra* note 1, at 63.

[5] *Id.* at 56.

[6] Center for Law and the Public's Health at Georgetown & Johns Hopkins Universities, *The Model State Emergency Health Powers Act*, 30 J. L. MED. & ETHICS 324 (2002).

[7] Wiley, *supra* note 1, at 66; Lawrence O. Gostin, *The Model State Emergency Health Powers Act: Public Health and Civil Liberties in a Time of Terrorism*, 13 HEALTH MATRIX 3, 26 (2003).

[8] Howard Markel et al., *Nonpharmaceutical Interventions Implemented by US Cities during the 1918–1919 Influenza Pandemic*, 298 JAMA 644, 653 (2007).

[9] CHRISTAKIS, *supra* note 2, at 96.

[10] 42 C.F.R. § 70, 42 C.F.R. § 71.

In the spring of 2020, individually focused measures were quickly outmatched by SARS-CoV-2. Although Korea and some other countries managed to contain the virus in 2020 with a robust program of testing, contact tracing, and quarantine,[11] the flawed rollout of testing in the United States doomed such strategies.[12] In their absence, social distancing measures were all that we had. Although far from perfect – and the details mattered – studies suggest that they saved lives.[13]

In theory, under the reasoning of *U.S. v. Carolene Products* footnote 4,[14] social distancing laws should raise fewer constitutional concerns than laws that target "discrete and insular" minorities or specific individuals. Precisely because social distancing laws affect broad classes – all residents, all retail businesses – they are more amenable to political accountability and less subject to abuse than laws that target minority populations or particular individuals. Indeed, political considerations led some governors to announce the lifting of restrictions in April 2020 and forgo new restrictions even as the virus resurged in the months and years that followed. In that sense, the political process "worked" to constrain government's ability to restrict negative liberty.

This is not to say that social distancing orders affected all groups equally. They did not. As Chapter 7 discusses, COVID was not an equal opportunity killer. Communities of color suffered disproportionately, especially in the pandemic's first year, as did immigrants, people with disabilities, and seniors. In addition, the lines that officials drew when designating which activities were "essential," and therefore allowed to stay open when other businesses were closed, sometimes seemed to reflect political and economic considerations as much as (or even more than) public health or the need to keep vital services functioning.

Despite several federal laws that softened the pandemic's economic bite – for example, by extending unemployment compensation and

---

[11] Paul Dyer, Policy and Institutional Responses to COVID-19: South Korea, Brookings Inst. (June 15, 2021), www.brookings.edu/research/policy-and-institutional-responses-to-covid-19-south-korea.

[12] Wiley, *supra* note 1, at 72.

[13] *See* "mbevand/npi-effectiness," GitHub, https://github.com/mbevand/npi-effectiveness?s=03 (listing studies) (last visited Apr. 18, 2022).

[14] United States v. Carolene Prods. Co., 304 U.S. 144, 152 n.4 (1938).

halting evictions – the country quickly fell into a deep recession.[15]
Many businesses and families suffered significant economic losses as
customers stayed away and businesses shuttered. Children and parents
were harmed as schools went online. All of this added to the pressure to
"reopen" the economy. But as economist Austan Goolsbee explained,
"the most important thing for the economy is [to] get control of this
virus."[16] As long as large numbers of people were dying and the health
care system was strained, the economy would suffer.

Controlling the virus while reducing the economic, mental health,
educational, and other harms caused by social distancing laws was not
easy. Still, the approach that many states took often seem guided as
much by short-term political grandstanding as by a careful attempt to
mitigate harms. As COVID polices became more politicized, several
states "reopened" even as health officials warned that they were acting
prematurely.

All told, the response to the pandemic consisted of a messy mix of
orders that seemed to come and go with little explanation. Restrictions
also varied by state, adding to the public's bewilderment. (Why are
restaurants closed here if they're open a few miles away?) In addition,
some industries (e.g., casinos in Nevada) seemed to get preferential
treatment, even as schools remained closed. President Trump's refusal
to embrace the guidance of his own health experts added to the confusion and distrust. So did his disparagement of public health orders. By
May 2020, the solidarity and shared sacrifice that Americans felt in
March had frayed.

Not surprisingly, many individuals and businesses took their
complaints to court. By mid-2021, plaintiffs had filed more than a
thousand lawsuits challenging state or local community mitigation
measures in federal and state courts.[17] These cases raised almost every
constitutional, statutory, and procedural claim imaginable. Plaintiffs
argued that their state had denied their rights to religious liberty, free

---

[15] *Here's Everything the Federal Government Has Done to Respond to the Coronavirus So
Far*, PETER G. PETERSON FOUNDATION (Mar. 15, 2021), www.pgpf.org/blog/2021/03/
heres-everything-congress-has-done-to-respond-to-the-coronavirus-so-far.

[16] Ailsa Chang et al., *When Will It Stop Being the "Pandemic Economy?,"* NPR (Oct. 27, 2021),
www.npr.org/2021/10/27/1049797074/when-will-it-stop-being-the-pandemic-economy.

[17] Michelle M. Mello & Wendy E. Parmet, *Public Health Law after COVID-19*, 385 N. ENG.
J. MED. 1153, 1153 (2021).

speech, and free assembly. They alleged violations of their Second Amendment right to buy guns as well as their rights to have an abortion and travel across state lines. Litigants also claimed that governors and health agencies had exceeded their statutory authority, and that broad grants of statutory authority were themselves unconstitutional.

These cases asked courts to reconcile *Jacobson* and the long tradition of *salus populi* with contemporary constitutional law's emphasis on negative liberty. More specifically, the COVID cases required courts to decide how to apply doctrines that had developed in the post-antibiotic era – ones that emphasize the nature of the individual's claim rather than the nature of the state's interest – to orders designed to mitigate a once-in-a-century pandemic.

Confronted with that challenge, most courts in the spring of 2020 upheld most state social distancing measures.[18] Nevertheless, as the pandemic progressed, many challenges succeeded. These decisions, which came more often from judges appointed by Republican presidents than from those appointed by Democratic presidents,[19] evinced a judiciary that was increasingly unwilling to defer to state health officials and that, in some important instances, weighed an individual's negative liberty over *salus populi*.

THE EARLY COVID CASES

Early in the pandemic, most courts deferred to state officials. In one of the first cases, *Binford v. Sununu* (2020), the plaintiffs argued that New Hampshire governor Chris Sununu had exceeded his statutory powers and violated their rights to free speech and free exercise of religion by limiting gatherings and closing businesses.[20] Although New Hampshire superior court justice John C. Kissinger considered each of the plaintiff's claims as required by the applicable contemporary doctrines, he articulated what Lindsay F. Wiley and Stephen I. Vladeck called

---

[18] Kenny Mok & Eric A. Posner, *Constitutional Challenges to Public Health Orders in Federal Courts during the COVID-19 Pandemic* (Aug. 1, 2021), https://papers.ssrn.com/sol3/papers.cfm?abstract_id=3897441.

[19] *Id.* at 3–4.

[20] Binford v. Sununu, No. 217-2020-CV-00152 (N.H. Sup. Ct. Mar. 25, 2020).

"the suspension principle" – the idea that judicial review should be significantly abridged during an emergency.[21]

A short time later, the US Court of Appeals for the Fifth Circuit seemed to adopt Kissinger's approach. In *In re Abbott*, plaintiffs argued that Texas governor Greg Abbott's order banning most abortions during the public health emergency violated the right to an abortion.[22] There was no question that the ban burdened a constitutionally protected right, as it was then understood. Abbott's claim that the ban was necessary to preserve health care resources was also dubious, in that childbirth utilizes more health care resources than abortion.[23] Nevertheless, in an opinion by Judge Stuart Kyle Duncan that the US Supreme Court later vacated, Duncan rejected plaintiffs' claims on the authority of *Jacobson*. According to Duncan, under *Jacobson*, during a public health emergency, judicial review is "'only' available" when the state law "has no real or substantial relation" to public health or "is beyond all question, a plain, palpable invasion of rights secured by fundamental law."[24]

Although Duncan did not slam the door shut on judicial review of constitutional claims during the pandemic, his opinion, like Kissinger's, suggested that review should be confined to egregious circumstances – in effect, the normal rules of constitutional review should not apply. Whether the conservative Duncan would have been quite so willing to limit judicial review if the first case before him had not concerned abortion rights is impossible to know. What is clear is that Duncan's interpretation of *Jacobson* was deeply problematic. *Jacobson*, after all, did not purport to declare a special rule for public health emergencies, and the Supreme Court had never treated it as doing so.[25] Instead, *Jacobson* emphasized public health's place in the social compact

---

[21] Lindsay F. Wiley & Stephen I. Vladeck, *Coronavirus, Civil Liberties, and the Courts: The Case against "Suspending" Judicial Review*, 133 HARV. L. REV. F. 179, 181–82 (July 13, 2020), https://harvardlawreview.org/2020/07/coronavirus-civil-liberties-and-the-courts.

[22] In re Abbott, 954 F. 3d 772, 793 (5th Cir. 2020), *vacated*, Planned Parenthood Ctr. for Choice v. Abbott, 141 S. Ct. 1261 (2021).

[23] *See, e.g.*, Daniel Grossman, *Abortions Don't Drain Hospital Resources*, BOS. REV. (Apr. 17, 2020), https://bostonreview.net/science-nature-politics-law-justice/daniel-grossman-abortions-dont-drain-hospital-resources.

[24] *In re* Abbott, 954 F. 3d at 784 (quoting Jacobson v. Mass., 197 U.S. 11, 31 (1905)).

[25] Wendy E. Parmet, *Rediscovering Jacobson in the Era of COVID-19*, 100 B.U. L. REV. ONLINE 117, 126–27 (2020), www.bu.edu/bulawreview/parmet.

and the deference that courts should give to elected and appointed officials. It also applied the police power jurisprudence of its time to affirm reasonable health regulations, while noting that courts should protect against "unreasonable, arbitrary, and oppressive" police power regulations.[26] In short, *Jacobson* provided a nuanced (if ambiguous) analysis of the tensions between positive and negative liberties and the role of courts in refereeing those tensions. The one thing it did not do was announce a two-part test for emergency orders.

Nevertheless, in early 2020, many courts were quick to adopt Duncan's reading of *Jacobson*. For example, in *In re Rutledge*, another abortion case, the US Court of Appeals for the Eighth Circuit relied on *Abbott*, stating that "while constitutional rights do not disappear during a public health crisis," they may be limited.[27] Likewise, in a freedom of assembly case, Judge Stephen Clark of the Eastern District of Missouri relied on *Abbott* and *Rutledge* to stress the limited nature of judicial review during a public health crisis.[28]

Not all courts agreed. Some cited *Abbott*'s reading of *Jacobson* but went on to analyze the plaintiff's constitutional claims just as they would have done in the absence of an emergency.[29] These courts, in effect, hedged their bets. They claimed that review was limited due to the public health emergency, but then dismissed the plaintiffs' claims using an analysis remarkably similar to the one they would have employed in the absence of an emergency. In most cases, such ordinary review led them to uphold the order in question.

To see why, consider free speech challenges to COVID restrictions. As Chapter 8 discusses more fully, courts today apply strict judicial scrutiny to most laws that regulate speech on the basis of its content.[30] So, for example, a law prohibiting speaking in opposition to but not in support of community-wide mitigation measures would be subject to strict scrutiny and almost assuredly held unconstitutional. In contrast, laws that impact speech but do not do so on the basis of

---

[26] Jacobson v. Massachusetts, 197 U.S. 11, 26 (1905).

[27] In re Rutledge, 956 F. 3d 1018, 1027 (8th Cir. 2020).

[28] SH3 Health Consulting, LLC v. Page, 459 F. Supp. 3d 1212, 1221 (E.D. Mo. 2020).

[29] Wendy E. Parmet, *The COVID Cases: A Preliminary Assessment of Judicial Review of Public Health Powers during a Partisan and Polarized Pandemic*, 57 S. DIEGO L. REV. 999, 1024 (2020).

[30] *E.g.*, Reed v. Town of Gilbert, 576 U.S. 155, 163 (2015).

content – often called "content-neutral" regulations – are subject to a type of intermediate scrutiny under which they will be upheld as long as they are narrowly tailored to serve a significant government interest and leave plaintiffs with other ways to communicate.[31] Hence, even though bans on mass gatherings including theaters affected speech, most courts concluded that they were content neutral and narrowly tailored to serve the important interest of protecting health.[32] Courts also upheld mask and vaccine mandates from free speech challenges, despite their incidental impact on speech.[33] In such cases, courts could avoid reconciling *Jacobson* with contemporary First Amendment doctrine, as the laws were constitutional under both.

Most other constitutional challenges to social distancing laws also failed to establish a violation of an established fundamental right.[34] COVID restrictions severely limited many people's ability to maintain their job or business. Since the New Deal, however, courts have not recognized a constitutional right to work or run a business in a particular manner.[35] Nor is there a constitutional right not to wear a face mask.[36] Such cases were relatively easy for the courts and did not require them to ponder the relationship between individual rights and public health. In a few cases, however, courts found that the state had infringed on a fundamental right but still concluded that the state law survived, or was likely to survive, strict scrutiny. *Bayley's Campground v. Mills* offers an illuminating example. In that May 2020 case, a federal district judge in Maine refused to enjoin an order requiring anyone arriving from out-of-state to quarantine for fourteen days.[37] The court accepted that the order might violate the fundamental right to travel but concluded that it would likely survive strict scrutiny due to the pandemic.[38]

---

[31] *E.g.*, Hill v. Colorado, 530 U.S. 703, 725–26 (2000).
[32] Parmet, *supra* note 29, at 1023.
[33] *E.g.*, Stepien v. Murphy, 574 F. Supp. 3d. 229 (D.N.J. 2021) (mask mandate); L.T. v. Zucker, 2021 WL 4775215 (N.D.N.Y. 2021) (mask mandate); Clementine Co. v. de Blasio, 2021 WL 5756398 (S.D.N.Y. 2021) (vaccine mandate).
[34] Mok & Posner, *supra* note 18, at 21, 23.
[35] *But see* Cnty. of Butler v. Wolf, 486 F. Supp. 3d 883, 928 (W.D. Pa. 2020), *stay granted pending appeal*, No. 20-2936, 2020 WL 5868393 (3d Cir. Oct. 1, 2020); Bols v. Newsom, 515 F. Supp. 3d 1120, 1132 (S.D. Cal. 2021).
[36] *E.g.*, Stepien v. Murphy, 574 F. Supp, 3d at 233.
[37] Bayley's Campground, Inc. v. Mills, 463 F. Supp. 3d 22 (D. Me. 2020), *aff'd* 985 F. 3d 153 (1st Cir. 2021).
[38] *Id.* at 33.

Not all claims were rejected. As the pandemic continued, free exercise claims in particular received a more favorable reception, especially from the Supreme Court.

FREE EXERCISE AND RELIGIOUS LIBERTY

In the spring of 2020, it became evident that indoor religious worship, particularly when accompanied by singing or chanting, could serve as a "super-spreader" event.[39] Despite the danger, most states exempted religious services from their social distancing orders.[40] Other states did place restrictions on religious services, but those restrictions were frequently looser than the rules for secular gatherings.[41]

The application of COVID mitigation measures to worship was extremely controversial. In late March 2020, Trump stressed that he wanted "packed churches" for Easter.[42] Later, Attorney General Bill Barr issued a memorandum stating that "government may not impose special restrictions on religious activity that do not also apply to similar nonreligious activity. ... Religious institutions must not be singled out for special burdens."[43]

Despite the controversy, there was little reason to believe that free exercise challenges to COVID restrictions would succeed. Not only did many courts cite *Jacobson* as requiring deferential review,

---

[39] *E.g.*, M. Koran, *California Megachurch Linked to Spread of More than 70 Coronavirus Cases*, GUARDIAN (Apr. 3, 2020), www.theguardian.com/world/2020/apr/03/california-church-coronvirus-outbreak-sacramento; Tangi Salaüm, *Special Report: Five Days of Worship That Set a Virus Time Bomb in France*, REUTERS (Mar. 30, 2020), www.reuters .com/article/us-health-coronavirus-france-church-spec/special-report-five-days-of-worship-that-set-a-virus-time-bomb-in-france-idUSKBN21H0Q2.

[40] *Most States Have Religious Exemptions to COVID-19 Social Distancing Rules*, PEW RSCH. CTR. (Apr. 27, 2020), www.pewresearch.org/fact-tank/2020/04/27/most-states-have-religious-exemptions-to-covid-19-social-distancing-rules.

[41] *Id.*

[42] *See, e.g.*, Kevin Breuninger, *Trump Wants "Packed Churches" and Economy Open Again on Easter Despite the Deadly Threat of Coronavirus*, CNBC (Mar. 24, 2020), www.cnbc .com/2020/03/24/coronavirus-response-trump-wants-to-reopen-us-economy-by-easter .html.

[43] Press Release, US Dept Justice, Attorney General William P. Barr Issues Statement on Religious Practice and Social Distancing; Department Files State of Interest in Mississippi Church Case (Apr. 14, 2020), www.justice.gov/opa/pr/attorney-general-william-p-barr-issues-statement-on-religious-practice-and-social-distancing-0.

but under a decision that Justice Antonin Scalia wrote for the Court in 1990, *Employment Division v. Smith,* state laws that are generally applicable and neutral (as to religion) were subject to rational basis review under the First Amendment's free exercise clause.[44] To give a simple example, a law requiring schoolchildren to receive the MMR (mumps, measles, and rubella) vaccine would not have been subject to strict scrutiny even though some individuals might have had a religious objection.[45] As long as the law applied to all schoolchildren, courts would apply rational basis review. Similarly, a law banning all gatherings should have been spared strict scrutiny even if it applied to religious services.

Another relevant precedent was the Court's 1993 decision in *Church of Lukumi Babalu Aye v. Hialeah,* which held that laws that target religious activity or are based on animus toward religion are subject to strict scrutiny.[46] Hence, if a state had kept its economy "open" while banning only Christian religious services, strict scrutiny would apply. Of course, determining if a law is neutral and generally applicable is not always easy. Consider a law that bars all gatherings of more than fifty people except in hospitals, which are allowed to continue to operate without any capacity limits. Is the law neutral and generally applicable, or does it discriminate against religion because it limits the capacity of religious gatherings while allowing hospitals to stay open? One might easily think that hospitals are quite distinct from, or – in the terms used by the courts – not comparable to religious worship, and that the exemption for hospitals does not mean that the state is treating worship differently than comparable secular activities. But in a 2016 dissent to the denial of review in *Stormans, Inc. v. Wiesman,* Justice Samuel Alito, who was joined by Justice Clarence Thomas, argued that the existence of *any* exemption for any secular activity should trigger strict scrutiny.[47] That reasoning would suggest that as long as hospitals stay open, churches, temples and mosques must be allowed to do likewise.

---

[44] Employ. Div. v. Smith, 494 U.S. 872, 889 (1990).
[45] *See, e.g.,* Brown v. Smith, 235 Cal. Rptr. 3d 218, 225–26 (Cal. Ct. App. 2018); Whitlow v. Cal. Dep't of Educ., 203 F. Supp. 3d 1079, 1087 (S.D. Cal. 2016); F.F. v. State of N.Y., 114 N.Y.S. 3d 852, 865–67 (N.Y. Sup. Ct. 2019).
[46] Church of the Lukumi Babalu Aye, Inc. v. City of Hialeah, 508 U.S. 520, 533 (1993).
[47] Stormans, Inc. v. Wiesman, 579 U.S. 942 (2016) (Alito, J., dissenting).

What's more problematic for public health laws is the fact that the protection afforded by the First Amendment is not limited to traditional worship. The religious activity in *Stormans*, for example, was a pharmacist's refusal to dispense Plan B, the emergency contraceptive commonly known as the "morning after pill." In other words, any activity or inactivity (e.g., not dispensing a drug) can be religious if someone sincerely believes it to be. As a result, if the existence of any secular exemption requires courts to apply strict scrutiny to any law that burdens any activity that an individual believes to be religious, almost every health law – including quarantines, food safety laws, and disease reporting requirements – could be subject to strict scrutiny under the free exercise clause.

Shortly before the pandemic struck in 2020, at least four justices seemed open to Alito's reasoning when the Court granted review in *Fulton v. City of Philadelphia* (which challenged Philadelphia's refusal to place children with foster care agencies that discriminate against same-sex couples) to consider whether *Smith* should be overruled.[48] Overruling *Smith* would presumably mean that *all* free exercise claims would be vulnerable to strict scrutiny. That would not necessarily mean that all claims would be victorious, but the threat of constitutional invalidation would hover over all public health laws.

Despite the uncertainty cast by the Court's grant of review in *Fulton*, in early 2020, most courts relied on *Jacobson* and *Smith* to reject free exercise challenges to social distancing laws. For example, in *Elim Romanian Pentecostal Church v. Pritzker*, the US Court of Appeals for the Seventh Circuit upheld Illinois's emergency COVID order, noting "it would be foolish to pretend that worship services are exactly like any of the possible comparisons, but they seem most like other congregate functions that occur in auditoriums, such as concerts and movies."[49]

At first, the Supreme Court also declined to block social distancing laws on free exercise grounds. As discussed in Chapter 1, in its first COVID case, *South Bay United Pentecostal Church v. Newsom*, the Court refused to block California governor Gavin Newsom's

[48] Fulton v. City of Philadelphia, 140 S. Ct. 1104 (2020) (mem.).
[49] Elim Romanian Pentecostal Church v. Pritzker, 962 F. 3d 341, 346 (7th Cir. 2020).

restrictions on in-person worship by a 5–4 vote from the shadow docket.[50] The majority did not publish an opinion, but in a concurring opinion, Chief Justice John Roberts stated that California's restrictions on worship "appear consistent with the Free Exercise Clause" given that "similar or more severe restrictions apply to comparable secular gatherings, including lectures, concerts, movie showings, spectator sports, and theatrical performances."[51] He added, "the precise question of when restrictions on particular social activities should be lifted during the pandemic is a dynamic and fact-intensive matter subject to reasonable disagreement," and that the Constitution "principally entrusts" such decisions to "politically accountable officials."[52] Although he cited *Jacobson* for that last point, he never claimed that it established a two-part test for determining the availability of judicial review during a pandemic.

Foreshadowing where the majority would later land, Justice Brett Kavanaugh wrote a biting dissent that Thomas and Justice Neil Gorsuch joined.[53] In it, Kavanaugh argued that California had discriminated against religion by placing a stricter cap on religious services than on some "comparable secular businesses" such as "factories, offices, supermarkets, restaurants, retail stores, pharmacies, shopping malls, pet grooming shops, bookstores, florists, hair salons, and cannabis dispensaries."[54] Tellingly, he offered no explanation as to how he determined that these activities were "comparable" to religious services.

In July 2020, again by a 5–4 vote, the Court refused to block Nevada's capacity limits on in-person religious worship.[55] Once again, the majority did not publish an opinion. However, in a dissent that Thomas and Kavanaugh signed, Alito explained that because *Jacobson* was a substantive due process case (recall that the Court had not yet applied the First Amendment to the states in 1905),[56] it had little to say about religious liberty claims.[57] In making this point, he ignored

---

[50] S. Bay United Pentecostal Church v. Newsom, 140 S. Ct. 1613 (2020).
[51] *Id.* at 1613 (Roberts, C. J., concurring).
[52] *Id.*
[53] *Id.* at 1614 (Kavanaugh, J., dissenting).
[54] *Id.*
[55] Calvary Chapel Dayton Valley v. Sisolak, 140 S. Ct. 2603 (2020).
[56] *See* Chapter 2.
[57] 140 U.S. at 2608 (Alito, J., dissenting).

the fact that the Court had frequently cited *Jacobson* for the point that the free exercise clause permits states to restrain an individual's exercise of religion when it endangered others.[58]

In his dissent, Kavanaugh conceded "that courts should be very deferential to the States' line-drawing in opening businesses and allowing certain activities during the pandemic" when "considering a substantive due process claim."[59] Nevertheless, he warned that "there are certain constitutional red lines that a State may not cross even in a crisis."[60] He added,

This Court's history is littered with unfortunate examples of overly broad judicial deference to the government when the government has invoked emergency powers and asserted crisis circumstances to override equal-treatment and free-speech principles. The court of history has rejected those jurisprudential mistakes and cautions us against an unduly deferential judicial approach, especially when questions of racial discrimination, religious discrimination, or free speech are at stake.[61]

Four months later, after Justice Amy Coney Barrett replaced Justice Ruth Bader Ginsburg on the Court, the views of the dissenters became those of the majority. *Roman Catholic Diocese v. Cuomo* (hereinafter referred to as *RCD*) concerned New York's order barring more than ten persons from attending religious services in "red zones" – areas that the state identified as COVID hot spots.[62] By the time the case reached the high court, the order no longer applied to the plaintiffs' facilities. For Roberts, that was reason enough for the Court not to intervene.[63] The new majority disagreed.

In an unsigned opinion, the majority noted that the order "imposes very severe restrictions on attendance at religious services in areas classified as 'red' or 'orange' zones."[64] The majority also found that the order was not a neutral rule of general applicability because

[58] Wendy E. Parmet, *From the Shadows: The Public Health Implications of the Supreme Court's COVID-Free Exercise Cases*, 49 J. L. MED. & ETHICS 564, 566 (2021).
[59] *Calvary Chapel Dayton Valley*, 140 S. Ct. at 2614 (Kavanaugh, J., dissenting).
[60] *Id.*
[61] *Id.* at 1615.
[62] Roman Cath. Diocese of Brooklyn v. Cuomo, 141 S. Ct. 63, 65–66 (2020) (per curiam) (hereinafter cited as *RCD*).
[63] *Id.* at 75–76 (Roberts, C. J., dissenting).
[64] *RCD*, 141 S. Ct. at 65–66.

the state had not imposed similar capacity limits on "acupuncture facilities, camp grounds, garages, as well as many whose services are not limited to those that can be regarded as essential, such as all plants manufacturing chemicals and microelectronics and all transportation facilities."[65] According to the Court, this meant that the state had regulated religious activity more strictly than comparable secular activities. Hence, the order was subject to strict scrutiny.

Applying strict scrutiny, the Court accepted that controlling COVID-19 was a compelling state interest, but nevertheless claimed that the order was not narrowly tailored to achieving that interest because there was "no evidence that the applicants have contributed to the spread of COVID-19."[66] This seemed to say that states could not try to prevent harm; they had to wait for it to happen. The Court also suggested that because many other states did not have regulations as strict as New York's, the regulations at issue were not necessary to protect the public's health.[67]

What was perhaps most important about the majority's opinion was what was omitted. First, the Court cited neither *Jacobson* nor Roberts's opinion in *South Bay*. It also did not grant any deference to state health officials. Nor did the majority consider *any* scientific evidence in determining which secular activities were comparable to religious services. Instead, the Court seemed to rely on the justices' own intuition about what activities were comparable to worship and which steps the state could take to reduce contagion. And the Court did all of that in the service of imposing an extraordinary remedy – enjoining a state law from the shadow docket.[68] In short, despite a raging pandemic and the long history of judicial deference to public health laws, the majority seemed eager to show that public health protection would no longer be given much weight in free exercise cases, nor would public health evidence.

Concurring opinions underscored that message. In his concurrence, Gorsuch complained, "At the flick of a pen, [governors] have

---

[65] *Id.* at 66.

[66] *Id.* at 67.

[67] *Id.*

[68] Stephen I. Vladeck, *The Most-Favored Right: COVID, the Supreme Court, and the (New) Free Exercise Clause*, 15 N.Y.U. J. L. & Lib. 1 (forthcoming 2022) (manuscript at 19), https://ssrn.com/abstract=3987461.

asserted the right to privilege restaurants, marijuana dispensaries, and casinos over churches, mosques, and temples. In far too many places, for far too long, our first freedom has fallen on deaf ears."[69] Gorsuch went on to call *Jacobson* a "modest decision" that concerned "an implied substantive due process" claim concerning a $5 fine.[70] Why, he wondered, did courts pay so much attention to it?[71] Perhaps because of "a particular judicial impulse to stay out of the way in times of crisis."[72] "Things never go well," he lamented, when courts follow that impulse.[73] Whether they go well when courts second-guess health experts during a pandemic, he did not say.

In his concurring opinion, Kavanaugh provided a fuller explanation of why he thought that strict scrutiny was required. "It does not suffice," he stated, "for a State to point out that, as compared to houses of worship, *some* secular businesses are subject to similarly severe or even more severe restrictions. ... Rather, once a State creates a favored class of businesses ... the State must justify why houses of worship are excluded from that favored class."[74] In effect, as in Alito's *Stormans* dissent, the existence of any exemption requires strict scrutiny in free exercise cases. In presenting this high – if not impossible – barrier, Kavanaugh gave little consideration to the public health crisis that was unfolding and was about to get a lot worse.

In dissent, Roberts accepted that the state's restrictions on worship raised serious constitutional questions and that courts should not give in to the "impulse to stay out the way in times of crisis."[75] Nevertheless, he stressed that there was no need for the Court to intervene given that the state's order no longer applied to the plaintiffs. He added that his citation to *Jacobson* in *South Bay* "should be uncontroversial."[76]

The three justices appointed by Democratic presidents also dissented. Justice Stephen Breyer, who was joined by Justices Elena Kagan and Sonia Sotomayor, argued that an injunction was not appropriate

---

[69] *RCD*, 141 S. Ct. at 69–70 (Gorsuch, J., concurring).

[70] *Id.* at 70–71.

[71] *Id.* at 71.

[72] *Id.*

[73] *Id.*

[74] *Id.* at 73 (Kavanaugh, J., concurring).

[75] *Id.* at 75 (Roberts, C. J., dissenting) (quoting *id.* at 71 (Gorsuch, J., concurring)).

[76] *Id.* at 76.

because the order at issue was no longer in effect. He also stressed the gravity of the pandemic and the need for courts to grant elected officials deference over questions "fraught with medical and scientific uncertainties."[77]

In a dissent that Kagan joined, Sotomayor noted the pandemic's toll and argued that New York had granted religious institutions more favorable treatment than comparable secular activities. She also warned that the Court "play[s] a deadly game in second guessing the expert judgment of health officials about the environment in which a contagious virus, now infecting a million Americans each week, spreads most easily."[78]

AFTER *ROMAN CATHOLIC DIOCESE V. CUOMO*

By itself, *RCD* might have had little impact. Although the Court's analysis was potentially far-reaching, there were ways to read it narrowly. For one thing, the New York order was especially draconian, and Governor Andrew Cuomo had made statements that could be read as reflecting animus toward the state's Orthodox Jewish community.[79] The Court could have relied on that. Alternatively, it could have limited its ruling to orders that explicitly identify worship. In addition, because the decision was rendered from the shadow docket, the Court could have – and should have – treated it as not setting a precedent.

Instead, the new majority treated *RCD* as an important precedent. In the weeks and months that followed the Thanksgiving Eve decision, the Court issued several more orders, all from the shadow docket, granting relief to plaintiffs who claimed that COVID restrictions burdened their exercise of religion.[80] Together, these decisions under-scored the majority's indifference to both *Jacobson* and public health

---

[77] *Id.* at 78 (quoting S. Bay United Pentecostal v. Newsom, 140 S. Ct. (Roberts, C. J., concurring)).

[78] *Id.* at 79 (Sotomayor, J., dissenting).

[79] *Id.* at 75.

[80] Tandon v. Newsom, 141 S. Ct. 1294 (2021) (per curiam); Gateway City Church v. Newsom, 141 S. Ct. 1460 (2021) (mem.); S. Bay United Pentecostal Church v. Newsom, 141 S. Ct. 716 (2021) (hereinafter cited as *South Bay II*); High Plains Harvest Church v. Polis, 141 S. Ct. 527 (2020) (mem.).

evidence, as well as its eagerness to intervene, even in procedurally dubious contexts, to limit state public health powers.[81] To the new majority, public health evidence is irrelevant; there is only one type of freedom, and it is freedom from government restrictions.

The Court's new attitude was evident in February 2021 in *South Bay United Pentecostal Church v. Newsom* (hereinafter referred to as *South Bay II*).[82] In a brief, unsigned order from the shadow docket, the Court blocked California's ban on indoor religious services but left in place – at least for a short time – a 25 percent capacity limit plus a ban on singing and chanting. The justices, who were divided over different aspects of the order, provided little explanation and cited no evidence to support the distinctions they drew. Gorsuch, however, was keen to show his annoyance with California's governor, admonishing, "So once more we appear to have a State playing favorites during a pandemic."[83]

A short time later, in *Gateway City Church v. Newsom*, the Court granted relief to a church that contested California's ban on indoor gatherings.[84] In contrast to the orders that the Court had previously blocked, this one did not specify worship by name. Hence, it could easily have been viewed as a neutral law of general applicability under *Smith*. Nevertheless, the Court blocked the order, claiming its decision was "clearly dictated by this Court's decision" in *South Bay II*.[85] With this, the Court made clear that decisions from the shadow docket – including those issued without any opinion by the Court – should be treated as binding precedent.

The Court hammered home those points in April 2021 in *Tandon v. Newsom*.[86] *Tandon* concerned limits that California set on the number of people from separate households who could gather in a private home. The plaintiffs, who wanted to gather in a residence for worship and Bible study, argued that the order violated the free exercise clause because it permitted more people to gather in certain

[81] Parmet, *supra* note 58, at 571–73.
[82] *South Bay II*, 141 S. Ct. at 716.
[83] *Id.* at 719 (statement of Gorsuch, J.).
[84] Gateway City Church v. Newsom, 141 S. Ct. at 1460.
[85] *Id.*
[86] Tandon v. Newsom, 141 S. Ct. at 1294.

secular settings, such as at train stations and shopping malls, than were allowed to congregate privately. The lower courts, finding that those settings were not comparable to private homes, disagreed and upheld the order using the rational basis test.[87]

In unsigned opinion, once again from the shadow docket, the Court by a 5–4 vote ruled that the state had not treated in-home religious meetings comparably to some secular activities, even though *all* secular in-person meetings in homes were similarly restricted. The majority declared that "it is no answer that a State treats some comparable secular businesses or other activities as poorly as or even less favorably than the religious exercise at issue."[88] The majority added that comparability must be determined by looking at the "risks various activities pose, not the reasons why people gather."[89] Then, without considering any evidence regarding the risks of the activities it pointed to, the majority concluded that the secular activities that were regulated less strictly than in-home religious meetings were comparable to such gatherings.

Applying strict scrutiny – again without any regard to any public health evidence – the Court then concluded that the state's order was not narrowly tailored because the state treated some out-of-home secular activities more leniently. In effect, the same analysis that the Court used to determine which activities were comparable to in-home religious activities led it to decide that the state's order failed strict scrutiny. In a dissent that Breyer and Sotomayor joined, Kagan lambasted the majority for ignoring the findings of the lower courts. She added that the Court "once more commands California 'to ignore its experts' scientific findings," hampering its ability to fight the pandemic.[90]

A few weeks later, the Supreme Court announced its decision in *Fulton v. City of Philadelphia*.[91] *Fulton* was not a COVID case; it concerned a challenge brought by a Catholic foster care agency to Philadelphia's requirement that agencies agree to place children with

---

[87] Tandon v. Newsom, 992 F. 3d 916 (2021) *rev'd* 141 S. Ct. 1294 (2021).
[88] Tandon v. Newsom, 141 S. Ct. at 1296.
[89] *Id.*
[90] *Id.* at 1299 (Kagan, J., dissenting) (quoting *South Bay II*, 141 S. Ct. 716, at 722 (Kagan, J., dissenting).
[91] Fulton v. City of Philadelphia, 141 S. Ct. 1868 (2021).

same-sex couples. The agency argued the antidiscrimination policy violated its religious liberty. In a unanimous decision written by Roberts, the Court agreed. Although five justices expressed concerns about *Smith*, the Court did not overrule that case. Instead, it held that the policy was not a generally applicable law under *Smith* because the city's contract with foster care agencies granted it sole discretion to exempt agencies from its nondiscrimination policy.[92] Thus, the Court followed the COVID cases in concluding that the existence – or even just the potential – for exemptions required the application of strict scrutiny in free exercise cases. In a lengthy concurring opinion that Thomas and Gorsuch joined, Alito argued for overruling *Smith*, claiming that the COVID cases showed that that decision had become unworkable.[93] In contrast, in her concurring opinion, Barrett, who was joined by Kavanaugh, worried that overruling *Smith* would raise difficult issues as to what should replace it and what strict scrutiny would look like in a range of cases.[94]

Although the Court did not overrule *Smith*, uncertainty abounds. Because all laws draw exceptions, all are now vulnerable to free exercise challenges. Further, as *Tandon* shows, the risk is not limited to laws that name or explicitly regulate worship. Rather, it applies to *any* law that burdens any litigant's ability to comport with their sincerely held religious beliefs.

To give a simple example, consider a law that sets a thirty-five-mile-per-hour speed limit but allows emergency vehicles to drive faster. Now, imagine an individual who sincerely believes that their religion requires them to drive sixty-five miles per hour to get to worship on time. Is that speed limit subject to strict scrutiny because it applies to people traveling to worship while exempting fire trucks and ambulances? Most people would say of course not, but after *Tandon* and *Fulton*, the answer is not clear. If, as *Tandon* suggests, the question of comparability depends solely on the nature of the risk posed rather than the benefit of the activity, then the litigant can argue that speeding worshipers are no more dangerous than speeding fire trucks and ambulances. Hence, strict scrutiny must apply.

[92] *Id.* at 1878–79.
[93] *Id.* at 1921–22 (Alito, J., concurring).
[94] *Id.* at 1882–83 (Barrett, J., concurring).

Who decides if speeding worshippers are more dangerous than speeding emergency vehicles? Under the COVID cases, the answer is the Court, and in doing so, it will grant no deference to motor vehicle safety experts or consider any scientific evidence. Instead, the justices' own intuition determines whether speeding to worship is comparable to speeding to a fire or a hospital. And even if the justices conclude that it is not, they might still decide that if the state grants police officers the discretion not to issue a ticket, strict scrutiny is required under *Fulton*.

True, strict scrutiny need not be fatal. As noted above, some early pandemic cases such as *Bayley's Campground* upheld COVID restrictions under strict scrutiny. However, the Supreme Court's shadow docket cases show that once strict scrutiny is applied, public health measures generally (if not always) fail. Indeed, the analysis the Court uses to determine if strict scrutiny applies is itself very close to strict scrutiny.

As a result, individuals who object to public health laws on free exercise grounds now hold a trump card. If they can convince the Court that a health order – whether applied to worship or driving – burdens their free exercise of religion, the Court is unlikely to grant deference to either the relevant experts or the factual findings of a lower court. Instead, as in *Lochner*, the Court will rely on its own intuitions to safeguard one type of liberty while ignoring the "real liberty" that Harlan tried to respect. In 2021 and 2022, this new approach complicated efforts to increase vaccination against COVID-19.

5   THE MANDATE WARS

During the second year of the COVID-19 pandemic, the focus of litigation shifted from social distancing laws, which tried to quell the pandemic by reducing human interaction, to vaccine and mask mandates, which tried to make such interactions less risky. Opponents argued that these laws violated negative liberty. Echoing John Stuart Mill, proponents claimed that no one has the liberty to spread a disease to others[1] and that mandates offered the chance to "reopen" safely.

The most contentious litigation concerned vaccine mandates. When the pandemic began, few could have imagined that safe and effective vaccines would be available within a year. That they were was a testament to decades of research on coronaviruses and vaccine technology, as well as numerous legal preparedness measures. For example, in the Project BioShield Act of 2003, Congress established the emergency use authorization (EUA) process, which allows for the emergency use of drugs and biologics that lack full approval by the FDA.[2] In 2005, Congress enacted the Public Readiness and Emergency Preparedness (PREP) Act,[3] offering immunity to individuals and entities that manufacture, sell, or administer medical countermeasures following a PREP Act emergency declaration. Once the COVID-19 pandemic began, Operation Warp Speed provided financial support to companies that developed COVID

---

[1] See JOHN STUART MILL, *On Liberty*, in JOHN STUART MILL: A SELECTION OF HIS WORKS 96–119 (John M. Robson ed., 1966) (1859).

[2] 21 U.S.C. § 360bbb-3.

[3] 42 U.S.C. § 247d-6d.

vaccines. The federal government also invoked the Defense Production Act of 1950[4] to ensure the availability of needed supplies.[5]

These efforts paid off with the record-breaking authorization of vaccines that dramatically reduce the risk of hospitalization or death from COVID-19.[6] The vaccines also lower, although they do not eliminate, the risk that someone will spread the virus.[7] And they do so with relatively few serious side effects (though short-term symptoms are common).[8] Remarkably, they remained highly effective in preventing serious disease even as new variants emerged.[9] The Commonwealth Fund estimated that through November 2021, COVID vaccines had prevented over more than 1 million deaths and more than 10 million hospitalizations in the United States.[10] Since then, the numbers saved have surely increased, even as the legal battles became more heated.

FROM SHORTAGES TO MANDATES

In early 2021, COVID vaccines were in short supply. News stories recounted crashed websites, winding lines at vaccination centers, and people traveling long distances for coveted appointments. But by late spring 2021, the vaccines were widely available to all adults; many Americans looked forward to a summer without having to worry about COVID.

---

[4] 15. U.S.C. § 4658.

[5] SIMI V. SIDDALINGAIAH, CONG. RSCH. SERV., IN11560, OPERATION WARP SPEED CONTRACTS FOR COVID-19 VACCINES AND ANCILLARY VACCINATION MATERIALS 1–2 (2021), https://crsreports.congress.gov/product/pdf/IN/IN11560.

[6] Phoebe Danza et al., *SARS-CoV-2 Infection and Hospitalization among Adults Aged ≥ 18 Years, by Vaccination Status, before and during SARS-CoV-2 B.1.1.529 (Omicron) Variant Predominance – Los Angeles County, California, November 7, 2021–January 8, 2022*, 71 MORBIDITY & MORTALITY WKLY. RPT. 177 (2022).

[7] Chris Stokel-Walker, *What Do We Know about Covid Vaccines and Preventing Transmission?*, 376 BMJ o298 (Feb. 4, 2022).

[8] *Safety of COVID-19 Vaccines*, CTRS. FOR DISEASE CONTROL & PREVENTION, www.cdc .gov/coronavirus/2019-ncov/vaccines/safety/safety-of-vaccines.html (last updated June 13, 2022).

[9] Andrew Joseph, *Early Data Indicate Vaccines Still Protect against Omicron's Sister Variant, BA.2*, STAT (Jan. 28, 2022), www.statnews.com/2022/01/28/ early-data-indicate-vaccines-still-protect-against-omicrons-sister-variant-ba-2.

[10] ERIC C. SCHNEIDER ET AL., COMMONWEALTH FUND, THE U.S. COVID-19 VACCINATION PROGRAM AT ONE YEAR: HOW MANY DEATHS AND HOSPITALIZATIONS WERE AVERTED? (2021), www.commonwealthfund.org/publications/issue-briefs/2021/dec/ us-covid-19-vaccination-program-one-year-how-many-deaths-and.

That was not to be. One problem was that supplies remained scarce in low-income countries. Although wealthy nations promised to share vaccines with poorer countries, and the United States provided more than 415 million doses,[11] wealthy countries tied up much of the world's supply with purchase contracts.[12] Intellectual property rights further impeded the development of low-cost generic vaccines.[13] These and other barriers added to COVID's toll in many countries while also magnifying the risk of new variants.[14] Two of those variants, delta and omicron, hit the United States hard. In each case, the vaccines were somewhat less effective in preventing infection and severe disease than they had been with the original, "wild" strain.[15]

Equity was also a problem within the United States. In early 2021, it was a challenge to get vaccinated. Getting a coveted appointment required good Internet access, and one often had to be willing (and able) to travel to a vaccination site, many of which were located in largely white communities that were inaccessible by public transportation.[16] Compounding the problem, many states did not provide workers with paid leave to get vaccinated or recuperate from side effects, making it difficult for low-wage workers to get the shot. Individuals with disabilities also faced formidable barriers getting to vaccination sites, and many people of color, who had strong reasons to distrust the health care system due to the long history of systemic racism,

[11] DOLORES ALBARRACIN ET AL., GETTING TO AND SUSTAINING THE NEXT NORMAL: A ROADMAP FOR LIVING WITH COVID 13 (2022), www.rockefellerfoundation.org/wp-content/uploads/2022/03/Getting-to-and-Sustaining-the-Next-Normal-A-Roadmap-for-Living-with-Covid-Report-Final.pdf.

[12] Felix Stein, *Risky Business: COVAX and the Financialization of Global Vaccine Equity*, 17 GLOBALIZATION & HEALTH (2021).

[13] Joia Mukherjee et al., *Global Vaccine Inequity Led to the COVID-19 Omicron Variant: It's Time for Collective Action*, HEALTH AFFS. FOREFRONT (Jan. 26, 2022), www.healthaffairs .org/do/10.1377/forefront.20220124.776516.

[14] *Id.*

[15] Joseph, *supra* note 9; Noah Higgins-Dunn, *From Escape Mutations to Wild Strains: Here's Everything You Need to Know about Covid Variants*, CNBC (Feb. 23, 2021), www.cnbc .com/2021/02/23/covid-variants-heres-everything-you-need-to-know.html.

[16] Natasha Williams et al., *Assessment of Racial and Ethnic Disparities in Access to COVID-19 Vaccination Sites in Brooklyn, New York*, 4 JAMA NETWORK OPEN e2113937 (2021), https://jamanetwork.com/journals/jamanetworkopen/fullarticle/2781195.

remained wary.[17] Although these problems did not disappear, over time, access improved in low-income communities, thanks in large measure to the hard work of community groups. Vaccine distrust among communities of color also declined,[18] and racial and ethnic gaps in vaccine coverage narrowed.[19]

Other problems arose, however. In April 2021, the CDC and the FDA recommended pausing use of Johnson & Johnson's vaccine as reports emerged about rare blood clots associated with it.[20] The agencies lifted the pause ten days later, but the damage was done, as the public lost confidence in that vaccine.[21] In July 2021, an outbreak among a highly vaccinated population in Provincetown, Massachusetts, showed that infections among those who were vaccinated were not as rare as initially thought.[22] That became more apparent as the months progressed, immunity waned, and new variants emerged. To many vaccine opponents, these developments demonstrated that the vaccines did not work.

Poor messaging about boosters made matters worse. After data showed that vaccine-induced immunity waned over time, the Biden administration began planning to offer booster shots to adults. The rollout, however, was confusing, with many experts initially questioning the need for boosters. In October 2021, after the FDA approved boosters for all frontline workers, CDC director Rochelle

[17] Hayley S. Thompson et al., *Factors Associated with Racial/Ethnic Group-Based Medical Mistrust and Perspectives on COVID-19 Vaccine Trial Participation and Vaccine Uptake in the US*, 4 JAMA Network Open e2111629 (2021), https://jamanetwork.com/journals/jamanetworkopen/fullarticle/2780402.

[18] Tasleem J. Padamsee et al., *Changes in COVID-19 Vaccine Hesitancy among Black and White Individuals in the US*, 5 JAMA Network Open e214470 (Jan. 21, 2022), https://jamanetwork.com/journals/jamanetworkopen/fullarticle/2788286.

[19] Nambi Ndugga et al., *Latest Data on COVID-19 Vaccinations by Race/Ethnicity*, Kaiser Fam. Found. (Apr. 7, 2022), www.kff.org/coronavirus-covid-19/issue-brief/latest-data-on-covid-19-vaccinations-by-race-ethnicity.

[20] Press Release, Food & Drug Admin., Joint CDC and FDA Statement on Johnson & Johnson COVID-19 Vaccine (Apr. 13, 2021), www.fda.gov/news-events/press-announcements/joint-cdc-and-fda-statement-johnson-johnson-covid-19-vaccine.

[21] Sy Mukherjee, *Public Confidence in the Johnson & Johnson Vaccine Has Dropped. What Will It Take to Restore Trust?*, Fortune (Apr. 16, 2021), https://fortune.com/2021/04/16/johnson-and-johnson-vaccine-covid-19-j-and-j-vaccination-public-trust-blood-clots.

[22] Ellen Barry & Beth Treffeisen, *"It's Nowhere Near Over": A Beach Town's Gust of Freedom, Then a U-Turn*, N.Y. Times (July 31, 2021), www.nytimes.com/2021/07/31/us/covid-outbreak-provincetown-cape-cod.html.

Walensky overruled the agency's advisory panel, which had rejected that proposal.[23] These disagreements among scientists added to the public's confusion and distrust.

As Chapter 8 discusses, the proliferation of misinformation and the increasingly partisan nature of views about vaccination further undermined efforts to vaccinate Americans. As of June 2022, only 67 percent of the US population was fully vaccinated and only 32 percent had received a booster.[24] In comparison, in Canada, 84 percent of the population was fully vaccinated and 58 percent was boosted.[25] Importantly, US vaccination rates varied dramatically by partisan affiliation: Republicans were far less likely to be vaccinated than Democrats.[26]

Governments, universities, and employers tried many strategies to increase vaccination rates, from public service campaigns to lotteries. In the spring of 2021, many universities that were anxious to resume in-person learning required students and staff to be vaccinated (often subject to exemptions).[27] In July 2021, New York City announced that it would require health care workers to be vaccinated or undergo weekly COVID testing.[28] Other jurisdictions soon imposed mandates on all or some public employees. Some required proof of vaccination to eat in restaurants or patronize other establishments.[29] Reflecting the

[23] Apoorva Mandavilli & Benjamin Mueller, *C.D.C. Chief Overrules Agency Panel and Recommends Pfizer-BioNTech Boosters for Workers at Risk*, N.Y. TIMES (Oct. 21, 2021), www.nytimes.com/2021/09/24/world/covid-boosters-vaccine-cdc-director.html.

[24] *See How Vaccinations Are Going in Your County and State*, N.Y. TIMES, www.nytimes.com/interactive/2020/us/covid-19-vaccine-doses.html (last updated June 15, 2022).

[25] Josh Holder, *Tracking Coronavirus Vaccinations around the World*, N.Y. TIMES, www.nytimes.com/interactive/2021/world/covid-vaccinations-tracker.html (last updated June 17, 2022).

[26] Ashley Kirzinger et al., *KFF COVID-19 Vaccine Monitor: The Increasing Importance of Partisanship in Predicting COVID-19 Vaccination Status*, KAISER FAM. FOUND. (Nov. 16, 2021), www.kff.org/coronavirus-covid-19/poll-finding/importance-of-partisanship-predicting-vaccination-status.

[27] Rukmini Callimachi, *For Colleges, Vaccine Mandates Often Depend on Which Party Is in Power*, N.Y. TIMES (Aug. 12, 2021), www.nytimes.com/2021/05/22/us/college-vaccine-universities.html.

[28] AJMC Staff, *A Timeline of COVID-19 Vaccine Developments for the Second Half of 2021*, AM. J. MANAGED CARE (Dec. 23, 2021), www.ajmc.com/view/a-timeline-of-covid-19-vaccine-developments-for-the-second-half-of-2021.

[29] *E.g.*, Press Release, City of New York, Mayor de Blasio Announces Vaccine Mandates for Private Sector Workers, and Major Expansions to Nation-Leading "Key to NYC" Program (Dec. 6, 2021), www1.nyc.gov/office-of-the-mayor/news/807-21/mayor-de-blasio-vaccine-mandate-private-sector-workers-major-expansions-to#.

partisan divide, the mandates were clustered in Democratic-leaning areas. Several Republican-leaning states blocked mandates for state workers and barred proof of vaccination requirements.[30]

As Chapter 2 discusses, states have long had vaccine mandates for schoolchildren. Originally, these mandates only covered the smallpox vaccine, but even as that mandate was lifted (after smallpox was eradicated, thanks to vaccines), states followed federal guidance and added other vaccines to the required list. Universities and health care facilities have also long required students and workers to be vaccinated for different diseases. Some mandates are fairly strict; others are relatively loose. Not surprisingly, the details impact their efficacy.[31]

The rationale for vaccine mandates is simple: Vaccines help everyone by reducing a communicable disease's prevalence within a community. With some diseases, this can create herd immunity, in which so few people remain susceptible to a disease that transmission cannot be sustained. Early on, many hoped that the COVID vaccines (and/or prior infection) would lead to herd immunity, but the virus's rapid mutation and the arrival of ever more variants quashed that hope.

Even so, vaccines can reduce contagion, and mandates are a time-tested way of increasing vaccination rates. Numerous studies show that prepandemic mandates improved vaccination rates among health care workers[32] and schoolchildren.[33] Early anecdotal reports suggested that workplace mandates increased COVID vaccination rates among employees. After instituting a mandate, Tyson Foods blogged, "over 96% of our active team members are vaccinated – or nearly 60,000 more than" when the mandate was announced.[34] In November 2021, the American Public Health Association and other leading health organizations called for mandates, stating, "We know

---

[30] *State Efforts to Ban or Enforce COVID-19 Vaccine Mandates and Passports*, NAT. ACAD. STATE HEALTH POL'Y (last updated June 10, 2022), www.nashp.org/ state-lawmakers-submit-bills-to-ban-employer-vaccine-mandates.

[31] Robert A. Bednarczyk et al. *Current Landscape of Nonmedical Vaccination Exemptions in the United States: Impact of Policy Changes*, 18 EXPERT REV. VACCINES 175 (2019).

[32] *E.g.*, Tiffany L. Wang et al., *Mandatory Influenza Vaccination for All Healthcare Personnel: A Review on Justification, Implementation and Effectiveness*, 29 CURRENT OPINION PEDIATRICS 606, 609 (2017).

[33] Devon Greyson et al., *Impact of School Vaccination Mandates on Pediatric Vaccination Coverage: A Systemic Review*, 7 CMAJ OPEN e524, e524 (2019).

[34] Donnie King, *Beating COVID-19, #TysonTogether*, TYSON: THE FEED BLOG (Oct. 26, 2021), https://thefeed.blog/2021/10/26/it-takes-a-team-to-fight-covid-19.

that vaccine mandates are effective. When employers require workers to get vaccinated, vaccination rates increase to over 90 percent."[35]

Despite such success, mandates are controversial, and opposition to them can rally antivaccination sentiment.[36] Workplace mandates can also backfire if many employees quit their jobs rather than get vaccinated. Traditionally, states have tried to thwart the backlash by allowing religious and personal belief exemptions to childhood vaccine mandates.[37] When opposition to vaccines is limited, exemptions have a relatively small impact on vaccination rates.

That can change in the face of a significant antivaccination movement. Starting in the late 1900s, a zealous antivaccination movement took off. Initially, it focused on alleged safety concerns, including the thoroughly refuted claim that the MMR vaccine causes autism.[38] Critics also linked vaccines to fetal cell lines and abortion. The proliferation of misinformation and the erosion of trust in science, coupled with the growth of a medical freedom movement, helped fuel the resistance.[39]

As opposition grew, more parents sought exemptions. Predictably, significant outbreaks of measles among unvaccinated children occurred, including in California in 2014[40] and New York in 2018 and 2019.[41] In response, both states eliminated nonmedical exemptions. Not surprisingly, these repeals were challenged in court on free exercise grounds. Before the pandemic, those were losing claims.[42]

---

[35] Press Release, Am. Pub. Health Ass'n, Leading Health Experts and Professional Organizations: Business Should Support OSHA's COVID Vaccine Mandate (Nov. 18, 2021), www.apha.org/News-and-Media/News-Releases/APHA-News-Releases/2021/Businesses-should-support-vaccine-mandate.

[36] See David I. Benbow, The Dizziness of Freedom: Understanding and Responding to Vaccine Anxieties, 49 J. L. MED. & ETHICS 580, 582 (2021).

[37] See WEN W. SHEN, CONG. RSCH. SERV., R46745, STATE AND FEDERAL AUTHORITY TO MANDATE COVID-19 VACCINATION, 5 (2021), https://crsreports.congress.gov/product/pdf/R/R46745.

[38] Autism and Vaccines, CTRS. FOR DISEASE CONTROL & PREVENTION, www.cdc.gov/vaccine-safety/concerns/autism.html (last visited May 10, 2022).

[39] Peter J. Hotez, America's Deadly Flirtation with Antiscience and the Medical Freedom Movement, 131 J. CLINICAL INVESTIGATION e149072 (2021).

[40] Cari Nierenberg, Disneyland Measles Outbreak Confirmed to Be Linked to Low Vaccination Rates, SCI. AM. (Mar. 17, 2015), www.scientificamerican.com/article/disneyland-measles-outbreak-confirmed-to-be-linked-to-low-vaccination-rates.

[41] Jane R. Zucker et al., Consequences of Undervaccination – Measles Outbreak, New York City, 2018–2019, 382 NEW ENG. J. MED. 1009, 1009 (2020).

[42] Wendy E. Parmet, From the Shadows: The Public Health Implications of the Supreme Court's Free Exercise Cases, 49 J. L. MED. & ETHICS 564, 567 (2021).

VACCINES AND RELIGIOUS LIBERTY

Between January 2021 and February 1, 2022, private employers, states, and local governments brought more than one hundred cases in state and federal courts challenging COVID vaccine mandates. Challengers raised every legal claim imaginable. Some argued that it was unlawful to mandate a vaccine that had only received EUA (a claim that was largely mooted once the Pfizer-BioNTech vaccine received full FDA approval in August 2021).[43] Others argued that mandates violated the due process clause of the Fourteenth Amendment (or the Fifth Amendment in relation to federal mandates) by infringing on their bodily integrity. Most claims received little traction.[44] Some free exercise claims fared better.

Although most organized religions do not oppose COVID-19 vaccination, many vaccine rejecters cite religious objections. Sometimes they claimed that the vaccines contained or were developed using cell lines from aborted fetuses. In actuality, the vaccines do not contain fetal cell lines, although the Johnson & Johnson vaccine was grown in a cell line that was derived from fetal cells and the Pfizer-BioNTech and Moderna vaccines were tested in experiments that used fetal cells. However, as former NIH director Francis Collins has explained, so, too, were "a very long list of current medicines, including aspirin and statins"[45] that are not usually met with religious objections. Nevertheless, in free exercise cases, courts demand neither logical consistency nor fidelity to established doctrines. (Doing so might raise problems under the First Amendment's establishment clause.) Instead, they usually defer to an individual's assertion that a law

---

[43] Press Release, U.S. Food & Drug. Admin., FDA Approves First COVID-19 Vaccine (Aug. 23, 2021), www.fda.gov/news-events/press-announcements/fda-approves-first-covid-19-vaccine.

[44] *See, e.g.*, Klaassen v. Trs. of Ind. Univ., 7 F. 4th 592 (7th Cir. 2021); Troogstad v. City of Chicago, 576 F. Supp. 3d 578 (N.D. Ill. 2021) *aff'd sub nom* Lukaszczyk v. Cook Cty, 47 F. 4th 587 (7 th Cir. 2022); Valdez v. Grisham, 559 F. Supp. 3d 1161 (D. N. M. 2021), *aff'd* No. 21-2105 2022 WL 2129071 (10th Cir. June 14, 2022).

[45] Michael Gerson, *Most Evangelical Objections to Vaccines Have Nothing to Do with Christianity*, Wash. Post (Dec. 30, 2021), www.washingtonpost.com/opinions/2021/12/30/vaccine-resistance-evangelical-christianity.

burdens their sincerely held religious beliefs, as they understand them.[46] This approach prevents courts from having to delve into questions of religious doctrine; it also makes it difficult for them to separate claims that are grounded in sincere religious objections from those that are not.[47]

Before COVID, most vaccine mandates have included religious exemptions. Some laws also demand them. For example, Title VII of the Civil Rights Act of 1964 requires private employers to accommodate an employee's religious practices as long as doing so does not create an undue burden.[48] The federal Religious Freedom Restoration Act (RFRA), which was enacted in response to *Employment Division v. Smith*,[49] compels courts to apply strict scrutiny to actions by the federal government that restrict religious liberty.[50]

Yet before the pandemic, courts read *Jacobson v. Massachusetts*[51] and *Smith* to hold that states need not provide religious exemptions to vaccine mandates. Although *Jacobson* was not a free exercise case, the Court often treated it as relevant in such cases. For example, in 1944, the Court cited *Jacobson* in rejecting a free exercise challenge to a child labor law, stating that a parent "cannot claim freedom from compulsory vaccination for the child more than for himself on religious grounds."[52] Later, in *Sherbert v. Verner* (1963), the Court cited *Jacobson* for the point that the Constitution does not protect religious actions that may harm others.[53]

Smith, which held that generally applicable laws that do not target religion are subject to rational basis review, further buttressed that conclusion.[54] Because vaccine laws do not single out religious believers,

---

[46] Samuel J. Levine, *The Supreme Court's Hands-Off Approach to Religious Questions in the Era of COVID-19 and Beyond*, 24 U. PA. J. CONST. L. 276, 281 (2022).

[47] Dorit Reiss, *People Lie about Their "Religious" Objections to Vaccines. Proving It Is Hard*, WASH. POST (Oct. 15, 2021), www.washingtonpost.com/outlook/religious-exemptions-law-vaccines-dishonesty/2021/10/15/df405c38-2d0d-11ec-8ef6-3ca8fe943a92_story.html.

[48] Mark A. Rothstein et al., *Employer-Mandated Vaccination for COVID-19*, 111 AM. J. PUB. HEALTH 1061, 1063 (2021).

[49] Emp. Div. v. Smith, 494 U.S. 872 (1990).

[50] 42 U.S.C. § 2000bb et seq.

[51] Jacobson v. Massachusetts, 197 U.S. 11 (1905).

[52] Prince v. Massachusetts, 321 U.S. 158, 166 n.12 (1944).

[53] Sherbert v. Verner, 374 U.S. 398, 403 (1963).

[54] *Smith*, 494 U.S. at 888–89.

pre-COVID, courts consistently held that strict scrutiny did not apply to free exercise challenges to vaccine laws.[55]

The legal climate changed significantly when the Court sidelined *Jacobson* in *Roman Catholic Diocese v. Cuomo*[56] and subsequent social distancing cases. As Chapter 4 discusses, these cases eviscerated *Smith*, even if they did not overrule it. Notably, *Tandon v. Newsom* held that strict scrutiny was required as long as the state treated any comparable secular activity more favorably than any regulated religious activity.[57] Mandate opponents used that to argue that if a vaccine mandate has a medical exemption (as all do), it must offer a religious exemption. In effect, they claimed that medical and religious exemptions are comparable, and that the presence of the former necessitates the latter.

Fulton v. City of Philadelphia created further challenges.[58] As Chapter 4 describes, *Fulton* held that strict scrutiny is required whenever a state retains discretion to grant individualized exemptions. Opponents of mandates used this to argue that as long as a state has discretion to grant exemptions, any refusal to grant a religious one is subject to strict scrutiny.

Dahl v. Board of Trustees of Western Michigan University (2021), which concerned a mandate for student athletes, is illustrative.[59] On paper, the mandate included a religious exemption; in actuality, the university never granted an exemption, nor did it establish a process for doing so. The US Court of Appeals for Sixth Circuit held that strict scrutiny was required by *Fulton* simply because the university had discretion to grant or deny an exemption. The court then held that the mandate failed strict scrutiny.[60]

The theoretical availability of a religious exemption also did not save the US military's mandate. Military immunization mandates date back to the Revolutionary War, when George Washington required

---

[55] Donna M. Gitter, *First Amendment Challenges to State Vaccine Mandates: Why the U.S. Supreme Court Should Hold That the Free Exercise Clause Does Not Require Religious Exemptions*, 71 Am. U. L. Rev. (forthcoming 2022).

[56] Roman Cath. Diocese of Brooklyn v. Cuomo, 141 S. Ct. 63 (2020).

[57] Tandon v. Newsom, 141 S. Ct. 1294, 1296 (2021).

[58] Fulton v. City of Philadelphia, 141 S. Ct. 1868 (2021).

[59] Dahl v. Bd. of Trs. of W. Mich. Univ., 15 F. 4th 728 (6th Cir. 2021) (per curiam).

[60] *Id.* at 733–35.

the Continental Army to be inoculated against smallpox.[61] Despite that history and the traditional deference that courts grant to the military, a federal district court in *U.S. Navy Seals 1–26 v. Biden* (2022) used an analysis similar to that in *Dahl* to find that the Navy violated both the free exercise clause and RFRA by denying plaintiffs' request for religious exemptions and refusing to deploy them while unvaccinated.[62] On appeal, the Fifth Circuit relied on RFRA to deny the Navy's request for a stay of the lower court's order.[63] The Navy then asked the Supreme Court to enable it to make deployment decisions while the litigation continued. Without ruling on the merits, the Supreme Court narrowed (but did not lift) the injunction, over the dissent of Justices Samuel Alito and Neil Gorsuch, who argued that the mandate violated RFRA.[64]

Cases like *Dahl* and *U.S. Navy Seals* create a type of catch-22: Once a religious exemption is offered, governments face constitutional peril if they deny it to anyone who seeks it. That might suggest that mandates should not include religious exemptions. But as noted above, other laws often preclude that option.[65] Nor does the lack of a religious exemption ensure that a mandate will escape strict scrutiny. That's because *Tandon* requires strict scrutiny as long as the state treats any *comparable* secular activity more favorably than the plaintiff's religious exercise, and every vaccine mandate allows for medical exemptions.[66] Indeed, the Americans with Disabilities Act demands them in some cases,[67] and *Jacobson* implies that the Constitution might do so as well.[68]

The U.S. Court of Appeals for the First Circuit in *Jane Does 1–6 v. Mills* (2021) considered a challenge to Maine's mandate for health care

---

[61] Stanley M. Lemon et al., Protecting Our Forces, Improving Vaccine Acquisition and Availability in the U.S. Military 4 (2002), https://perma.cc/E545-TQ9G.

[62] U.S. Navy Seals 1–26 v. Biden, 578 F. Supp. 3d 822 (N.D. Tex. 2022, *aff'd*, No. 27 F. 4th 336 (5th Cir. 2022) (denying a partial stay on the preliminary injunction that precludes the Navy from considering the plaintiffs' vaccination status in making deployment and assignment decision), *stayed in part sub nom*, Austin v. U.S. Navy Seals 1–26, 142 S. Ct. 1301 (2022).

[63] U.S. Navy Seals, at 350-52.

[64] Austin v. U.S. Navy Seals 1–26, 142 S. Ct. at 1301, 1307 (Alito, J., dissenting).

[65] Rothstein et al., *supra* note 48, at 1063.

[66] Tandon v. Newsom, 141 S. Ct. 1294, 1296 (2021).

[67] Rothstein et al., *supra* note 48, at 1062.

[68] Jacobson v. Massachusetts, 197 U.S. 11, 30 (1905).

workers that was based on the availability of medical exemptions.[69] Writing for the court, Judge Sandra Lynch found that medical exemptions were not comparable to religious exemptions because the former serve the state's interest in protecting health by excusing those who cannot be vaccinated safely. Religious exemptions, in contrast, do not protect health. Then, after determining that strict scrutiny was inapplicable, she ruled that the mandate would nevertheless survive such review because Maine had no less restrictive means for protecting patient health.[70]

The plaintiffs then sought emergency review from the Supreme Court. On October 29, 2021, the Court, by a 6–3 vote from the shadow docket, rejected their petition.[71] Although there was no majority opinion, Justice Amy Coney Barrett, in a concurring opinion that Justice Brett Kavanaugh joined, explained that the decision to deny an emergency petition includes a discretionary component that "counsels against a grant of extraordinary relief in this case, which is the first to address the questions presented."[72] In short, without affirming that the state could deny religious exemptions, Barrett signaled that she did not believe that the Court should use its shadow docket, at least at that moment, to enter the fray.

Gorsuch felt no such compunction. In a dissent that Justices Clarence Thomas and Alito joined, he argued that because Maine allowed for medical exemptions, strict scrutiny was required.[73] Applying that test, he warned that slowing the spread of COVID-19 should not qualify as a compelling state interest "forever."[74] He added that "Maine's decision to deny a religious exemption in these circumstances doesn't just fail the least restrictive means test, it borders on the irrational."[75]

In the weeks that followed, the Supreme Court continued to refuse to hear free exercise challenges to state mandates, even as Gorsuch,

---

[69] Does 1–6 v. Mills, 16 F. 4th 20, 31 (1st Cir. 2021).
[70] Id. at 33–34.
[71] Does 1–3 v. Mills, 142 S. Ct. 17 (2021).
[72] Id. at 18 (Barrett, J., concurring).
[73] Id. at 19 (Gorsuch, J., dissenting).
[74] Id. at 21.
[75] Id. at 22.

Thomas, and Alito continued to argue that the lack or denial of a religious exemptions was unconstitutional.[76]

THE SCOPE OF FEDERAL AUTHORITY

In December 2020, President-elect Joe Biden stated that he "wouldn't demand [that vaccination] be mandatory."[77] Instead, he promised to "encourage people to do the right thing."[78] Nine months later, as efforts to vaccinate Americans faltered and after the FDA granted full approval to the Pfizer-BioNTech vaccine, Biden changed his position, and his administration began requiring vaccination in a number of sectors subject to federal oversight. On August 18, 2021, the federal Centers for Medicare and Medicaid Services (CMS) announced that it would require that staff in nursing homes that receive federal funds be vaccinated.[79] A week later, the Pentagon announced that active-duty military personnel would have to be vaccinated.[80] Then, on September 9, Biden ordered all federal workers – who previously faced a vaccinate-or-test requirement – plus all federal contractors to be vaccinated.[81] He also directed the Occupational Safety and Health Administration (OSHA) to develop an emergency temporary standard (ETS) requiring employers with more than one hundred employees to mandate either vaccination or masking and weekly testing.[82]

Together, these federal mandates had the potential to significantly increase vaccination rates, including in sectors (such as health care and frontline workplaces) that faced high rates of COVID transmission.

---

[76] Dr. A. v. Hochul, 142 S. Ct. 552, 556 (2021) (Gorsuch, J., dissenting).

[77] Jacob Jarvis, *Fact Check: Did Joe Biden Reject Idea of Mandatory Vaccines in December 2020?*, NEWSWEEK (Sept. 10, 2020), www.newsweek.com/fact-check-joe-biden-no-vaccines-mandatory-december-2020-1627774.

[78] *Id.*

[79] AJMC Staff, *supra* note 28.

[80] *Id.*

[81] Exec. Order No. 14043, 86 Fed. Reg. 50,989 (Sept. 9, 2021); Exec. Order No. 14042, 86 Fed. Reg. 50,985 (Sept. 9, 2021), www.whitehouse.gov/briefing-room/presidential-actions/2021/09/09/executive-order-on-ensuring-adequate-covid-safety-protocols-for-federal-contractors.

[82] Katie Rogers & Sheryl Gay Stolberg, *Biden Mandates Vaccines for Workers, Saying, "Our Patience Is Wearing Thin,"* N.Y. TIMES (Sept. 9, 2021), www.nytimes.com/2021/09/09/us/politics/biden-mandates-vaccines.html.

OSHA estimated that the workplace rules alone would save 6,500 lives and prevent 250,000 hospitalizations over six months.[83]

Not surprisingly, the mandates were met by a barrage of legal challenges. To understand these cases, it is important to recall that the federal government, unlike the states, lacks a police power. Hence, all federal regulations must rest on one of the constitutionally enumerated bases for federal action. For health regulations, the most common sources of authority are Congress's powers under Article I to regulate international or interstate commerce, or to tax and spend for the general welfare.[84] Actions by federal administrative agencies, such as the CDC or OSHA, must also be authorized by acts of Congress.

Congress has traditionally given administrative agencies broad powers to carry out its objectives. In 1989, the Supreme Court explained, "Congress simply cannot do its job absent an ability to delegate power under broad general directives."[85] This seems especially true when it comes to public health for which scientific expertise and the ability to act swiftly can be crucial. If Congress had to predict every health threat and explicate every specific response, the federal government would be impotent to protect the nation's health. Nor can states alone respond effectively to threats – such as pandemics – that cross state lines.

States have also long recognized the benefits of giving their own health agencies broad authority. In 1868, the New York Court of Appeals upheld the authority of the new Metropolitan Board of Health by stating, "from the earliest organization of the government, the absolute control over persons and property, so far as the public health was concerned, was vested in boards or officers, who exercised a summary jurisdiction over the subject."[86] In *Jacobson*, Justice John Marshall Harlan agreed, stating,

> The authority to determine for all what ought to be done in such an emergency must have been lodged somewhere or in some body; and surely it was appropriate for the legislature to refer that

[83] COVID-19 Vaccination and Testing Emergency Temporary Standard, 86 Fed. Reg. 61402, 61408 (2021).
[84] Michelle M. Mello & Wendy E. Parmet, *Perspective: U.S. Public Health Law – Foundations and Emerging Shifts*, 386 N. Eng. J. Med. 805, 805 (2022).
[85] Mistretta v. United States, 488 U.S. 361, 372 (1989).
[86] Metro. Bd. of Health v. Heister, 37 N.Y. 661, 670 (1868).

question, in the first instance, to a board of health composed of persons residing in the locality affected and appointed, presumably, because of their fitness to determine such questions.[87]

Despite that history, in 1935, the Supreme Court blocked two New Deal statutes that dealt with economic (not health) matters, declaring that Congress's delegation of authority to the executive branch was impermissibly broad.[88] In *A.L.A. Schechter Poultry Corp. v. United States*, the Court stated, "Congress cannot delegate legislative powers to the President to exercise an unfettered discretion to make whatever laws he thinks may be needed or advisable."[89] Since then, the Court has not struck another federal statute on nondelegation grounds. Instead, it has accepted that delegations are constitutional as long as Congress supplies an "intelligible principle" to cabin administrative authority.[90] In 2001, the Court held that requiring an agency to set standards to protect the public's health satisfied that requirement.[91] Such rulings have allowed the federal government to address a wide range of health threats.

That doesn't mean that the Court has totally abstained from checking the reach of administrative agencies. Despite the much-debated "*Chevron* doctrine," under which courts grant deference to an agency's own interpretation of its authority when it does not violate a statute's plain meaning,[92] the Court has sometimes read broad grants of authority narrowly. For example, in 2000 in *Food and Drug Administration v. Brown and Williamson Tobacco Corp.*, the Court held that the FDA's claim of authority over tobacco was inconsistent with the structure of the Food, Drug, and Cosmetic Act and other federal statutes relating to tobacco.[93] And in 2014 in *Utility Air Regulatory Group v. Environmental Protection Agency*, the Court ruled that the EPA lacked authority over greenhouse gases, stating, "We expect

---

[87] Jacobson v. Massachusetts, 197 U.S. 11, 27 (1905).
[88] A.L.A. Schechter Poultry Corp. v. United States, 295 U.S. 495, 541–42 (1935); Panama Refining Co. v. Ryan, 293 U.S. 388, 430–32 (1935).
[89] *Schechter*, 295 U.S. at 537–38.
[90] Whitman v. Am. Trucking Ass'ns, 531 U.S. 457, 472 (2001) (quoting J. W. Hampton, Jr. & Co. v. U.S., 276 U.S. 394, 409 (1928)).
[91] *Id.* at 474–76.
[92] Chevron U.S.A., Inc. v. Nat'l Res. Def. Council, 467 U.S. 837, 842–43 (1984).
[93] FDA v. Brown & Williamson Tobacco Corp., 529 U.S. 120, 126 (2000).

Congress to speak clearly if it wishes to assign to an agency decisions of vast 'economic and political significance.'"[94]

These precedents gave rise to what has become known as the "major questions doctrine," under which courts require specific statutory authorization for regulations about so-called major questions. The doctrine can be viewed as a mode of statutory construction, or as a way of reining in broad delegations of authority without explicitly reviving *Schechter*, a step that at least five currently serving justices of the Supreme Court have expressed interest in taking.[95]

This approach to statutory construction and delegation became salient in 2020 as state health officials used their emergency powers to impose social distancing laws. Because few statutes explicitly mention all of the measures that officials took in response to COVID, challengers argued that officials had overstepped their authority, and that the broad reading of the statutes that health officials relied on would raise nondelegation concerns. Most state courts rejected these claims, interpreting public health powers broadly, as courts have traditionally done.[96] But some courts took a different approach.

The Wisconsin Supreme Court led the way in a case that the state's Republican legislature brought against Andrea Palm, the secretary-designee of the state's Department of Health Services. By a 4–3 vote in May 2020, the court ruled that Palm lacked authority to issue emergency orders without going through the rulemaking process that state law demands for most regulations.[97] The court added that even if rulemaking was not required, the emergency orders were unlawful because they were not explicitly authorized by the state's communicable disease act.[98] A few months later, the same court held that the governor lacked authority under the state's emergency laws to issue successive emergency declarations and impose a mask mandate.[99] Concurring,

[94] Util. Air Regul. Grp. v. EPA, 573 U.S. 302, 324 (2014) (quoting Brown & Williamson, 529 U.S. at 160).

[95] Julian Davis Mortenson & Nicholas Bagley, *Delegation at the Founding*, 121 COLUM. L. REV. 277, 284 (2021).

[96] *See, e.g.*, Desrosiers v. Governor, 486 Mass. 369, 385–86 (2020).

[97] Wis. Legislature v. Palm, 942 N.W. 2d 900, 912–13 (Wis. 2020).

[98] *Id.* at 916–18.

[99] Fabick v. Evers, 956 N.W. 2d 856, 864–65 (Wis. 2021).

Justice Rebecca Grassl Bradley cited *Schechter* for the "fundamental principle underlying the foundation of our government."[100]

The same perspective was apparent in litigation concerning the CDC's moratorium on evictions. Early in the pandemic, Congress passed a 120-day pause on evictions to reduce hardship and the spread of COVID-19 that would occur if people lost their homes and had to move in with other families or rely on homeless shelters.[101] After that moratorium expired, the CDC issued its own moratorium. Then, in December 2020, Congress extended the moratorium. When that also expired, the CDC extended its own order several times.[102] Litigation ensued.

The issue before the courts was whether the CDC had authority under Section 361(a) of the Public Health Service Act to issue the moratorium.[103] The 1944 act grants the CDC the power to "make and enforce such regulations as in [its] judgment may be necessary to prevent the introduction, transmission, or spread of communicable diseases" into the country or across state lines.[104] The statute adds that "for purposes of carrying out and enforcing such regulations," the CDC "may provide for such inspection, fumigation, disinfection, sanitation, pest extermination, destruction of animals or articles found to be infected or contaminated ... and other measures, as in [its] judgement may be necessary."[105]

Initially, most courts upheld the CDC's moratorium, focusing on the language in Section 361(a) that gives the CDC the authority to do what it finds to be "necessary" to prevent the spread of communicable diseases into the country or across state lines.[106] But in 2021, some courts read the statute to limit the CDC to the specific measures that

[100] *Id.* at 871 (Bradley, J., concurring).
[101] Mahathi Vemireddy & Faith Khalik, *Eviction Moratorium Cases Reveal Court's Misunderstanding of Public Health*, BILL OF HEALTH (July 29, 2021), https://blog.petrieflom.law.harvard.edu/2021/07/29/eviction-moratorium-public-health-courts.
[102] *Id.* The statute grants the power to the surgeon general, but the authority has since been shifted to the CDC.
[103] Public Health Service Act of 1944, 58 Stat. 682, 703 (codified as amended at 42 U.S.C. §§ 201-300mm-61 (West 2021)).
[104] *Id.* at § 264(a).
[105] *Id.*
[106] *See, e.g.*, Brown v. Azar, 497 F. Supp. 3d 1270, 1299 (N.D. Ga. 2020), *aff'd* Brown v. Sec't U.S. Dep't of Health & Hum. Servs., 4 F. 2d 1220 (11th Cir. 2021), *vacated* 20 F. 4th 1385 (11th Cir. 2021); Chambless Enters. v. Redfield, 508 F. Supp. 3d 101, 123–24 (W.D. La. 2020).

are enumerated in Section 361(a), arguing that a broader reading of the CDC's powers would raise federalism and separation of powers issues.[107]

In June 2021, the moratorium came before the Supreme Court. By a 5–4 vote, from the shadow docket, the Court refused to block the moratorium.[108] Concurring, Kavanaugh (whose vote was essential to the decision not to block the moratorium) stated that he voted as he did only because the moratorium was set to expire at the end of July.[109] After the decision, Biden announced that the CDC would issue a new, narrower moratorium, which it did on August 6, 2021.[110] This time, the Court was less forgiving. On August 26, by a 6–3 vote from the shadow docket, the Supreme Court blocked the new moratorium.[111]

In the unsigned opinion in *Alabama Association of Realtors v. Department of Health and Human Services*, the majority argued that the CDC's interpretation of its authority reached too far. According to the Court, all the measures enumerated in Section 361(a) "directly relate to the interstate spread of disease," whereas there was only a "downstream connection between eviction and the interstate spread of disease."[112] Citing *Brown and Williamson*, the Court added that even if the "text were ambiguous," the CDC claimed a "breathtaking amount of authority," and that "'precedents require Congress to enact exceedingly clear language if it wishes to significantly alter the balance between federal and state power and the power of the Government over private property.'"[113] With that, the Court warned Congress that it had to speak with specificity if it wanted to give federal agencies broad authority over significant issues that touch on the states' police power.

---

[107] *See, e.g.*, Tiger Lily, LLC. v. U.S. Dep't of Hous. & Urb. Dev., 5 F. 4th 666 (6th Cir. 2021). *See also* Skyworks, Ltd. v. Ctrs. for Disease Control & Prevention, 524 F. Supp. 3d 745 (N.D. Ohio 2021).

[108] Ala. Ass'n of Realtors v. Dep't of Health & Hum. Servs., 141 S. Ct. 2320 (2021) (per curiam).

[109] *Id.* at 2321 (Kavanaugh, J., concurring).

[110] *Temporary Halt in Residential Evictions in Communities with Substantial or High Transmission of COVID-19 to Prevent the Further Spread of COVID-19*, 86 FED. REG. 43244 (Aug. 6, 2021).

[111] Ala. Ass'n of Realtors v. Dep't of Health & Human Servs., 141 S. Ct. 2485 (2021) (per curiam).

[112] *Id.* at 2488.

[113] *Id.* at 2489 (quoting U.S. Forest Serv. v. Cowpasture River Preservation Ass'n, 140 S. Ct. 1837, 1850 (2020)).

Alabama Association of Realtors offered a tempting roadmap for those challenging federal vaccine and mask mandates. Because no federal statute explicitly stated that masks or vaccines could be compelled, litigants could and did argue that explicit statutory authorization was required. Many lower courts agreed, enjoining the federal government's vaccine mandates for health care workers,[114] federal contractors,[115] and large employers.[116] In April 2022, one federal court in Florida enjoined the CDC's mask mandate for public transportation.[117]

The courts in these cases read the authority of federal agencies as narrowly as possible. In the Florida mask case, for example, federal district judge Kathryn Kimball Mizelle invoked the major questions doctrine and held that the CDC could not mandate masking in public transportation because Section 361(a) does not specifically mention masking, and masking could not fall within the enumerated term "sanitation" because the most common definition of that term, in the years before the statute was enacted, focused on cleaning.[118] In so doing, Mizelle discarded the definition of sanitation that related most closely to public health, even though she was construing the Public Health Service Act. She also ignored the fact that the Supreme Court in *Alabama Association of Realtors* seemed to suggest that the CDC could act to stop the direct interstate spread of disease, as masking in transportation does.

Many of the judges who blocked the various federal orders also sounded constitutional alarms. For example, in reviewing OSHA's requirement that large employers mandate vaccination or testing and masking, the US Court of Appeals for the Fifth Circuit stated that the Occupational Safety and Health Act of 1970 (hereinafter referred to as the OSH Act) "likely *could* not be, under the Commerce Clause and nondelegation doctrine – intended to authorize a workplace safety administration in the deep recesses of the federal bureaucracy to make

---

[114] Missouri v. Biden, 571 F. Supp. 3d 516 (E.D. Mo. 2021), *stay denied*, 2021 WL 5631736 (E.D. Mo. Dec. 1, 2021), *stayed* Biden v. Missouri, 142 S. Ct. 647 (2022).

[115] Kentucky v. Biden, 23 F. 4th 585 (6th Cir. 2022).

[116] BST Holdings, LLC v. OSHA, 17 F. 4th 604, 619 (5th Cir. 2021).

[117] Health Freedom Def. Fund v. Biden, No. 8:21-cv-1693-KKM-AEP, 2022 WL 1134138 (M.D. Fla. Apr. 18, 2022).

[118] *Id.* at *4–*7.

sweeping pronouncements on matters of public health affecting every member of society in the profoundest of ways."[119]

Not all lower courts blocked all mandates. For example, another federal judge in Florida relied on *Chevron* and deferred to the CDC's own interpretation of Section 361(a) to uphold the masking mandate.[120] In another case, a split panel of the Sixth Circuit called the major questions doctrine a "seldom-used … canon of statutory interpretation that has been described as an exception to *Chevron* deference,"[121] ruling that the OSH Act granted OSHA "clear" authority to protect workers against infectious diseases, as it has long done.[122] Similarly, a split panel of the US Court of Appeals for the Eleventh Circuit concluded that the major questions doctrine did not apply to the mandate for health care workers, finding that the relevant statutes authorized the secretary of health and human services to impose conditions that are "necessary in the interest of health and safety."[123] The panel added, "To suggest [that Congress had to explicitly authorize vaccine mandates] would mean that Congress had to have anticipated both the unprecedented COVID-19 pandemic and the unprecedented politicization of the disease to regulate vaccination against it."[124]

The Supreme Court also took divergent approaches in the two federal vaccine mandate cases that it decided on January 13, 2022. Perhaps burned by criticism of deciding important cases from the shadow docket without the benefit of argument, the Court decided both cases following expedited argument. In the first case, *Biden v. Missouri* (hereinafter referred to as *Biden*), the Court upheld CMS's mandate (subject to exemptions) for health care workers by a 5–4 vote in an unsigned opinion.[125] In the second case, *National Federation of Independent Businesses v. Department of Labor* (hereinafter referred to as *NFIB*), the Court, by a 6–3 vote in another unsigned opinion, stayed OSHA's rule requiring employers with more than one hundred

---

[119] *BST Holdings,* 17 F. 4th at 611.
[120] Wall v. Ctrs. For Disease Control & Prevention, No. 6:21-cv-00975-PGB-DCI, 2022 WL 1619516 (M.D. Fla. Apr. 29, 2022).
[121] In re MCP No. 165, 21 F. 4th 357, 372 (6th Cir. 2021).
[122] *Id.* at 371.
[123] Florida v. Dep't of Health & Hum. Servs., 19 F. 4th 1271, 1287 (11th Cir. 2021).
[124] *Id.* at 1288.
[125] Biden v. Missouri, 142 S. Ct. 647 (2022).

employees to either mandate vaccination (subject to exemptions) or institute a policy of testing and masking.[126]

Biden was undoubtedly the stronger case for the government. For one thing, CMS's authority derived from the Constitution's spending clause, which the Court has usually read to give Congress broad powers. For another, Congress had explicitly authorized the secretary of health and human services to impose conditions on facilities receiving federal funds that they find "necessary in the interests of the health and safety of individuals who are furnished services."[127] Furthermore, CMS had long used that power to protect patients from hospital-acquired infections. Finally, the idea that health care workers must be vaccinated was, as the majority explained, "consistent with the fundamental principle of the medical profession: first, do no harm."[128] Thus, the Court majority seemed to accept that health care workers, as a class, could be compelled to act to protect *patients* who, as a class, are especially vulnerable to COVID-19.

For the dissenters, even that was a bridge too far. In a dissent that Alito, Gorsuch, and Barrett joined, Thomas argued that the "government has not made a strong showing that this hodgepodge of [statutory] provisions authorizes a nationwide vaccine mandate."[129] He then invoked the major questions doctrine, quoting *Alabama Association of Realtors* for the point that Congress must speak with "exceedingly clear language if it wishes to significantly alter the balance between state and federal power."[130] In doing so, he did not mention the many cases that he had joined limiting the *states'* capacity to respond to the pandemic. Nor did he consider that the mandate was limited to workers in federally funded programs.

In his dissent, which Thomas, Gorsuch, and Barrett joined, Alito focused on the fact that CMS issued the mandate as an emergency measure, bypassing the typical lengthy administrative process. He also offered a broad critique of the administrative state's impact on the lives of Americans, lamenting, "Today, however, most federal

---

[126] Nat'l Fed'n of Indep. Bus. v. Dep't of Lab., 142 S. Ct. 661, 662 (2022).
[127] *Biden,* 142 S. Ct. at 650 (quoting 42 U.S.C. § 1395x(e)(9))
[128] *Id.* at 652.
[129] *Id.* at 656 (Thomas, J., dissenting).
[130] *Id.* at 658 (quoting *Ala. Ass'n of Realtors,* 141 S. Ct. at 2485, 2489).

law is not made by Congress. It comes in the form of rules issued by unelected administrators."[131]

The majority in *NFIB* shared that critique. In striking OSHA's emergency temporary standard, the Court tied the question of statutory authority to the preservation of negative liberty, stating, "This is no 'everyday exercise of federal power,'" but rather "a significant encroachment into the lives—and health—of a vast number of employees."[132] With that, the majority invoked (without naming) the major questions doctrine and concluded that the OSH Act did not plainly authorize the ETS. In reaching that conclusion, the Court relied on a problematic distinction between occupational health – which OSHA is authorized to address – and public health. According to the Court, the OSH Act allows OSHA "to set *workplace* standards, not broad public health measures."[133] Because COVID-19 "can and does spread at home, in schools, during sporting events, and everywhere else that people gather," it is a "universal risk ... no different from day-to-day dangers that all face from crime, air pollution, or any number of communicable diseases."[134]

In making this argument, the majority ignored the fact that many hazards that OSHA regulates also occur outside the workplace.[135] The majority did concede that OSHA might have authority to "regulate occupation-specific risks related to COVID-19," such as those that occur in research facilities where workers study COVID-19.[136] But that narrow example would leave out most workplaces – meatpacking plants, retail stores, prisons, – where workers were exposed and vulnerable to SARS-CoV-2.

The majority also downplayed the fact that the ETS allowed employers to opt for testing and masking instead of requiring vaccination. To the majority, that fact was irrelevant because under the ETS, employers could compel vaccination even in states that had

---

[131] *Id.* at 659 (Alito, J., dissenting).
[132] *Nat'l Fed'n of Indep. Bus.*, 142 S. Ct. 661, 665 (quoting In re MCP No. 165, 20 F. 4th 264, 272 (6th Cir. 2021) (Sutton, C. J., dissenting)).
[133] *Id.*
[134] *Id.*
[135] *Id.* at 673 (Breyer, J., dissenting).
[136] *Id.* at 665–66.

prohibited vaccine mandates.[137] The real problem, as Alito suggested in *Biden*, was the mandates' impact on workers' freedom to reject vaccination, which "cannot be undone at the end of the day."[138]

By reading OSHA's authority narrowly to further workers' liberty to reject vaccination, the majority, as in the social distancing cases, privileged one aspect of liberty (the freedom to reject vaccination) over another (the freedom to work in a safe environment). Ironically, the latter freedom was one that the justices sought for themselves.[139]

Concurring, in *NFIB*, Gorsuch remarked, "The central question we face today is: Who decides?"[140] He then emphasized the limited nature of the federal government's authority over public health, explaining that "there is no question that state and local authorities possess considerable power to regulate public health."[141] This statement was curious, given Gorsuch's eagerness to strike state laws relating to the pandemic. But with it, Gorsuch underscored that the major questions doctrine and the Court's approach to statutory interpretation served not only to cabin the reach of administrative agencies, but more broadly to limit the federal government's capacity to protect health. Or perhaps, given his other opinions, one might say "*any* government's capacity to protect health."

WHO DECIDES?

The COVID cases offer two emphatic answers to Gorsuch's question. The obvious one is the courts. Through its decisions, the Court has made clear that federal courts rather than state or federal health officials, or even Congress, are the institutions that determine how the nation can respond to a pandemic. And courts will make those decisions without granting deference to elected or appointed officials, and with little concern for what the science shows.

---

[137] *Id.* at 664.

[138] *Id.* at 665 (quoting *In re* MCP No. 165, 20 F. 4th at 274 (Sutton, C. J., dissenting)).

[139] David Michaels, *The Supreme Court Has Strict Covid Rules. Will It Let OSHA Protect Other Workers?*, Wash. Post (Jan. 7, 2022), www.washingtonpost.com/outlook/2022/01/07/osha-supreme-court-mandate.

[140] *Nat'l Fed'n of Indep. Bus.*, 142 S. Ct. at 667 (Gorsuch, J., concurring).

[141] *Id.*

Yet in seizing that power, the Court's COVID cases offer another answer: individuals. Taken together, the COVID cases suggest that individuals who are (or think they are) healthy and invulnerable get to decide what steps – if any – they are willing to take to keep others safe. Call it the freedom of the epidemiologically privileged. Left unprotected is the freedom of those who are more vulnerable due to age, health conditions, occupation, or myriad other social or economic conditions.

The Court has also shown little concern for the public's liberty to attain a healthier environment. With a high court making it increasingly difficult for state and federal governments to protect the public's health, citizens' capacity for self-governance becomes increasingly anemic. And both legislatures and executive officials have fewer tools with which to respond to health problems and less ability to effectuate the public's will.

Did these cases and the shifting judicial landscape that underlay them add to COVID's death toll to a significant degree? Looking back at the mandate cases, one can't help but wonder how many lives they cost. To be sure, opposition to mandates had grown long before the courts intervened. By the fall of 2021, the politics had become increasingly divisive; many red states were barring vaccine mandates even as blue states imposed them. In that climate, it's possible that the court cases striking mandates made little difference. Opposition to mandates might have been undermined their efficacy even if courts had not intervened.

Alternatively, it is possible that the many cases striking the mandates helped to propel the contestation over them, validating opponents' view that the mandates violated their freedom. Whether this hardened antivaccine and antimask sentiment and left more Americans vulnerable to the omicron surge is impossible to know. What is clear is that while these battles raged, Americans continued to die in startling numbers. And if a new surge or pandemic arises, officials at all levels of government will have few tools with which to respond. Personal responsibility will be all that we have.

It's also clear that the Court's decisions in the COVID cases will resonate beyond COVID and future pandemics. The Court's disregard of *Jacobson* and its application of strict scrutiny to seemingly neutral laws of general applicability have created a mortal threat to long-standing childhood vaccine laws.[142] Both state laws that allow for exemptions and those that do not will be challenged. Denying any claim for a religious exemption will become legally risky. Childhood vaccination rates may well fall, giving rise to outbreaks of measles, chicken pox, and pertussis, among old killers.

But a resurgence of once-tamed or newly emerging infectious diseases is not the only risk. The Court's reasoning in *Alabama Association of Realtors* and *NFIB* paved the way for the Court to strike other health-related regulations. In June 2022, the Supreme Court did just that, relying on the major questions doctrine and the COVID mandate cases to strike EPA's Affordable Clean Energy Rule.[143] Thus, the Court used a pandemic that has killed more than a million Americans to significantly erode the federal government's capacity to protect the public from the risks associated with climate change.

---

[142] Nahid Bhadelia, *We're Losing Ground against Diseases We've Already Defeated*, WASH. POST (Nov. 7, 2021), www.washingtonpost.com/opinions/2021/11/07/were-losing-ground-against-diseases-weve-already-defeated.

[143] West Virginia v. EPA, 142 S. Ct. 2587 (2022).

6   AN ASYMMETRY OF RIGHTS

As in-person schooling resumed in the summer of 2021, the legal battles over COVID orders took a new turn. Following thousands of lawsuits claiming that public health measures were unlawful, often on constitutional grounds, some parents went to court challenging laws that prohibited mask mandates in public schools. In a few instances, they won.

In Arkansas, a state circuit court judge ruled that a law barring mask mandates, which the governor later said he regretted signing,[1] violated separation of powers provisions in the state's constitution.[2] Several courts also found that bans on mask requirements denied children with disabilities equal access to public schools in violation of federal disability rights statutes.[3] The US Court of Appeals for the Sixth Circuit explained,

> Plaintiffs provided ample evidence in the district court that, without reasonable accommodations to mitigate the risk of contracting COVID-19 while attending public school, they will be denied the benefits of a public education because of their disabilities. Plaintiffs also put forth evidence that universal mask wearing is an effective way to mitigate the spread of COVID-19.[4]

Other courts were less hospitable to such claims. The US Court of Appeals for the Fifth Circuit, for example, stayed a lower court's

---

[1] Josie Fischels, *Arkansas Governor Wants to Reverse a Law That Forbids Schools to Require Masks*, NPR (Aug. 4, 2021), www.npr.org/2021/08/04/1024939859/arkansas-governor-reverse-law-let-schools-require-masks.
[2] McClane v. Arkansas, 60 CV-21-4692 (Pulaski Cnty. Cir. Ct Aug. 6, 2021).
[3] Arc of Iowa v. Reynolds, 24 F. 4th 1162 (8th Cir. 2022), *vacated,* 33 F. 4th 1042 (8th Cir. 2022).
[4] G.S. ex rel. Schwaigert v. Lee, No. 21-5915, 2021 WL 5411218 (6th Cir. Nov. 19, 2021). *See also* M.B. v. Lee, No. 21-6007, 2021 WL 6101486 (6th Cir. Dec. 20, 2021).

preliminary injunction, ruling that parents' concerns about their children contracting COVID-19 in school were too speculative to confer standing, and that the parents were in any event unlikely to succeed on the merits of their claims.[5] The US Court of Appeals for the Fourth Circuit dismissed a challenge to South Carolina's ban on mask mandates in school with similar reasoning.[6]

Such cases illustrate the challenges that litigants faced when they tried to demand rather than resist public health protection. In sharp contrast to the plaintiffs in the free exercise cases, parents who sought a safe education for their children had an uphill climb. They also had to rely on federal and state statutes rather than the Constitution. This chapter looks at why this was so, and the impact of decisions that see the Constitution as limiting but not ensuring public health protection.

WHAT MAKES US HEALTHY?

During a pandemic, health officials focus on and respond to the causes that are most proximal to the danger. During the first year of the COVID-19 pandemic, the problem was contagion, and the response was to impose social distancing measures. After vaccines became available, a key problem was getting shots into arms. The response was to bring vaccines to where people were and, in some instances, to mandate them.

These responses made a difference. As Chapters 4 and 5 discuss, social distancing measures and the distribution of vaccines saved enormous numbers of lives.[7] That's why judicial decisions that limited public health measures without careful consideration of the public health evidence or consequences were so troubling. Nevertheless, it is a mistake to think that pandemic mitigation measures on their own could have prevented the catastrophe that befell the United States during the pandemic. The calamity was far more deeply rooted.

---

[5] E.T. v. Paxton, 19 F. 4th 760 (5th Cir. 2021).

[6] Disability Rts. S.C. v. McMaster, 24 F. 4th 893 (4th Cir. 2022).

[7] Charlie B. Fischer et al., *Mask Adherence and Rate of COVID-19 across the United States*, 16 PLOS One e0249891 (2021), https://journals.plos.org/plosone/article?id=10.1371/journal.pone.0249891.

As earlier chapters relate, a substantial body of scientific research has established that a broad array of social conditions, commonly called the social determinants of health, help to shape both individual and population health. These SDOH are "the conditions in which people are born, grow, live and age, and the wider set of forces and systems shaping the conditions of daily life."[8] They include education, employment and economic stability, access to housing, health care, education, and a safe and healthy natural and built environment.[9] Structural racism and other forms of systemic discrimination also operate as SDOH.[10] So does law. As public health law expert Scott Burris explains, law "helps structure and perpetuate the social conditions that we describe as 'social determinants.'"[11] Thus, to understand Americans' vulnerability to COVID-19, we need to understand how law influenced the distribution of other SDOH.

Even before the pandemic, Americans were less healthy than people in other wealthy countries. Although the United States spends more per capita than any other nation on health care,[12] it invests far less than other high-income countries on social programs that can improve the SDOH.[13] In addition, and again in sharp contrast to other wealthy countries, the United States fails to guarantee paid sick leave,[14] paid family leave,[15] or health insurance.

---

[8] *Social Determinants of Health*, World Health Org., www.who.int/health-topics/social-determinants-of-health (last visited June 16, 2022).

[9] *Social Determinants of Health*, Healthy People 2030, https://health.gov/healthypeople/objectives-and-data/social-determinants-health (last visited Apr. 29, 2022).

[10] Gilbert C. Gee, Racism as a Social Determinant of Health Inequities (June 1–2, 2016), https://healthequity.globalpolicysolutions.org/wp-content/uploads/2016/12/Racismas SDOH.pdf.

[11] Scott Burris, *From Health Care Law to the Social Determinants of Health: A Public Health Law Research Perspective*, 159 U. Pa. L. Rev. 1649, 1655 (2011).

[12] Roosa Tikkanen & Melinda K. Abrams, Commonwealth Fund, U.S. Health Care from a Global Perspective, *2019: Higher Spending, Worse Outcomes?* (2020), www.commonwealthfund.org/publications/issue-briefs/2020/jan/us-health-care-global-perspective-2019.

[13] *Social Spending (Indicator)*, OECD (2021), https://doi.org/10.1787/7497563b-en (last visited Apr. 29, 2022).

[14] Paid Sick Leave to Protect Income, Health and Jobs through the COVID-19 Crisis, OECD (2020), www.oecd.org/coronavirus/policy-responses/paid-sick-leave-to-protect-income-health-and-jobs-through-the-covid-19-crisis-a9e1a154.

[15] Paid Family Leave Across OECD Countries, Bipartisan Policy Center, https://bipartisanpolicy.org/explainer/paid-family-leave-across-oecd-countries (last visited June 16, 2022).

Such gaps in the social safety net, alongside growing economic inequality and persistent and systematic racial inequities, undermined Americans' health long before COVID. In 2017, economists Anne Case and Angus Deaton used the term "deaths of despair" to capture the loss of life from substance use disorders, suicides, and alcohol-related disease among non-Hispanic white Americans who lack a college degree.[16] Persistent disinvestment in public health exacerbated the toll of these diseases, as health departments lacked the resources to tackle worsening health problems.[17]

Prior to 2020, the danger signs were everywhere. Prepandemic, the United States had "a higher infant mortality rate, a higher prevalence of obesity and lower life expectancy compared with most OECD countries."[18] Life expectancy was actually declining *before the pandemic*, as diseases of despair mounted.

Critically, as Chapter 7 describes more fully, these problems were not evenly distributed. In 2019, life expectancy for non-Hispanic white Americans was more than four years greater than for non-Hispanic Black Americans (Hispanic Americans had the longest life expectancy).[19] In 2020, once the pandemic hit, the difference in life expectancies between non-Hispanic Black Americans' and white Americans' increased to six years, evincing COVID's disparate toll on Black Americans.[20] Health also varied by education[21] and geography. In 2018, the average life expectancy in West Virginia was 74.4 years; in Hawaii, it was 81.0 years.[22] There were also dramatic variations within

[16] Anne Case & Angus Deaton, *Mortality and Morbidity in the 21st Century*, in BROOKING PAPERS ON ECON. ACTIVITY 397, 398 (2017), www.brookings.edu/wp-content/uploads/2017/08/casetextsp17bpea.pdf.

[17] Nason Maani & Sandro Galea, *COVID-19 and Underinvestment in the Public Health Infrastructure of the United States*, 98 MILBANK Q. 250 (2020).

[18] AMERICA'S HEALTH RANKINGS, INTERNATIONAL COMPARISON 2019 ANNUAL REPORT, www.americashealthrankings.org/learn/reports/2019-annual-report/international-comparison (last visited Jan. 4, 2022).

[19] Elizabeth Arias et al., *Provisional Life Expectancy Estimates for January through June, 2020*, 10 VITAL STATISTICS RAPID RELEASE (Feb. 2021), www.cdc.gov/nchs/data/vsrr/VSRR10-508.pdf.

[20] *Id.*

[21] Anna Zajacova & Elizabeth M. Lawrence, *The Relationship between Education and Health: Reducing Disparities through a Contextual Approach*, 39 ANN. REV. PUB. HEALTH (Apr. 1, 2018), www.ncbi.nlm.nih.gov/pmc/articles/PMC5880718.

[22] Elizabeth Arias et al., *U.S. State Life Tables, 2018* 70 NAT'L VITAL STAT. REP. 3 (2021), www.cdc.gov/nchs/data/nvsr/nvsr70/nvsr70-1-508.pdf.

states. According to the Robert Wood Johnson Foundation, "people living just a few blocks apart may have vastly different opportunities to live a long life in part because of their neighborhood."[23] Critically, at a population level, the differences are not due to the choices people make, but the choices they have and the environments they face.

These preexisting problems left the United States especially susceptible to COVID. Although it ranked first among wealthy nations in a Global Health Security Index prepandemic scorecard on "preparedness" in 2019,[24] the United States did far worse than other wealthy countries during the pandemic. For example, as of June 2022, the United States had experienced over 300 deaths per 100,000 as compared with France, which had slightly less than 230 deaths per 100,000, Germany, which experienced less than 170 deaths per 100,000, and Canada, which had less than 110 deaths per 100,000.[25] All countries made mistakes during the pandemic, and all suffered grievous losses. Yet no other high-income country fared as poorly as the United States.

Much of the blame is attributable to President Trump's failure to take the pandemic seriously, the bungled messaging by the Biden administration over masks and vaccine boosters, and the political clashes over pandemic policies. The previous chapters have also argued that court decisions stymied mitigation efforts. Although each of these factors played a role, preexisting social vulnerabilities were also central to the United States' failure during COVID.[26] Economically insecure individuals could not stay safe at home during the pandemic. Housing instability caused overcrowded living arrangements that allowed contagion to flare.[27] High rates of

[23] *Life Expectancy: Could Where You Live Influence How Long You Live?*, ROBERT WOOD JOHNSON FOUNDATION, www.rwjf.org/en/library/interactives/whereyouliveaffectshow-longyoulive.html (last visited Apr. 29, 2022).

[24] Enoch J. Abbey et al., *The Global Health Security Index is not Predictive of Coronavirus Pandemic Responses among Organization for Economic Cooperation and Development Countries*, 15 PLOS ONE e0239398 (2020), www.ncbi.nlm.nih.gov/pmc/articles/PMC7540886.

[25] *Mortality Analyses*, JOHNS HOPKINS CORONAVIRUS RES. CTR., https://coronavirus.jhu.edu/data/mortality (last visited Apr. 29, 2022).

[26] *E.g.*, Elissa M. Abrams & Stanley J. Szefler, *COVID-19 and the Impact of Social Determinants of Health*, 8 LANCET RESPIRATORY MED. 659 (2020).

[27] Gracie Himmelstein & Matthew Desmond, *Eviction and Health: A Vicious Cycle Exacerbated by a Pandemic*, HEALTH AFFS. HEALTH POL'Y BRIEF (Apr. 1, 2021), www.healthaffairs.org/do/10.1377/hpb20210315.747908/full.

incarceration and detention created "tinderbox[es]" of infection,[28] as did overcrowded and underfunded nursing homes[29] and poor working conditions in meatpacking and other plants. Individuals who lacked paid sick leave were reluctant to be tested, stay home, or seek treatment when they were ill.[30] They also had trouble taking time off to be vaccinated or to deal with the common side effects of the vaccines. Individuals without health insurance were also less likely to seek treatment, and more likely to have untreated comorbidities. (One study estimated that over 338,000 COVID deaths in the United States could be attributed to the lack of universal health insurance.[31]) High rates of obesity, diabetes, and chronic lung disease – all of which are associated with adverse SDOH and are unevenly distributed across populations – made many Americans who contracted COVID-19 more likely to require hospitalization or to die.[32]

We generally attribute such problems to nature (i.e., bad genes), the choices of individuals, or the decisions of elected leaders. Despite the frequent rhetorical claim that health is a "human right," we do not usually think of lack of access to sick pay or safe housing as violating our constitutional rights. As discussed below, there are some compelling reasons for that position. There is also a high cost, which is magnified by the robust protection that courts grant to many forms of negative liberty. Although courts increasingly strike public health laws as unconstitutional, they rarely conclude that the government's failure to protect health is unconstitutional. In a pandemic, this asymmetry of judicial intervention can be deadly.

---

[28] Valentine v. Collier, 141 S. Ct. 57, 58 (2020) (Sotomayor, J., dissenting) (quoting Valentine v. Collier, 455 F. Supp. 3d 308, 322 (S.D. Tex. 2020)).

[29] Eric Reinhart, *Why U.S. Pandemic Management Has Failed: Lack of Attention to America's Epidemic Engines*, STAT (Oct. 5, 2021), www.statnews.com/2021/10/05/jails-prisons-schools-nursing-homes-america-epidemic-engines.

[30] Daiquiri J. Steele, *Preserving Pandemic Protections*, 42 BERK. J. EMPL. & LAB. L. 321, 323–25 (2021).

[31] Alison P. Galvani et al., *Universal Healthcare as Pandemic Preparedness: The Lives and Costs That Could Have Been Saved during the COVID-19 Pandemic*, 119 PROCED. NAT'L ACAD. SCI. e2200536119 (June 2022), www.pnas.org/doi/full/10.1073/pnas.2200536119.

[32] *People with Certain Medical Conditions*, CTRS. FOR DISEASE CONTROL & PREVENTION (last updated May 2, 2022), www.cdc.gov/coronavirus/2019-ncov/need-extra-precautions/people-with-medical-conditions.html.

THE REJECTION OF POSITIVE RIGHTS

To understand the roots of this asymmetry, recall that before the New Deal, courts identified public health protection with the states' police power and held that reasonable public health laws did not violate individual rights.[33] Courts, as in *Jacobson*, also seemed to understand that "real liberty" comprised not only freedom from government but also freedom from disease.[34]

A few courts went further, suggesting that states not only had the power to protect public health, but also the duty to do so. For example, in 1830 in *Hazen v. Strong*, the Vermont Supreme Court quoted a statute stating that where there was the possibility of contagion, "it becomes the duty of the selectman to take the most prudent measures to prevent the spreading of the disease."[35] Such statements by courts were rare; for the most part, judges were content to protect "real liberty" by granting broad deference to elected and appointed officials who acted (or failed to act) to protect the public's health.

As judicial protection of negative rights expanded in the twentieth century, liberals began to argue that the Constitution guaranteed positive, legally enforceable rights, sometimes termed "second-generation rights,"[36] to the conditions necessary to live a healthy life. In 1941, President Franklin Roosevelt proclaimed four freedoms. These included the negative freedoms of speech and religion and the positive freedoms from want and fear.[37] Three years later, as World War II raged, he proposed a "second Bill of Rights" that would guarantee Americans numerous positive rights, including the right to "adequate health care," to "a decent home," to "good education," and to a "useful and remunerative job."[38]

---

[33] *See* Chapter 2.

[34] Jacobson v. Massachusetts, 197 U.S. 11, 26 (1905).

[35] Hazen v. Strong, 2 Vt. 427, 433 (1830).

[36] Edward Rubin, *The Affordable Care Act, The Constitutional Meaning of Statutes, and the Emerging Doctrine of Positive Constitutional Rights*, 53 Wm. M. L. Rev. 1639, 1687 (2012).

[37] Paul M. Sparrow, *The "Four Freedoms" Speech Remastered*, Franklin D. Roosevelt Presidential Libr. & Museum (Jan. 6, 2016), https://fdr.blogs.archives.gov/2016/01/06/four_freedoms/.

[38] Franklin D. Roosevelt, *"Economic Bill of Rights" in the 1944 Annual Message to Congress*, reprinted in The Public Papers and Addresses of Franklin D. Roosevelt 40–42 (Samuel I. Roseman ed., 1950).

Roosevelt did not live to see those rights recognized in American law. But after World War II, the United Nations adopted the Universal Declaration of Human Rights. Article 25 states:

> Everyone has the right to a standard of living adequate for the health and well-being of himself and of his family, including food, clothing, housing and medical care and necessary social services, and the right to security in the event of unemployment, sickness, disability, widowhood, old age or other lack of livelihood in circumstances beyond his control.[39]

In the years that followed, positive rights received further endorsement in international law. For example, the International Covenant on Economic, Social, and Cultural Rights, which the United Nations General Assembly adopted in 1966, required nations to respect rights to social benefits and health.[40] The United States did not ratify that treaty, though it did sign it. Still, many Americans adopted the language of rights to argue for greater access to health care and other positive SDOH.[41] Indeed, by the mid-twentieth century, the claim that there is a "right to health," usually understood as a right to affordable health insurance, became commonplace.

For a brief time, it seemed as if the Supreme Court might conclude that the Constitution guarantees some rights to social goods. Notably, in 1970, in *Goldberg v. Kelly*, the Court held that welfare benefits were a form of "property" that entitled individuals to procedural due process protections prior to their termination.[42] Likewise, in *Shapiro v. Thompson* (1969)[43] and *Memorial Hospital v. Maricopa County* (1974),[44] the Court ruled that laws limiting welfare or publicly funded health benefits to long-time state residents violated equal protection and the "right to travel."

[39] Universal Declaration of Human Rights, G.A. Res. 217 (III) A, U.N. Doc. A/RES/217(III) (Dec. 10, 1948).

[40] *See* International Covenant on Economic, Social and Cultural Rights, G.A. Res. 2200 (XXI) A, U.N. Doc. A/RES/2200 (XXI) (Dec. 16, 1966).

[41] *E.g.*, Susan Bandes, *The Negative Constitution: A Critique*, 88 MICH. L. REV. 2271 (1990); Frank L. Michelman, *Foreword: On Protecting the Poor through the Fourteenth Amendment*, 83 HARV. L. REV. 7 (1968); Frank L. Michelman, *Welfare Rights in a Constitutional Democracy*, 1979 WASH. U. L. Q. 659 (1979).

[42] Goldberg v. Kelly, 397 U.S. 254, 261 (1970).

[43] Shapiro v. Thompson, 394 U.S. 618, 630–31 (1969).

[44] Memorial Hosp. v. Maricopa Cnty., 415 U.S. 250, 269 (1974).

Although such cases showed how courts could construe social benefits as "rights" triggering constitutional protections, the Court never held that the Constitution compelled the government to establish social benefits. Indeed, in the few cases that hinted at welfare rights, the Court pegged its analysis to the denial of already recognized liberties. This approach was evident in *Estelle v. Gamble* (1976), in which the Court held that deliberate indifference to a prisoner's medical care violated the Eighth Amendment's prohibition on cruel and unusual punishment.[45] As the Court explained, "An inmate must rely on prison authorities to treat his medical needs; if the authorities fail to do so, those needs will not be met."[46] Thus, because the state deprives a prisoner of their negative liberty, leaving them wholly dependent on the state, the state must provide for their health care.

In other cases, the connection between the deprivation of positive rights and the violation of other established rights was more subtle, but still critical. For example, in *Goldberg*, the Court did not announce a "right to welfare"; it only held that once a state created a welfare program, it could not take away a particular individual's benefits without offering procedural protections. In *Shapiro* and *Maricopa County*, the Court tied welfare rights to the negative right to travel. In each case, the Court hinted at the recognition of a positive right but was careful not to proclaim one.

The justices' refusal to embrace welfare rights likely has many causes. Historically, support for social benefits has been undermined by racism and the belief among many white Americans that such benefits disproportionately benefit Black Americans.[47] Indeed, opposition to welfare rights seemed to harden in the late 1960s, as the backlash to the civil rights movement intensified. It is surely no coincidence that the Court's flirtation with positive rights ended as public support for such rights declined and a more conservative Court pulled back from its support for claims brought by racial minorities.[48] The justices, however, offered other rationales. Most importantly, they

---

[45] Estelle v. Gamble, 429 U.S. 97 (1976).

[46] *Id.* at 103.

[47] *E.g.*, KENNETH J. NEUBECK & NOEL A. CAZENAVE, WELFARE RACISM: PLAYING THE RACE CARD AGAINST AMERICA'S POOR 3 (2001).

[48] *See* Chapter 7.

noted that the recognition of positive welfare rights might embroil them in the type of policy decisions that the New Deal Court had left to the political branches. Dissenting in *Shapiro*, Justice John Marshall Harlan II (the grandson of *Jacobson*'s author) wrote, "I know of nothing which entitles this Court to pick out particular human activities, characterize them as 'fundamental,' and give them added protection under an unusually stringent equal protection test."[49]

Harlan's views prevailed in *Dandridge v. Williams* (1970), in which the plaintiffs argued that Maryland's policy of capping welfare payments violated the equal protection rights of large families.[50] The Court, in an opinion by Justice Potter Stewart, rejected the plaintiffs' argument, stating, "We deal with state regulation in the social and economic field, not affecting freedoms guaranteed by the Bill of Rights, and claimed to violate the Fourteenth Amendment only because the regulation results in some disparity in grants of welfare payments to the largest ... families."[51] Validating the plaintiffs' claim, Stewart argued, "would be far too reminiscent of an era when the Court thought the Fourteenth Amendment gave it power to strike down state laws 'because they may be unwise, improvident, or out of harmony with a particular school of thought.'"[52]

Two years later, in *Lindsey v. Normet* (1972), the Court disposed of an equal protection challenge to Oregon's eviction procedures, stating,

> We do not denigrate the importance of decent, safe, and sanitary housing. But the Constitution does not provide judicial remedies for every social and economic ill. We are unable to perceive in that document any constitutional guarantee of access to dwellings of a particular quality, or any recognition of the right of a tenant to occupy the real property of his landlord beyond the term of his lease without the payment of rent or otherwise contrary to the terms of the relevant agreement.[53]

Then, in *San Antonio Independent School District v. Rodriguez* (1973), the Court rejected an equal protection challenge to Texas's

---

[49] *Shapiro*, 394 U.S. at 662 (Harlan, J., dissenting).
[50] Dandridge v. Williams, 397 U.S. 471 (1970).
[51] *Id.* at 484.
[52] *Id.* (quoting Williamson v. Lee Optical, Inc., 348 U.S. 483, 488 (1955)).
[53] Lindsey v. Normet, 405 U.S. 56, 74 (1972).

school financing system, which relied heavily on local property taxes and left schools in poorer communities with far fewer resources than those in wealthier communities.[54] Writing for the Court, Justice Lewis F. Powell, Jr., stated that the financing system did not "operate to the peculiar disadvantage of any suspect class," and that "the Equal Protection Clause does not require absolute equality or precisely equal advantages."[55] He added that the judiciary would be "assuming a legislative role and one for which the Court lacks both authority and competence" if it treated education as a fundamental right.[56]

The Court later applied such reasoning to health care, even when it related to a recognized fundamental right such as abortion. In *Maher v. Roe* (1977), the Court rejected an equal protection challenge to a Connecticut law banning Medicaid coverage for abortions that were not medically necessary.[57] Writing for the Court, Powell was blunt: "The Constitution imposes no obligations on the States to pay the pregnancy-related medical expenses of indigent women, or indeed to pay any of the medical expenses of indigents."[58] The difficulties that poor individuals face in paying for abortions, he asserted, "[are] neither created nor in any way affected by the Connecticut regulation."[59] Three years later, the Court extended *Maher*, ruling that the Hyde Amendment, which bars federal funding of abortions (even when they are medically required), was constitutional.[60]

These rulings slammed the door on the recognition of a constitutional right to health care or other SDOH. Their outcome was unequivocal: Congress or the states can establish programs to support health, but they are not required to do so. It followed that the political branches had broad discretion to limit or even repeal any benefits that were granted. Case in point: Congress could offer tax credits to support paid sick leave during the pandemic, as it did in the American Rescue Plan Act (or ARPA, the COVID-19 stimulus

---

[54] San Antonio Indep. Sch. Dist. v. Rodriguez, 411 U.S. 1 (1973).
[55] *Id.* at 24, 28.
[56] *Id.* at 31.
[57] Maher v. Roe, 432 U.S. 464 (1977).
[58] *Id.* at 469.
[59] *Id.* at 474.
[60] Harris v. McRae, 448 U.S. 297 (1980).

package passed in 2021),[61] but it could also allow those credits to
expire in a few months, as it did.

POOR JOSHUA

The Court's rejection of positive constitutional rights was not confined
to claims for publicly funded benefits, such as health insurance,
welfare, or housing support. Viewing the Constitution as "a charter of
negative rather than positive liberties," as Judge Richard Posner called
it in an opinion for the US Court of Appeals for Seventh Circuit,[62] the
Supreme Court also rebuffed the notion that the Constitution requires
states to use their police power to protect health or safety.

The key case was the 1989 decision in *DeShaney v. Winnebago
County Department of Social Services.*[63] Joshua DeShaney was four
years old when a beating by his father caused him permanent brain
damage. In the two years before that near-fatal assault, the Winnebago
County Department of Social Services knew that Joshua's father was
abusing him and was deeply involved with the family. At one point,
after a beating landed Joshua in the hospital, the department obtained a
court order placing him in the hospital's temporary custody, but he was
eventually returned to his father. Later, even after the department had
learned of further instances of abuse, it failed to act until it was too late.

Through his mother, Joshua sued the county, arguing that it had
violated the Fourteenth Amendment by depriving him of his liberty
interest in his bodily integrity. By a 6–3 vote, the Court disagreed.[64] In
an opinion by Chief Justice William Rehnquist, the Court ruled that
the Constitution imposed no affirmative duty of care on the states.
Rehnquist asserted,

> Nothing in the language of the Due Process Clause itself requires
> the State to protect the life, liberty, and property of its citizens

---

[61] *Under the American Rescue Plan, Employers Are Entitled to Tax Credits for Providing
Paid Leave to Employees Who Take Time Off Related to COVID-19 Vaccinations,*
INTERNAL REVENUE SERV. (last updated July 28, 2021), www.irs.gov/newsroom/
employer-tax-credits-for-employee-paid-leave-due-to-covid-19.

[62] Jackson v. City of Joliet, 715 F. 2d 1200, 1203 (7th Cir. 1983).

[63] DeShaney v. Winnebago Cnty. Dep't of Soc. Servs., 489 U.S. 189 (1989).

[64] *Id.* at 195.

against invasion by private actors. The Clause is phrased as a limitation on the State's power to act, not as a guarantee of certain minimal levels of safety and security. It forbids the State itself to deprive individuals of life, liberty, or property without "due process of law," but its language cannot fairly be extended to impose an affirmative obligation on the State to ensure that those interests do not come to harm through other means.[65]

Rehnquist was equally disdainful of *DeShaney*'s attempt to tie the state's obligation to the care that it had already provided Joshua. Distinguishing Joshua's predicament from that of the prisoner in *Estelle v. Gamble*, Rehnquist wrote, "While the State may have been aware of the dangers that Joshua faced in the free world, it played no part in their creation, nor did it do anything to render him any more vulnerable to them."[66] In short, the Constitution did not compel the state to protect Joshua from private actors.

In dissent, the liberal justices accepted that the Constitution "creates no general right to basic governmental services."[67] But Justice William Brennan, who was joined by Justices Thurgood Marshall and Harry Blackmun, questioned the majority's framing of the case, arguing that when the state "displace[s] private sources of protection," it cannot "shrug its shoulders and turn away from the harm that it has promised to try to prevent."[68] He also argued that by returning Joshua to his father, the state had not simply failed to act, it had acted in a way that endangered Joshua. Thus, Brennan saw the claim as one for negative liberty rather than a positive right to protection.

In his own dissent, Blackmun was indignant. Comparing the ruling to antebellum cases that upheld fugitive slave laws, he urged the Court to "adopt a 'sympathetic' reading, one which comports with dictates of fundamental justice and recognizes that compassion need not be exiled from the province of judging."[69] He concluded, "Poor Joshua! ... It is a sad commentary upon American life, and constitutional principles – so full of late of patriotic fervor and proud proclamations about 'liberty

[65] *Id.*
[66] *Id.* at 201.
[67] *Id.* at 203 (Brennan, J., dissenting).
[68] *Id.* at 212.
[69] *Id.* at 212–13 (Blackmun, J., dissenting).

and justice for all' – that this child, Joshua DeShaney, now is assigned
to live out the reminder of life profoundly retarded."[70]

A CHARTER OF NEGATIVE RIGHTS

Since *DeShaney*, the Court has continued to reject attempts to find
constitutional rights to protection. For example, in 2005 in *Castle Rock
v. Gonzales*, the Court rebuffed the claims of a mother whose children were murdered by her husband when the state failed to enforce a
restraining order.[71] In an opinion by Justice Antonin Scalia, the Court
asserted, "the Due Process Clause does not protect everything that
might be described as a 'benefit.'"[72] As long as the government retains
discretion to "grant or deny" a benefit, the individual has no property
right in it, thus the negligent deprivation of the benefit does not violate
the Due Process clause's prohibition on taking property "without due
process of law."

Jurists and commentators have offered many justifications for viewing the Constitution as a charter of negative rights. One explanation
points to the common law's traditional (but inconsistent) rejection of
affirmative duties to act. Another points to the lack of any clear textual
support in the Constitution for positive rights. Although many state
constitutions[73] as well as the constitutions of some nations[74] explicitly guarantee rights to education and health, no such language exists
in the US Constitution. Nevertheless, as constitutional law specialist
Edward Rubin argues, "the text of the Constitution, and specifically
the Fourteenth Amendment, is certainly capacious enough to include
positive rights."[75] Further, many negative rights, including the rights
of privacy and interstate travel, also lack clear textual foundations.

[70] *Id.*
[71] Castle Rock v. Gonzales, 545 U.S. 748 (2005).
[72] *Id.* at 756.
[73] *See* Areto A. Imoukhuede, *Enforcing the Right to Public Education*, 72 Ark. L. Rev. 443,
445–46 (2019); Elizabeth Weeks Leonard, *State Constitutionalism and the Right to Health
Care*, 12 U. Pa. J. Const. L. 1325, 1402–5 (2010).
[74] Curt Bentley, Comment, *Constrained by the Liberal Tradition: Why the Supreme Court
Has Not Found Positive Rights in the American Constitution*, 2007 B.Y.U. L. Rev. 1721,
1721–22 (2007); *see* Rubin, *supra* note 36, at 1685.
[75] Rubin, *supra* note 36, at 1689.

Another justification focuses on the status of such rights when the Bill of Rights and the Fourteenth Amendment were ratified. Both ratifications predate the development of modern social welfare programs. Nevertheless, as Chapter 2 discusses, states had many public health laws during the Constitution's early years. Yet because constitutional protections did not generally limit the actions of the states before Reconstruction, courts had little occasion to consider the constitutionality of the states' failure to use their police power to protect the health of their residents.

With Reconstruction, the relationship between the federal Constitution and the states changed. It became possible to imagine that federal constitutional rights limited actions by the states. The idea that it might also establish some positive duties was not totally far-fetched. After all, the establishment of the Freedmen's Bureau demonstrated the Reconstruction Congress's recognition of the need for the government to undertake some affirmative measures to assist individuals who were formerly enslaved.[76] From this, one can argue that the original understanding of the Fourteenth Amendment allowed for the recognition of some positive rights. Still, with the rapid end of Reconstruction, the onset of Jim Crow, and the development of the jurisprudence of constitutional limitations, the Reconstruction Amendments were quickly interpreted as protecting negative liberties. The idea of rights to protection never developed.

Critics of positive rights have also offered many conceptual and pragmatic reasons for reading the Constitution solely as a charter of negative liberty. One criticism, building on Harlan's concerns in *Dandridge*, emphasizes the threat that the judicial recognition of positive rights may pose to self-governance.[77] After all, if courts view education, health care, public health protection, or even child protective services as "rights," judges may become far more involved in decisions over which public programs will be established, how well they must be funded, and what shape they will take. This would reduce the electorate's capacity to influence public policy, thereby thinning democratic

---

[76] Mark A. Graber, *The Second Freedmen's Bureau Bill's Constitution*, 94 TEX. L. REV. 1361, 1392–95 (2016).

[77] *E.g.*, Jenna MacNaughton, *Positive Rights in Constitutional Law: No Need to Graft, Best Not to Prune*, 3 *U. PA. J. CONST. L.* 750, 764–66 (2001).

decision-making as occurred during the *Lochner* era. Hence, if respect for self-governance means, as Justice Oliver Wendell Holmes's dissent in *Lochner* suggested, that majorities are free to reject laissez-faire,[78] then they should also be able to reject any particular social welfare program or public health policy.

There are also practical reasons to reject positive constitutional rights.[79] First, courts lack the power of the purse. Without it, how can they fund the positive rights they proclaim? To be sure, the recognition of negative rights can also cost money. For example, judicial decisions requiring religious exemptions for vaccine mandates require states to provide a mechanism to review requests for an exemption. Such decisions also indirectly require states to bear the costs that arise when unvaccinated workers become sick and miss work. Still, there is no doubt that the recognition of a right to health – or any other positive socioeconomic right – could have more immediate and significant fiscal implications than courts ordinarily confront.

Perhaps more importantly, the recognition of positive rights, at least if accompanied by the type of robust judicial review that the Court uses for fundamental rights, would require courts to tackle difficult trade-offs.[80] Consider a constitutional "right to health." Should it be read as demanding that states provide health insurance? If so, must any particular set of services be covered? And must the insurance program take any particular shape? Or should courts follow international human rights law and interpret a right of health as encompassing a "standard of living adequate for … health," as well as a wide array of other goods, services, and supports that ensure social conditions that are conducive to health? What would such a "right to health" mean during a pandemic? Would it compel a particular set of public health interventions? Would courts read the right as demanding strict scrutiny when a state decides not to require masking? Or would the courts decide that the right is not fundamental, and that therefore rational basis review applies?

---

[78] Lochner v. New York, 198 U.S. 45, 75–76 (1905) (Holmes, J., dissenting).
[79] *See, e.g.*, Cass R. Sunstein, *Why Does the American Constitution Lack Social and Economic Guarantees?*, 56 SYRACUSE L. REV. 1, 5–8 (2005).
[80] Bandes, *supra* note 41, at 2329.

The difficulties posed by such questions may help to explain why many courts outside the United States have been reluctant to enforce rights to health even when their constitutions offer explicit textual support. Nevertheless, as legal scholar and Brazilian jurist Pedro Felipe de Oliveira Santos describes, courts in some nations, including Brazil and South Africa, have relied on constitutional provisions protecting the right to health to issue important decisions that advance health.[81] In addition, courts face many of the same difficulties when they protect negative liberties. Recall that in cases such as *Roman Catholic Diocese v. Cuomo*[82] and *Tandon v. Newsom*,[83] the Supreme Court discarded deference to the politically accountable branches in deciding that the religious activities barred by the state were comparable in terms of risk to the secular activities that faced looser restrictions. In so doing, the Court implicitly made health policy – concluding, for example, that religious worship could not be curtailed if shopping malls were left open. Such decisions, made to safeguard negative liberty, can have as profound an impact on health policy as decisions supporting positive liberty. The current Court, however, only sees the problem of judicial policymaking when it comes to positive rights.

THE TROUBLING ASYMMETRY

The Court's rejection of positive rights becomes especially problematic for health when juxtaposed against the Court's aggressive protection of fundamental negative rights. When only some types of liberties are constitutionally protected, then all the legitimacy that judicial decisions confer falls on the side of not protecting health.[84] Policymakers who act to promote public health may be viewed as violating constitutional rights; those who take no action are spared such condemnation. Thus, during the pandemic, policymakers who decided to let COVID-19

---

[81] Pedro Felipe de Oliveira Santos, *Beyond Minimalism and Usurpation: Designing Judicial Review to Control the Mis-Enforcement of Socio-Economic Rights*, 18 WASH. U. GLOBAL STUDIES L. REV. 493, 497 (2019).

[82] Roman Cath. Diocese of Brooklyn v. Cuomo, 141 S. Ct. 63 (2020) (per curiam).

[83] Tandon v. Newsom, 141 S. Ct. 1294 (2021) (per curiam).

[84] *See* Joseph Daniel Ura, *Backlash and Legitimation: Macro Political Responses to Supreme Court Decisions*, 58 AM. J. POL. SCI. 110 (2014).

surge faced no constitutional risk. Likewise, although individuals who rejected COVID-related orders had viable – if not always successful – constitutional claims, those who needed assistance or were at elevated risk from the lack of mitigation measures had none. All the power and force of constitutional law pushed *against* public health interventions.

Such asymmetries undermined the government's scope of action during the pandemic. They also weakened government's ability before the pandemic to address the social determinants that made Americans so vulnerable to COVID-19. The Supreme Court's 2012 decision regarding the Affordable Care Act offers an especially stark example.[85]

Although health care is far less important to health than most Americans think, access to affordable, high-quality health care is widely recognized as an important SDOH.[86] Medicaid, the joint federal and state program that provided health insurance to more than seventy-two million low-income Americans in 2019, has been especially important to health.[87] A 2020 report by the Kaiser Family Foundation on the literature regarding the impact of Medicaid's expansion under the Affordable Care Act noted that although some studies found no effect, "a growing body of research has found an association between Medicaid expansion and mortality, either population-level rates overall, for particular populations, or associated with certain health conditions."[88] The report further observed that Medicaid expansion was followed by "improvements in measures of self-reported health physical and mental health, as well as increases in healthy behaviors such as self-reported diabetes management."[89] A 2021 report also by the Kaiser Family Foundation found that the Medicaid expansion "was associated with significant declines in mortality related to specific conditions, in some instances limited to certain subgroups. These findings include decreased mortality associated with different types of

---

[85] Nat'l Fed'n of Indep. Bus. v. Sebelius, 567 U.S. 519 (2012).

[86] *Social Determinants of Health, supra* note 9.

[87] *Analysis of Recent Declines in Medicaid and CHIP Enrollment,* KAISER FAM. FOUND. (Nov. 25, 2019), www.kff.org/medicaid/fact-sheet/analysis-of-recent-declines-in-medicaid-and-chip-enrollment.

[88] MADELINE GUTH ET AL., KAISER FAMILY FOUND., THE EFFECTS OF MEDICAID EXPANSION UNDER THE ACA; UPDATED FINDINGS FROM A LITERATURE REVIEW 11 (2020), https://files.kff.org/attachment/Report-The-Effects-of-Medicaid-Expansion-under-the-ACA-Updated-Findings-from-a-Literature-Review.pdf.

[89] *Id.*

cancer, cardiovascular disease, and liver disease" as well as "decreased maternal mortality."[90] Such studies hint that access to Medicaid may help protect low-income Americans from some of the chronic diseases, such as diabetes, cardiovascular disease, and cancer, that place people at high risk for hospitalization and death from COVID-19.

In 2012, however, the Supreme Court barred the federal government from requiring states to expand their Medicaid programs. *National Federation of Independent Business v. Sebelius* (hereinafter referred to as *Sebelius*) considered constitutional challenges to several parts of the ACA.[91] Technically, the issues related to federalism: The ACA's opponents argued that the federal government overstepped its constitutional authority by requiring individuals to carry health insurance (through the so-called individual mandate) and compelling states to expand Medicaid. Yet, as in *NFIB*,[92] the Court in *Sebelius* seemed more concerned with negative liberty than either federalism or health.

The first question before the Court – and the one that got most of the public's attention – was whether Congress had authority under the Constitution's commerce clause to require that individuals be insured. Under post–New Deal doctrine, the Court should have granted Congress broad deference to determine that the individual mandate was reasonably related to the regulation of interstate commerce.[93] The Rehnquist Court, however, had issued several decisions interpreting Congress's authority under the commerce clause more narrowly. In so doing, the Court connected federalism to "the protection of 'our fundamental liberties.'"[94] In other words, by the late twentieth century, the Court began to police the boundaries of federal authority to preserve negative liberties rather than to protect the states' police power.

This use of federalism to protect negative liberty was also evident in the opinions of the more conservative justices in *Sebelius*. In his

---

[90] Madeline Guth & Meghana Ammula, Kaiser Family Found., Building on the Evidence Base: Studies on the Effects of Medicaid Expansion, February 2020 to March 2021 5 (2021), https://files.kff.org/attachment/Report-Building-on-the-Evidence-Base-Studies-on-the-Effects-of-Medicaid-Expansion.pdf.
[91] *Sebelius*, 567 U.S. at 519.
[92] Nat'l Fed'n Indep. Bus. v. Dep't Labor, 142 S. Ct. 661 (2022); *see* Chapter 5.
[93] *E.g.*, Gonzales v. Raich, 545 U.S. 1 (2005); Wickard v. Filburn, 317 U.S. 111 (1942).
[94] Gregory v. Ashcroft, 501 U.S. 452, 458 (1991) (quoting Atascadero State Hosp. v. Scanlon, 473 U.S. 234, 242 (1985)).

opinion, Chief Justice John Roberts explained that the language in
the Constitution granting Congress the power to regulate commerce
"presupposes the existence of commercial activity to be regulated."[95]
Because the ACA required individuals who did not have insurance to
obtain it, the act regulated activity that had yet to occur. From this,
Roberts concluded that Congress could not mandate insurance, lest
it be able to mandate a healthy diet or any number of other beneficial
behaviors.[96] Left unsaid – but strongly implied – was that such unlikely
laws would limit individual autonomy. In other words, Roberts read
the commerce clause narrowly to protect an individual's liberty not to
have health insurance even though there is no recognized fundamental
right to be uninsured. Equally, despite his later counseling of deference during the pandemic,[97] he was unwilling to show any deference
to Congress's health policy choices in his *Sebelius* opinion, stating,
"Our deference in matters of policy cannot, however, become abdica-
tion in matters of law."[98]

In his own opinion, which Justices Anthony Kennedy, Clarence
Thomas, and Samuel Alito joined, Scalia also saw the ACA as violating
individual liberty. "Congress," he argued "has impressed into service
third parties, healthy individuals who could be but are not customers of the relevant industry."[99] Treading into health policy, he added
that there were "many ways other than this unprecedented Individual
Mandate" through which Congress could achieve its goal of making
health insurance affordable.[100]

Even though five justices concluded that the mandate exceeded
Congress's commerce power, the mandate survived thanks to Roberts's
decision to join the four liberal justices in ruling that Congress had the
power to impose the mandate as a tax penalty. As a result, Roberts's
discussion of the commerce clause could be considered "dicta"
(language unnecessary to the Court's decision). Nevertheless, it
was important in two ways. First, it helped to keep the controversy
of the ACA alive, inviting new litigation (that ultimately failed) over

[95] *Sebelius*, 567 U.S. at 550.
[96] *Id.* at 553.
[97] S. Bay United Pentecostal Church v. Newsom, 140 S. Ct. 1613 (Roberts, C. J., concurring).
[98] *Sebelius*, 567 U.S. at 538.
[99] *Id.* at 652 (Scalia, J., dissenting).
[100] *Id.* at 654.

the entire law's constitutionality after Congress, during Trump's presidency, repealed the tax penalty.[101] In that sense, the Court helped to amplify contestation over a measure designed to benefit health just as it did during the pandemic. Second, the commerce clause discussion in *Sebelius* foreshadowed the Court's decisions during the pandemic in the eviction and OSHA vaccine mandate cases[102] by showing how the Court can use federalism to protect negatives liberties and weaken Congress's ability to promote health. The irony, of course, is that although the justices have pointed to the problem of judicial policymaking as a rationale for not recognizing positive rights, they found no such compunction when protecting negative liberties.

The Court's ruling in *Sebelius* about the Medicaid expansion probably had an even greater impact on the nation's vulnerability to COVID-19. When it was established in 1965, Medicaid was almost an afterthought to Medicare. In contrast to Medicare, which is available to almost all seniors regardless of income, Medicaid was created as a means-tested program available only to some categories of low-income individuals, the so-called "deserving poor."[103] In addition, and again unlike Medicare, Medicaid was designed as a joint federal-state program through which the federal government helped to pay for health care for eligible individuals via a formula based on a state's own Medicaid spending and per capita income. States were free to opt in or opt out; they also had substantial leeway to set, within broad federal parameters, the terms of their own state plans.[104] Theoretically, the Centers for Medicare and Medicaid Services, the federal agency that oversees Medicaid, can withhold federal money when it finds that states fail to comply with federal requirements. In practice, CMS avoids taking such drastic action.

Over the years, Congress has frequently revisited Medicaid, often to expand coverage and services.[105] Nevertheless, prior to the ACA, low-income, childless adults in most states remained ineligible for

---

[101] California v. Texas, 141 S. Ct. 2104 (2021).

[102] *Nat'l Fed'n Indep. Bus.*, 142 S. Ct. 661; Ala. Ass'n Realtors v. Dep't Health & Hum. Servs., 141 S. Ct. 2485 (2021) (per curiam).

[103] Kevin Outterson et al., *Plunging into Endless Difficulties: Medicaid and Coercion in National Federal of Independent Business v. Sebelius*, 93 B.U. L. REV. 1, 13 (2013).

[104] *Id.* at 17–18.

[105] *See id.* at 21–25.

coverage. The ACA sought to remedy that by requiring states to cover all citizens and otherwise eligible residents, regardless of family or disability status, with incomes up to 133 percent of the federal poverty level.[106] To ease the burden on states, the ACA required that the federal government pay 100 percent of the new costs for the first three years, and up to 90 percent of the costs after 2020.[107]

Although "significant," the expansion was, according to health law specialist Kevin Outterson and colleagues, "just another step in a regular process of incrementalist modification to the existing program, akin to prior amendments over the past half century."[108] Still, it was expected to provide coverage to sixteen million more Americans, marking a major step toward expanding access to health insurance.[109] The Supreme Court made sure that that did not happen.

In his opinion about the Medicaid expansion, Roberts accepted that Congress can "provide for the … general Welfare" by granting funds to the states, and that when it does so, it can attach conditions to those grants.[110] But that power, he warned, needs to be checked in order to preserve political accountability.[111] Hence, he explained, the Court had long imposed limits on Congress's capacity to impose conditions on the states. The ACA, he claimed, violated those limits by threatening states with the loss of all their federal Medicaid funding if they did not expand their programs.

Roberts was correct that the Court had long hinted at some limits on Congress's power to impose conditions on states in order to receive federal funds. Nevertheless, since the New Deal, the Court had never held that Congress had exceeded those limits. Nor had the Court found previous Medicaid expansions unconstitutional. So why did this one expansion go too far? Roberts answered that the "Medicaid expansion … accomplishes a shift in kind, not merely degree," because by offering coverage to the "entire nonelderly population" with incomes

---

[106] *Id.* at 25.
[107] *Id.* at 27–28.
[108] *Id.* at 29.
[109] Lawrence R. Jacobs & Theda Skocpol, Health Care Reform and American Politics: What Everyone Needs to Know 132 (2010).
[110] *Sebelius*, 567 U.S. at 576.
[111] *Id.* at 578.

under 133 percent of the federal poverty level, the ACA transformed
Medicaid into "an element of a comprehensive national plan to provide
universal health coverage."[112]

After deciding that Congress could not tie all Medicaid funding
to the expansion, Roberts went on to conclude that the constitutional
defect was severable, meaning that it did not nullify all the ACA provisions relating to the expansion. Instead, he held that the expansion
could survive, but only as a choice available to each state.[113] Because
two justices (Stephen Breyer and Elena Kagan) agreed with him and
two others (Ruth Bader Ginsburg and Sonia Sotomayor) would have
found the entire expansion constitutional, the expansion survived, but
only as a state option. Shortly before the pandemic, fourteen states had
rejected that option, leaving more than two million people uninsured[114]
and more vulnerable to the preexisting chronic health problems that
heightened the risk of hospitalization and death from COVID-19.

To both his critics and his supporters, Roberts's opinion in
Sebelius exemplified his pragmatism and institutionalism. In his opinion, Roberts gave something to everyone, finding that Congress had
exceeded its authority in two instances, yet permitting most of the ACA
to remain in effect. Less charitably, Roberts amended the statute, leaving the health of the nation's poorest and most vulnerable residents on
the chopping block. Further, by agreeing that Congress had crossed
lines that endangered negative liberty, he and his fellow justices helped
to legitimize political opposition to the ACA.

It is impossible to know what would have happened if the *Sebelius*
Court had followed the approach that the New Deal Court adopted
and had stated unequivocally that it deferred to Congress's rational
decisions regarding the scope of its authority under the commerce
clause. Perhaps litigants would have continued to challenge particular
aspects of the ACA and its regulations (such as treating contracep-
tion as an essential benefit).[115] Republicans might have continued to

---

[112] *Id.* at 583.

[113] *Id.* at 586.

[114] Nicole Huberfeld, *Medicaid's Vital Role in Addressing Health and Economic Emergencies,*
in ASSESSING LEGAL RESPONSES TO COVID-19, 104 (Scott Burris et al. eds., 2020),
https://static1.squarespace.com/static/5956e16e6b8f5b8c45f1c216/t/5f4d65782257052
85562d0f0/1598908033901/COVID19PolicyPlaybook_Aug2020+Full.pdf.

[115] *E.g.*, Burwell v. Hobby Lobby Stores, Inc., 573 U.S. 682 (2014).

push for the act's repeal. It is also possible, however, that the law's detractors would have gotten the message that the ACA, like Social Security and Medicare, was "settled law."

What is clear is that *Sebelius*, like many other cases, illustrates the constitutional risks that governments face when they try to protect health. Even before the pandemic, the Supreme Court was not content to forgo the recognition of positive rights that might promote health. Rather, it actively impeded the political branches' efforts to formulate effective health policies.

7   AN UNEQUAL PANDEMIC

On May 25, 2020, as the United States began to "reopen" from the strict social distancing laws that were imposed during the first wave of the COVID-19 pandemic, Minneapolis police officer Derek Chauvin killed George Floyd, an unarmed Black man, while arresting him for allegedly using a counterfeit $20 bill.[1] After a video showing the murder went viral, protesters took to the streets, first in Minneapolis and then around the country, waving the banner "Black Lives Matter."

Although the protests focused on police killings of unarmed Black Americans, the cry that "Black Lives Matter" was especially powerful during a pandemic that disproportionately ravaged communities of color.[2] COVID-19 could and did kill anyone, but African American, Latinx, and Native American individuals were especially hard hit. A 2022 analysis by the Kaiser Family Foundation that analyzed federal, state, and local data found that as of February 22, 2022, "people of color have experienced a disproportionate burden of cases and death."[3] The disparities were particularly glaring when the data was adjusted for age: "Hispanic, Black, and AIAN [American Indian and Alaska Native] people are about twice as likely to die from COVID-19 as their White counterparts and ... Hispanic and AIAN people are at one and a half times greater risk

---

[1] Evan Hill et al., *How George Floyd Was Killed in Police Custody*, N.Y. TIMES (May 31, 2020), www.nytimes.com/2020/05/31/us/george-floyd-investigation.html.

[2] Latoya Hill & Samantha Artiga, *COVID-19 Cases and Death by Race/Ethnicity: Current Data and Changes Over Time*, KAISER FAM. FOUND. (Feb. 22, 2022), www.kff .org/coronavirus-covid-19/issue-brief/covid-19-cases-and-deaths-by-race-ethnicity-current-data-and-changes-over-time.

[3] *Id.*

of COVID-19 infection that White people."[4] There were also "large disparities in COVID-19 hospitalizations for AIAN, Black, and Hispanic people."[5] These differences narrowed at times, but "the underlying structural inequities in health and health care and social and economic factors that placed people of color at increased risk at the outset of the pandemic" persisted.[6]

The pandemic has also increased disparities in life expectancy. In 2020, Black Americans – who prepandemic had a lower life expectancy than white Americans – saw an almost three-year decline in life expectancy, and Hispanic Americans also experienced a three-year decline. For non-Hispanic white Americans, the decline was only a little over a year.[7] This pattern changed in 2021, when white Americans experienced a greater decline in life expectancy than people of color. Nevertheless, in a preprint released in 2022 that analyzed data from the National Center for Health Statistics, Ryan K. Masters and colleagues found that during the pandemic's first two years, "Hispanic and Black populations clearly experienced much larger losses in life expectancy than did the White population."[8]

Researchers who studied these racial and ethnic disparities pointed to many interrelated factors, most of which long predated the pandemic, which help to explain why pre-COVID, African Americans and Native Americans had lower life expectancies and higher rates of numerous chronic health conditions.[9] Among the factors implicated are segregation,[10] immigration/citizenship status,[11] socioeconomic

---

[4] *Id.*

[5] *Id.*

[6] *Id.*

[7] ELIZABETH ARIAS ET AL., NAT'L VITAL STATISTICS SYS., PROVISIONAL LIFE EXPECTANCY ESTIMATES FOR 2020 (2021), www.cdc.gov/nchs/data/vsrr/vsrr015-508.pdf.

[8] Ryan K. Masters et al., *Changes in Life Expectancy between 2019 and 2021: United States and 19 Peer Countries*, MEDRXIV (Apr. 7, 2022, preprint), www.medrxiv.org/content/10 .1101/2022.04.05.22273393v1.full.pdf.

[9] Nambi Ndugga & Samantha Artiga, *Disparities in Health and Health Care: 5 Key Questions and Answers*, KAISER FAM. FOUND. (May 11, 2021), www.kff.org/racial-equity-and-health-policy/issue-brief/disparities-in-health-and-health-care-5-key-question-and-answers.

[10] Elizabeth L. Tung et al., *Association of Neighborhood Disadvantage with Racial Disparities in COVID-19 Positivity in Chicago*, 40 HEALTH AFFS. 1784, 1784 (2021).

[11] Jose F. Figueroa et al., *Community-Level Factors Associated with Racial and Ethnic Disparities in COVID-19 Rates in Massachusetts*, 39 HEALTH AFFS. 1984, 1990 (2020).

status,[12] and structural racism,[13] the latter of which has long infected the health care system.[14] The sorry history of systemic racism within public health itself, as exemplified by the infamous Tuskegee syphilis study discussed in Chapter 3, amplified the problem. Also important are constitutional law decisions that have thwarted efforts to address past racial inequities while perpetuating current ones.

A MISSION UNFULFILLED

To generations of idealistic Americans, the Supreme Court stood as the guarantor of equality. Despite its shameful history supporting slavery and upholding Jim Crow, the Supreme Court during the New Deal proposed the protection of "discrete and insular minorities" from discrimination as part of its mission.[15] Yet only a few years later, the Court failed that mission by upholding the internment of Japanese Americans during World War II.[16]

Despite that infamous ruling, the Court cemented its reputation as a defender of racial justice with its 1954 decision in *Brown v. Board of Education*.[17] The landmark case ruled that legally imposed (de jure) segregation in public education violated the equal protection clause of the Fourteenth Amendment. That clause, which was added to the Constitution during Reconstruction, was designed to protect the rights of formerly enslaved individuals. Yet less than

---

[12] Monita Karmakar et al., *Association of Social and Demographic Factors with COVID-19 Incidence and Death Rates in the US*, 4 JAMA NETWORK OPEN e2036462 (2021), https://jamanetwork.com/journals/jamanetworkopen/fullarticle/2775732.

[13] Yin Paradies et al., *Racism as a Determinant of Health: A Systematic Review and Meta-Analysis*, 10 PLOS ONE e0138511 (2015), https://journals.plos.org/plosone/article?id=10.1371/journal.pone.0138511; Keith Churchwell et al., *Call to Action: Structural Racism as a Fundamental Driver of Health Disparities – A Presidential Advisory from the American Heart Association*, 142 CIRCULATION e454 (2020), https://doi.org/10.1161/CIR.0000000000000936.

[14] DAYNA BOWEN MATTHEW, JUST MEDICINE: A CURE FOR RACIAL INEQUALITY IN AMERICAN HEALTH CARE 1–2 (2015).

[15] United States v. Carolene Prod. Co., 304 U.S. 144, 152 n.4 (1938).

[16] Korematsu v. United States, 323 U.S. 214 (1944).

[17] Brown v. Bd. of Educ., 347 U.S. 483, 495 (1954).

thirty years later, in *Plessy v. Ferguson* (1896), the Court failed to see how Jim Crow laws violated equal protection.[18]

Brown overruled *Plessy*, launching a new era in civil rights cases. Its impact on the Court's reputation was dramatic. As legal scholar and civil rights activist Derrick Bell wrote, most civil rights professionals "believed with an almost religious passion that the *Brown* decision was the equivalent of the Holy Grail of racial justice."[19] *Brown* not only seemed to promise the unwinding of Jim Crow, it also granted constitutional legitimacy to the civil rights movement's quest for equality. Still, as Bell and other scholars have shown, if racial equality was *Brown*'s promise, then that promise remained unfulfilled. Following *Brown*, the Court's approach to school desegregation was halting.[20] Six decades later, American schools remain largely segregated by race.[21] Further, Black children are more likely than white children to learn in poorly funded, poorly performing schools.[22]

Brown and the cases that followed it also created "confusion and conflict" and with the Civil Rights Act of 1964, sparked a backlash.[23] In 1968, Richard Nixon was elected president employing a "Southern strategy" that sought to attract white voters by opposing civil rights and stirring white racial resentment.[24] Once in office, Nixon reshaped the Supreme Court, nominating Warren Burger to replace Earl Warren as chief justice and later Lewis Powell and William Rehnquist (who would go on to be named chief justice under Ronald Reagan) as associate justices.

In 1976, a more conservative court decided *Washington v. Davis*, which slammed the door on whatever promise of racial justice *Brown* had offered.[25] As it did so, *Brown*'s rejection of de jure discrimination was transformed into a formalistic equal protection doctrine that

---

[18] Plessy v. Ferguson, 163 U.S. 537 (1896).

[19] DERRICK BELL, SILENT COVENANTS: BROWN V. BOARD OF EDUCATION AND THE UNFULFILLED HOPES FOR RACIAL REFORM 14 (2004).

[20] Brown v. Bd. of Educ., 349 U.S. 294, 300–1 (1955).

[21] EMMA GARCÍA, ECON. POL'Y INST, SCHOOLS ARE STILL SEGREGATED, AND BLACK CHILDREN ARE PAYING A PRICE (2020), www.epi.org/publication/schools-are-still-segregated-and-black-children-are-paying-a-price.

[22] *Id.*

[23] BELL, *supra* note 19, at 16.

[24] Bruce H. Kalk, *Wormley's Hotel Revisited: Richard Nixon's Southern Strategy and the End of the Second Reconstruction*, 71 N.C. HIST. REV. 85, 94–95 (1994).

[25] Washington v. Davis, 426 U.S. 229, 239 (1976).

employed the tiers of scrutiny that Chapter 3 discussed. With that, the equal protection clause ceased offering the possibility of redressing systemic racism and improving the social determinants of health.

The facts in *Washington* were simple. The plaintiffs argued that the District of Columbia had violated the equal protection clause by requiring would-be police officers to pass a test that Black candidates failed at a far higher rate than white candidates. Importantly, the exam did not utilize any explicit racial classifications. The plaintiffs nevertheless argued that it violated equal protection by creating racially unequal outcomes. The Supreme Court disagreed. In an opinion authored by Justice Byron White, the Court ruled that the fact that a law disproportionately harms a racial minority does not justify heightened judicial scrutiny.[26] Rather, White stated, strict scrutiny under the equal protection clause was appropriate only when a law utilized racial or other suspect classifications, or when the plaintiff was able to prove that the law resulted from racial animus. That is a very difficult showing to make.

In one sense, the Court's decision reflected the post–New Deal Court's reluctance to subject most social and economic laws to heightened scrutiny. Given the nation's racist history, and the unequal distribution of wealth, education, and other social goods that permeates American society, most if not all laws have a racially disparate impact. After all, a law applied equally to an unequal playing field will have an unequal result. If that alone triggered strict scrutiny, *every* (or almost every) law would be subject to heightened review, granting the Court an ever larger say over the nation's economic and social welfare policies.

Nevertheless, the Court's refusal in *Washington* to consider a law's racially disparate effect decimated *Brown*'s promise of equality. Because most laws that perpetuate long-sown racial inequalities no longer rely on explicit racial classifications, constitutional remediation is seldom available to unwind deep-seated disparities that jeopardize health.[27] Hence, capital sentences,[28] zoning regulations,[29] and decisions to site polluting

---

[26] *Id.* at 242.

[27] *See* Haley M. Lane et al., *Historical Redlining Is Associated with Present-Day Air Pollution Disparities in U.S. Cities*, 9 ENVIRON. SCI. TECH. LETTERS 345 (2022).

[28] *E.g.*, McCleskey v. Kemp, 481 U.S. 279, 313 (1987).

[29] Vill. of Arlington Heights v. Metro. Hous. Dev. Corp., 429 U.S. 252, 254 (1977).

factories in minority neighborhoods[30] are subject only to rational basis review, despite their adverse disparate impact on communities of color and their ties to systemic racism. Courts treat those harms – much like those suffered by Joshua DeShaney – as private wrongs beyond the scope of society's responsibility.[31] In that sense, *Washington* foreshadowed the focus on individualism and personal responsibility that was evident in the Court's post-*RCD* COVID cases. That focus, in turn, magnified health disparities. Hence, "for many BIPOC [Black, Indigenous and people of color], controlling risk of exposure was nearly impossible, since both places of employment, necessary for financial stability, and the home, necessary for survival, became key sites of exposure."[32] In this way, COVID exemplified the fact that a policy that emphasizes personal choice inevitably disadvantages those less privileged to choose safer options.

Although *Washington* presaged the individualism evident in the Court's post-*RCD* free exercise cases, it differed from those cases in an important way. As Chapter 4 discusses, the Court in the free exercise cases did not require that plaintiffs show either explicit or intentional discrimination against religion in order to receive strict scrutiny. Instead, the Court held that strict scrutiny was applicable as long as plaintiffs could point to some comparable (in the Court's view) secular activity that was regulated less strictly than the religious activity at issue. In that sense, the free exercise cases looked beyond a law's text to consider its impact. This is precisely what the Court in *Washington* refused to do for equal protection claims.

The Court has, however, looked more favorably upon claims brought by white plaintiffs who challenge race-conscious laws that seek to benefit minorities. To some extent, this view simply follows from the Court's formalistic approach to equal protection, where the existence of a racial classification triggers strict scrutiny, and the absence usually leads to rational basis review. Because most laws that

---

[30] *E.g.*, S. Camden Citizens in Action v. N.J. Dep't of Env't Prot., 274 F. 3d 771, 774 (3d Cir. 2001).

[31] DeShaney v. Winnebago Cnty. Dep't of Soc. Servs., 489 U.S. 189, 195–96 (1989).

[32] Aziza Ahmed & Jason Jackson, *Race, Risk, and Personal Responsibility in the Response to COVID-19*, 121 COLUM. L. F. (2021), https://columbialawreview.org/content/race-risk-and-personal-responsibility-in-the-response-to-covid-19.

are silent as to race favor white Americans, and most laws that mention race seek to redress long-seated racial inequities, the Court's formalistic approach consistently favors those who challenge efforts to *reduce* existing racial inequities.

Without reviewing the evolution and permutations of the Supreme Court's affirmative action or reverse discrimination jurisprudence, suffice it to say that the Court has made clear that laws that grant preferences to minorities can survive strict scrutiny only in a very narrow set of circumstances.[33] For example, policies that give preferences to minorities in public contracting are permissible only when they are narrowly tailored to remedy past invidious discrimination of the kind that would be found unconstitutional under *Washington*.[34] That means that governments cannot use racial preferences to redress workforce disparities unless they can show that those disparities resulted from past intentional discrimination – which is very difficult to do.

The Court has also treated race-conscious laws and policies that seek to integrate K–12 schools with skepticism. Chief Justice John Roberts's 2007 plurality opinion in *Parents Involved in Community Schools v. Seattle School District No. 1* is illustrative.[35] Claiming *Brown*'s mantle, Roberts wrote, "The way to stop discrimination on the basis of race is to stop discriminating on the basis of race."[36] Although Roberts in that opinion did not speak for the majority, the Court's changed composition makes it likely that the current Court will share his sentiment. The Court's 2022 decision to hear two challenges to the use of race to enhance diversity in higher education offers further reason to believe that race-conscious admissions programs in that sector will soon be barred.[37]

The insistence on "color-blind" policies impeded efforts during the pandemic to channel relief to the communities most affected. Although many states and localities were able, without legal pushback,

---

[33] Adarand Constructors, Inc. v. Pena, 515 U.S. 200, 236–37 (1995).
[34] *See id.*
[35] Parents Involved in Cmty. Schs. v. Seattle Sch. Dist. No. 1, 551 U.S. 701, 730–33 (2007).
[36] *Id.* at 748.
[37] Adam Liptak & Anemona Hartocollis, *Supreme Court Will Hear Challenge to Affirmative Action at Harvard and U.N.C.*, N.Y. Times (Jan. 24, 2022), www.nytimes.com/2022/01/24/us/politics/supreme-court-affirmative-action-harvard-unc.html.

to target communities of color for vaccine clinics – and at least one state, Montana, gave preferential placement to American Indians and people of color in their 2020 vaccination queues[38] – efforts to redress the pandemic's disparate economic impact on communities of color faced the judiciary's wrath. Consider an ARPA provision that prioritized funding for small, privately owned restaurants to those that were at least 51 percent owned and controlled by women, veterans, or the "socially and economically disadvantaged."[39] Small Business Administration regulations created a presumption (that could be rebutted) that "'Black Americans,' 'Hispanic Americans,' 'Asian Pacific Americans,' 'Native Americans,' and 'Subcontinent Asian Americans'" were socially disadvantaged.[40] As a result, the government utilized an explicit racial classification to allocate funding. According to the US Court of Appeals for the Sixth Circuit, that meant that the ARPA provision at issue was subject to strict scrutiny and in violation of the equal protection clause.[41]

A federal court in Florida applied a similar analysis to another ARPA provision that offered debt relief to "socially disadvantaged farmers and ranchers."[42] Once again, the definition of "socially disadvantaged" included farmers and ranchers who were "Black, American Indian/ Alaskan Native, Hispanic, Asian and Pacific Islander."[43] On review, a federal district court acknowledged the history of discrimination against minority farmers but nevertheless ruled that the government had failed to prove that it had a compelling interest in redressing past discrimination, or that the preference in ARPA was narrowly tailored to meet a compelling state interest.[44] The *New York Times* wrote that such decisions "created new and unexpected financial strains for Black farmers."[45]

---

[38] Doron Dorfman, *Pandemic "Disability Cons,"* 49 J. L. MED. & ETHICS 401, 404 (2021).

[39] American Rescue Plan Act of 2021, Pub. L. No. 117-2, 135 Stat. 88 (2021) at § 5003(c)(1).

[40] Vitolo v. Guzman, 999 F. 3d 353, 357 (6th Cir. 2021) (quoting 13. C.F.R § 124,103).

[41] *Id.* at 360–64.

[42] Wynn v. Vilsack, 545 F. Supp. 3d 1271, 1279, 1283 (M. D. Fla. 2021) (discussing ARPA § 1005, 135 Stat. at 12–13 (2021)).

[43] *Wynn,* 545 F. Supp. 3d at 1275.

[44] *Id.* at 1278–83.

[45] Alan Rappeport, *Black Farmers Fear Foreclosures as Debt Relief Remains Frozen,* N.Y. TIMES (Feb. 21, 2022), www.nytimes.com/2022/02/21/us/politics/black-farmers-debt-relief.html.

Reverse discrimination lawsuits also threatened efforts to ensure that racial minorities had access to lifesaving treatments. In one interesting case, plaintiffs challenged a New York Health Department recommendation that was designed to reduce disparities in access to monoclonal antibodies (used to treat COVID-19) by recommending that clinicians consider a patient's race.[46] That case was dismissed by the trial court for lack of standing.[47] Still, the message that such cases send is clear: Efforts to redress racial inequities risk constitutional peril; laws that perpetuate past disparities do not.

IMMUNIZING POLICE VIOLENCE

The police killing of George Floyd and many other Black people before and during the pandemic shone a light on police violence and the systemic racism that too often underlies it. Studies show that African Americans experience such violence disproportionately,[48] and that it leads to excessive morbidity and mortality, including adverse maternal and neonatal outcomes.[49] Importantly, police violence not only harms the direct victims; it traumatizes communities, jeopardizing their collective mental health.[50]

Despite the glaring exception of the murder conviction of Derek Chauvin, Floyd's murderer, criminal convictions and civil redress remain rare. One recent study found that the arrest (not conviction) rate for fatal police shootings over a fifteen-year period was under 2 percent,[51] and convictions were rarer still. As criminal justice expert

[46] Jacobson v. Bassett, No. 3:22-CV-00033, 2022 WL 1039691, at *1–2 (N.D.N.Y Mar. 25, 2022).

[47] Id., at *5.

[48] David G. Maxted, *The Qualified Immunity Litigation Machine: Eviscerating the Anti-Racist Heart of § 1983, Weaponizing Interlocutory Appeal, and the Routine of Police Violence against Black Lives*, 98 DEN. L. REV. 629, 640–41 (2021).

[49] Sirry Alang et al., *Police Brutality and Black Health: Setting the Agenda for Public Health Scholars*, 107 AM. J. PUB. HEALTH 662, 662 (2017); Yuki Noguchi, *How Police Violence Could Impact the Health of Black Infants*, NPR (Nov. 13, 2020), www.npr.org/2020/11/13/933084699/how-police-violence-could-impact-the-health-of-black-infants.

[50] Jordan DeVylder et al., *Impact of Police Violence on Mental Health: A Theoretical Framework*, 110 AM. J. PUB. HEALTH 1704, 1705 (2020).

[51] German Lopez, *Police Officers Are Prosecuted for Murder in Less than 2 Percent of Fatal Shootings*, VOX (Apr. 2, 2021), www.vox.com/21497089/derek-chauvin-george-floyd-trial-police-prosecutions-black-lives-matter.

Philip Matthew Stinson explains, many juries are "very reluctant to second-guess the split-second, life-or-death decisions of a police officer."[52] Civil redress is also elusive. A major reason is the Supreme Court's qualified immunity doctrine.

Strictly speaking, qualified immunity is not a doctrine of substantive constitutional law. Rather, it is a judge-made procedural doctrine that makes it difficult for plaintiffs to prevail in constitutional claims against police officers and other government officials. The doctrine's modern roots trace to the Court's 1982 decision in *Harlow v. Fitzgerald*,[53] which held that public officials who are sued under 42 U.S.C. § 1983, the Reconstruction era statute that created a remedy for violations of constitutional rights, are entitled to "qualified or 'good faith'" immunity.[54] The Court explained that this immunity had both objective and subjective elements, with the objective element involving "a presumptive knowledge of and respect for 'basic, unquestioned constitutional rights.'"[55]

In the years that followed, the hurdle imposed by the objective element grew ever higher. For example, in 2017 in *White v. Pauly*, the Court stated that in order to overcome immunity, plaintiffs have to establish that a defendant's actions violated a constitutional right that was clearly established by past precedent that was "'particularized' to the facts of the case."[56] In other words, to escape immunity, plaintiffs have to show that there was a precedential decision ruling that actions almost identical to the ones at issue in their case was unconstitutional. What makes this so difficult is that in in 2009, the Court in *Pearson v. Callahan* held that lower courts could decide whether a defendant violated a clearly established precedent relating to similar facts before considering if the defendant's actions were in fact unconstitutional.[57] This allowed lower courts to avoid deciding the merits of cases that could be dismissed due to qualified immunity. It also created a type of catch-22: Plaintiffs can only avoid immunity by showing that a clearly

---

[52] *Id.* (quoting Philip Matthew Stinson).

[53] Harlow v. Fitzgerald, 457 U.S. 800 (1982).

[54] *Id.* at 815.

[55] *Id.* (quoting Wood v. Strickland, 420 U.S. 308, 322 (1975)).

[56] White v. Pauly, 137 S. Ct. 548, 552 (2017) (quoting Anderson v. Creighton, 483 U.S. 635, 640 (1987)).

[57] Pearson v. Callahan, 555 U.S. 223, 236 (2009).

established constitutional right was violated, but constitutional rights relating to police violence are rarely established because the cases that might do so can be dismissed on qualified immunity grounds before the court turns to the merits.[58] Thus, qualified immunity forestalls the development and exposition of constitutional protections against police violence.

For a brief time in 2020, it seemed as if the Court might modestly readjust its approach to qualified immunity. On November 2, 2020, Justice Amy Coney Barrett's first day on the bench, the Court, in an unsigned per curiam ruling, held that the US Court of Appeals for the Fifth Circuit had erred in dismissing a case on the basis of qualified immunity due to a lack of precedent clearly on point where the facts were "particularly egregious," such that "any reasonable officer should have realized" that their actions "offended the Constitution."[59] Yet the Court soon made clear that it was not loosening its approach to qualified immunity. In 2021, in *Rives-Villegas v. Cortesluna*, the Court, once again from the shadow docket, reiterated that "specificity is especially important in the Fourth Amendment context," and that to defeat qualified immunity, plaintiffs must show that existing precedent "placed the statutory or constitutional question beyond debate."[60] More ominously, the Court added that the plaintiff had failed to make such a showing, "[e]ven assuming that controlling Circuit precedent clearly establishes law for purposes of §1983."[61] This hinted that plaintiffs might only be able to overcome immunity by pointing to a right that had been clearly established by the Supreme Court itself. As legal scholar Ian Millhiser noted, that would make qualified immunity "something much closer to absolute immunity."[62] If that happened, redressing police violence would become even harder.

---

[58] Wendy E. Parmet, *Quarantining the Law of Quarantine: Why Quarantine Law Does Not Reflect Contemporary Constitutional Law*, 9 WAKE FOREST J. L. & POL'Y 1, 26–27 (2018).
[59] Taylor v. Riojas, 141 S. Ct. 52, 54 (2020) (per curiam).
[60] Rives-Villegas v. Cortesluna, 142 S. Ct. 4, 8 (2021) (per curiam) (quoting Mullenix v. Luna, 577 U.S. 7, 12 (2015) and *White*, 137 S. Ct. at 551).
[61] *Id.* at 7.
[62] Ian Millhiser, *The Supreme Court Floats a Startling Expansion to Police Immunity from the Law*, Vox (Oct. 20, 2021), www.vox.com/2021/10/20/22733467/supreme-court-police-qualified-immunity-rivas-villegas-cortesluna-criminal-justice.

IMMIGRATION LAW'S IMPACT ON HEALTH

Chelsea, Massachusetts, is a small, densely packed city with just under forty thousand residents less than five miles from downtown Boston. In 2020, it was a hot spot for COVID-19, at times suffering the highest infection rate in the state.[63] By June 2022, Chelsea had an astonishing case rate of close to 43 percent – compared to 28 percent in Boston and 25 percent in nearby Cambridge.[64] Chelsea's residents also endured enormous economic hardship during the pandemic; at one point, up to 24 percent of the city's residents were unemployed.[65]

Like the other hardest-hit communities in Massachusetts, Chelsea is a majority–minority city. More than two-thirds of its population are Latinx; almost half of its residents are foreign-born, and fewer than 70 percent are US citizens.[66] Many live in large, multigenerational, mixed-status households comprised of newcomers of varied immigration statuses along with native-born residents. Many are frontline or "essential workers" who had little choice but to continue going to work during the pandemic, often using public transportation, while other workers were able to work safely from home.

The disproportionate toll experienced by Chelsea's residents was common among Latinx communities (that frequently have large numbers of immigrants) throughout the United States.[67] Interestingly, despite significant heterogeneity among subpopulations, immigrants have historically been healthier than native-born Americans, a phenomenon that is sometimes called the "healthy immigrant" (or, more

---

[63] Figueroa et al., *supra* note 11, at 1987.

[64] Ryan Huddle & Peter Bailey-Wells, *Town-by-Town COVID-19 Data in Massachusetts*, Bos. Globe (last updated June 16, 2022), www.bostonglobe.com/2020/04/15/nation/massachusetts-confirmed-coronavirus-cases-by-city.

[65] *The Impact of COVID-19 on Underserved Communities: Chelsea, MA and Healthy Chelsea*, Mass. Gen. Hosp. (Oct. 15, 2020), www.massgeneral.org/news/coronavirus/covid-19-impact-underserved-communities-part-1.

[66] *Chelsea MA, Census Place*, Data USA, https://datausa.io/profile/geo/chelsea-ma (last visited May 11, 2022).

[67] Michael Poulson et al., *Intersectional Disparities among Hispanic Groups in COVID-19 Outcomes*, 23 J. Immigr. & Minority Health 4, 9 (2020); Marissa B. Reitsma et al., *Racial/Ethnic Disparities in COVID-19 Exposure Risk, Testing, and Cases at the Subcounty Level in California*, 40 Health Affs. 870, 872–73 (2021).

narrowly, the "healthy Hispanic") paradox.[68] Nevertheless, even before the pandemic, scholars identified immigration status as an adverse social determinant of health. More specifically, they noted that laws that disadvantage noncitizens – for example, by denying them access to publicly funded health insurance or state tuition benefits – can undermine health.[69] Immigration enforcement policies have also been shown to have adverse health effects, not only for those who are or could be deported but also for members of their family.[70]

During the pandemic, these immigration-related vulnerabilities amplified contagion. Many noncitizens and members of mixed-status households (more than two-thirds of noncitizens live with one or more citizens) avoided seeking health care, including testing and vaccination, due to fear of immigration enforcement and the application of the Trump administration's "public charge rule," which is discussed below.[71] Immigrants – especially those who were undocumented – were also at greater risk due to their vulnerability in the labor market and their ineligibility for many of the economic benefits and protections that Congress provided during the pandemic.[72] Immigrants who were detained either at the border or in facilities that failed to take adequate safety precautions faced especially high risks.[73]

Once again, courts played an important role in allowing COVID's inequitable bite. Without providing a full review of the Supreme Court's approach to immigration law, it is worth noting that in the nineteenth century, even as the courts identified the states' police power with the

---

[68] Stacey A. Teruya & Shahrzad Bazargan-Hejazi, *The Immigrant and Hispanic Paradoxes: A Systematic Review of Their Predictions and Effects*, 35 Hisp. J. Behav. Sci. 486, 486 (2013).

[69] Heide Castañeda et al., *Immigration as a Social Determinant of Health*, 36 Ann. Rev. Pub. Health 375, 381–82 (2015).

[70] Abigail S. Friedman & Atheendar S. Venkataramani, *Chilling Effects: US Immigration Enforcement and Health Care Seeking among Hispanic Adults*, 40 Health Affs. 1056, 1061 (2021).

[71] Wendy E. Parmet, *Reversing Immigration Law's Adverse Impact on Health*, in COVID-19 Policy Playbook II: Legal Recommendations for a Safer, More Equitable Future 217–18 (Scott Burris et al. eds., 2021), https://static1.squarespace.com/static/5956e16e6b8f5b8c45f1c216/t/60995942ea2dbf3f3bc31788/1620662599928/COVIDPolicyPlaybook-v2_May2021.pdf.

[72] *Id.*

[73] Nicole Narea, *It's Only a Matter of Time before Omicron Spreads through Immigration Detention*, Vox (Dec. 26, 2021), www.vox.com/policy-and-politics/22848851/ice-immigration-detention-omicron-vaccine-booster.

protection of public health, the Court held that the federal government had exclusive power over immigration and could use that power to exclude immigrants who were thought to carry dangerous diseases. For example, in upholding the Chinese Exclusion Act in *Chae Chang Ping v. United States* (1889), the Court affirmed Congress's power to exclude "paupers, criminals and persons afflicted with incurable diseases."[74] This ruling condoned a dangerous conflation of race and ethnicity with ill health, under which immigrants who were not from northern Europe were viewed as carriers of disease.[75]

This conflation continued throughout the twentieth century and into our own as the federal government barred non-nationals who were HIV-positive from entering the country, even though HIV was well established within American communities. This policy led the United States in the 1990s to detain HIV-positive Haitian refugees under harsh conditions and without adequate health care in Guantanamo Bay, Cuba. Their confinement ended only after a lower federal court, in a decision later vacated, ruled it unconstitutional.[76] The congressionally imposed entry ban on HIV-positive non-nationals, however, continued until 2008, long after effective HIV treatments became widely available.[77]

When COVID-19 first appeared, the United States once again focused on excluding non-nationals as if the pandemic could be kept out by barring those with foreign passports. In early 2020, the Trump administration's first major response to the pandemic was to ban travel by non-nationals from China. President Trump later imposed similar bans on foreign nationals traveling from Europe.[78] His administration also used a provision of the Public Health Service Act of 1944, commonly referred to as Title 42, to bar entry from Mexico.[79] The

---

[74] Chae Chang Ping v. United States, 130 U.S. 581, 608 (1889).

[75] PATRICIA ILLINGWORTH AND WENDY E. PARMET, THE HEALTH OF NEWCOMERS: IMMIGRATION, HEALTH POLICY, AND THE CASE FOR GLOBAL SOLIDARITY, 31–44 (2017).

[76] *Id.* at 39–40.

[77] *Id.*

[78] Parmet, *supra* note 71, at 218–19; Allison Aubrey, *Trump Declares Coronavirus a Public Health Emergency and Restricts Travel from China* NPR (Jan. 31, 2020), www.npr.org/sections/health-shots/2020/01/31/801686524/trump-declares-coronavirus-a-public-health-emergency-and-restricts-travel-from-c.

[79] 42 U.S.C. § 265.

Biden administration kept that ban in place, with an exemption for unaccompanied minors, until May 2022, though supporters of the rule have gone to court to keep it in place.[80]

As epidemiologist Jennifer Nuzzo explains, nationality-based exclusions offer a misleading sense of security.[81] They do not and cannot keep a virus out. Yet under current legal doctrine – and in sharp contrast to many other COVID-19 mitigation measures – travel bans that are based on passport status are almost certainly constitutional.[82] Indeed, in upholding Trump's so-called Muslim ban, the Supreme Court suggested that the president's power over immigration was so vast as to permit measures that might otherwise be viewed as discrimination on the basis of religion.[83]

The Court has also condoned discrimination against noncitizens within the country, including those who are lawfully present. For a brief time, it appeared that the Court would apply strict scrutiny to state laws that discriminate against lawfully present noncitizens. In 1971, in *Graham v. Richardson*, the Court explained that classifications based on alienage (the legal term for noncitizenship) "are inherently suspect and subject to close judicial scrutiny."[84] Later cases, however, limited that holding, ruling that states can deny lawfully present non-citizens numerous benefits and opportunities that are deemed to serve a political function.[85] The Court has also held that laws that discriminate against undocumented immigrants are subject only to rational basis review.[86]

The 1976 decision in *Mathews v. Diaz* was especially significant.[87] *Diaz* concerned a challenge to a federal law limiting some

[80] Raja Razek & Devan Cole, *GOP-Led States Sue over Decision to End Trump-Era Pandemic Restrictions at the US Border*, CNN (Apr. 4, 2022), www.cnn.com/2022/04/04/politics/republican-states-lawsuit-biden-administration-title-42/index.html.

[81] Benjamin Mueller & Declan Walsh, *As Omicron Variant Circles the Globe, African Nations Face Blame and Bans,* NY Times (Nov. 30, 2021) (paraphrasing Jennifer Nuzzo), www.nytimes.com/2021/11/27/world/africa/coronavirus-omicron-africa.html.

[82] Trump v. Hawaii, 138 S. Ct. 2392, 2417–20 (2018).

[83] *Id.* at 2420–21.

[84] Graham v. Richardson, 403 U.S. 365, 372 (1971).

[85] Cabell v. Chavez-Salido, 454 U.S. 432, 439–40 (1982) (upholding constitutionality of state law requiring peace officers to be citizens); Ambach v. Norwick, 441 U.S. 68, 73–74 (1979); *but see* Bernal v. Fainter, 467 U.S. 216, 225–27 (1984).

[86] Plyler v. Doe, 457 U.S. 202, 212–13, 224–25 (1982).

[87] Mathews v. Diaz, 426 U.S. 67 (1976).

permanent residents' access to supplemental medical insurance through Medicare Part B. The Court rejected the challenge, stating that "Congress regularly makes rules that would be unacceptable if applied to citizens. ... The fact that an Act of Congress treats aliens differently from citizens does not in itself imply that such disparate treatment is 'invidious.'"[88] The Court added that because decisions relating to immigration "implicate our relations with foreign powers," they should generally be left to the political branches and be subject only to "a narrow standard of review."[89]

As a result of *Diaz*, the federal government has a relatively free hand in excluding noncitizens from many government benefits and programs. Congress has taken advantage of that latitude. In the 1996 Personal Responsibility and Work Opportunity Reconciliation Act (PRWORA), Congress barred undocumented immigrants from receiving most federally funded benefits, including Medicaid, the Children's Health Insurance Program, and the Supplemental Nutrition Assistance Program (SNAP).[90] PROWRA also requires most lawfully present immigrants to have had that status for five years before becoming eligible for most federally funded benefits, though public health programs are exempted. By denying many noncitizens access to health insurance, food assistance, and other public benefits, PRWORA increased immigrants' vulnerability to infectious and other diseases.

Other state and federal laws also discriminate against various classes of noncitizens. For example, the Affordable Care Act bars undocumented immigrants from receiving subsidies or purchasing insurance on the ACA's health insurance exchanges.[91] In addition, many of the pandemic-relief measures that Congress enacted in 2020 and 2021 limited some of their benefits to immigrants with Social Security numbers.[92] Without economic support during the pandemic, undocumented workers had little choice but to keep working even when it was not safe to do so. Of course, the infections that followed

---

[88] *Id.* at 80.

[89] *Id.* at 81–82.

[90] 1996 Personal Responsibility and Work Opportunity Reconciliation Act, 8 U.S.C. § 1611–13.

[91] Parmet, *supra* note 71, at 218.

[92] *Id.*

could be – and often were – transmitted to others. During a pandemic, measures that harm the health of some groups threaten the health of all.

One of the greatest immigration-related threats to public health during the pandemic came from the Trump administration's public charge rule. Briefly, the Immigration and Nationality Act of 1952 (INA) has long required most noncitizens who seek admission to the country or legal permanent residency status (a green card) to prove that they are not likely "at any time to become a public charge."[93] Under long-standing practice, the use of noncash public benefits, such as Medicaid or SNAP, was not considered during the public charge determination. As a result, noncitizens could use whatever (limited) benefits were available to them without fear of adverse immigration consequences.

Shortly after Trump took office, his administration began exploring ways to deter noncitizens from using public benefits.[94] Following several informal administrative actions, in August 2019, the Department of Homeland Security (DHS) published regulations that defined a public charge as "an alien who receives one or more designated public bene-fits," which included Medicaid and SNAP, "for more than 12 months in the aggregate within any 36 month period."[95] In another words, a "public charge" was someone who used public benefits for 12 out of 36 months. Further, past receipt of the designated public benefits was treated as a "heavily weighted negative factor" in determining whether the noncitizen was likely to become a public charge (i.e., someone who would use public benefits) in the future.[96] Another heavily weighted negative factor was having a serious medical condition "that is likely to require extensive medical treatment or institutionalization or that will interfere with the alien's ability to provide for himself or herself, attend school, or work."[97]

The public charge rule made it risky for noncitizens to use public benefits or even be diagnosed with a medical condition. Indeed, in

---

[93] Immigration and Nationality Act of 1952, 8 U.S.C. § 1182(a)(4).

[94] Wendy E. Parmet, *Immigration Law as a Social Determinant of Health*, 92 TEMPLE L. REV. 932, 939 (2020).

[95] Inadmissibility on Public Charge Grounds, 84 Fed. Reg. 41292, 41295 (Aug. 14, 2019).

[96] *Id.* at 41,298.

[97] *Id.* at 41,504.

proposing the rule, DHS recognized that it would result in "worse health outcomes" and an "increased prevalence of communicable diseases, including among members of the U.S. citizen population who are not vaccinated."[98] DHS nevertheless argued that those health dangers were necessary to promote self-sufficiency. In effect, DHS accepted that SDOH could adversely impact health but determined that those effects should be ignored to promote "personal responsibility."

After the rule was promulgated, immigration advocates and several blue states went to court, arguing that it exceeded the scope of the INA and that DHS had acted arbitrarily and capriciously in violation of the Administrative Procedure Act. The plaintiffs also argued that the rule would jeopardize the health of noncitizens and their families. Tellingly, most plaintiffs did not raise a constitutional claim. Given the Supreme Court's past precedent regarding the president's broad powers over immigration, to do so would have been futile.

Several lower courts enjoined the rule, finding that DHS had failed to adequately justify the departure from past precedent.[99] Some courts also noted that the department had neglected to consider the rule's adverse impact on health. However, on January 27, 2020, the Supreme Court, by a 5–4 vote from the shadow docket, stayed a nationwide injunction pending review in the Court of Appeals.[100] The majority did not write an opinion, but concurring, Justices Neil Gorsuch and Clarence Thomas criticized the lower court for issuing a nationwide injunction.[101] However, less than a month later, Gorsuch and Thomas joined the majority in another order from the shadow docket blocking an injunction that was limited to the state of Illinois.[102] This time Justice Sonia Sotomayor dissented, criticizing the majority's willingness to use the shadow docket to grant relief to the Trump administration.[103]

That was not the end of the story. Just a few days later, as the pandemic upended Americans' lives, DHS published guidance claiming that the use of Medicaid to support testing of and treatment for

---

[98] Inadmissibility on Public Charge Grounds, 83 Fed. Reg. 51,114, 51,270 (Oct. 10, 2018).
[99] Parmet, *supra* note 94, at 949–50.
[100] Dep't of Homeland Sec. v. New York, 140 S. Ct. 599 (2020).
[101] *Id.* at 600 (Gorsuch, J., concurring).
[102] Wolf v. Cook Cnty., 140 S. Ct. 681 (2020).
[103] *Id.* (Sotomayor, J., dissenting).

COVID-19 would not be counted in the public charge determination.[104] Yet because this exemption was limited to treatment for COVID-19, it could not reassure noncitizens who sought health care that doing so would not result in adverse immigration consequences if the illness they sought care for turned out *not* to be COVID-19.[105] Nor did the guidance promise an exemption for noncitizens who used other public benefits to compensate for loss of income during the pandemic. Instead, the guidance only offered immigrants the option of documenting how their economic needs related to the pandemic. In short, DHS was unwilling to suspend a rule that threatened to deter people from receiving needed health care and critical benefits even as the pandemic raged.

The story was not yet over. Citing the pandemic, in April 2020, New York asked the Supreme Court to reinstate the nationwide injunction of the public charge rule. The Court refused to do so, but it suggested that the plaintiffs go back to the district court.[106] They did. By the end of 2020, several lower courts had enjoined the rule and the Trump administration again sought review by the Court.

In February 2021, after President Biden took office, the Court granted review. The new administration then announced that it would not defend the Trump era rule.[107] As a result, the Court dismissed the cases that were pending before it, allowing the injunctions to remain in place.[108] DHS then vacated the rule, at which point states that supported it tried to intervene to defend it because the Biden administration would not. On October 29, 2021, the Court granted review to determine if those states could do so.[109] A few months later, the Biden administration proposed a new rule that would essentially return the definition of public charge to what it was before the Trump administration.[110] Several months later,

---

[104] Medha D. Makhlouf & Jasmine Sandhu, *Immigrants and Interdependence: How the COVID-19 Pandemic Exposes the Folly of the New Public Charge Rule*, 115 Nw. U. L. Rev. 146, 163 (2020).

[105] *Id.*

[106] Dep't of Homeland Sec. v. New York, 140 S. Ct. 2709 (2020) (mem.).

[107] Public Charge Ground of Inadmissibility, 87 Fed. Reg. 10,570, 10,587 (Feb. 24, 2022) (to be codified at 8 C.F.R. pts. 212, 245).

[108] *Id.*

[109] San Francisco v. U.S. Citizen and Immigr. Servs., 992 F. 3d 742 (9th Cir. 2021), *cert. granted*, 142 S. Ct. 417 (U.S. Oct. 29, 2021) (No. 20-1775).

[110] Public Charge Ground of Inadmissibility, 87 Fed. Reg. at 10,571.

the Supreme Court revoked its grant of review to the states' case, likely ending the litigation saga, at least until the DHS's new rule is finalized.[111]

As all the litigation continued, damage accrued. Confusion was sown and fear was inflicted. Immigrants, including those who were not subject to the rule, declined to use public benefits during the pandemic, including benefits – such as Emergency Medicaid (which covers uninsured immigrants in the event of a medical emergency) – that were not subject to the rule.[112] Immigrants also avoided seeking benefits for their citizen children.[113] Even several months into the Biden administration, many immigrants remained unaware that the public charge rule was no longer in force.[114] As legal scholars Medha D. Makhlouf and Jasmine Sandhu explain, the rule left "noncitizens and the people with whom they live, including U.S. citizens, disproportionately vulnerable to suffering and possibly dying from untreated COVID-19. It also [left] them at heightened risk of food insecurity, homelessness, and other maladies linked with a sudden loss of income and increased exposure to infectious disease."[115]

BEYOND CONSTITUTIONAL LAW

Constitutional law was not the sole cause of the inequities that exacerbated the pandemic. Nor does their remediation depend primarily on constitutional litigation. Indeed, the story of the public charge rule shows the salience of other legal remedies, including statutory and administrative law claims. And of course, the rule was vacated following a presidential election. Politics matter.

---

[111] Arizona v. City & Cnty San Francisco, 142 S. Ct. 1926 (June 15, 2022) (per curiam).

[112] Sharon Touw et al., *Immigrant Essential Workers Likely Avoided Medicaid and SNAP Because of a Change to the Public Charge Rule*, 40 HEALTH AFFS. 7 (2021); Randy Capps et al., *Anticipated "Chilling Effects" of the Public-Charge Rule Are Real: Census Data Reflect Steep Decline in Benefits Use by Immigrant Families*, MIGRATION POL'Y INST. (Dec. 2020), www.migrationpolicy.org/news/anticipated-chilling-effects-public-charge-rule-are-real.

[113] Public Charge Ground of Inadmissibility, 87 Fed. Reg. at 10,587.

[114] *Immigrant Mixed Status Families Toplines Summary*, BSP RSCH. & PROTECTING IMMIGRANT FAMILIES (Dec. 8, 2021), https://protectingimmigrantfamilies.org/wp-content/uploads/2021/12/PIF-Poll-Toplines-Memo-FINAL-1.pdf.

[115] Makhlouf & Sandhu, *supra* note 104, at 152.

Still, constitutional decisions contributed to the inequities upon which COVID feasted. The Supreme Court's approach to equality has not only allowed structural racism and xenophobia to infect many of our laws and policies, it has also given credence to a hyperindividualism (termed "self-sufficiency" in the public charge rule) in which individuals alone are held responsible for their own fates. Constitutional law in particular permits social harms to be neglected as long as they are not perpetuated by "bad actors" who overtly display invidious intent, and even that is tolerated when it comes to immigration.

Further, the same individualism that permits the disregard of the social determinants of health works its way through other doctrines, from limitations on racial preferences to the rejection of positive rights to the preferences granted to religious objectors. From the start, this viewing of the pandemic as a matter of individual choice and personal responsibility disadvantaged people of color and other less privileged members of society, including those who were old or medically vulnerable. It also hampered efforts by the political branches to redress inequities and mitigate the pandemic. By fostering this individualist framing, judicial decisions facilitated contagion.

8 THE INFODEMIC

Early in the COVID-19 pandemic, Tedros Adhanom Ghebreyesus, director general of the World Health Organization, warned that we were not "just fighting an epidemic, we're fighting an infodemic."[1] By that, he meant that the proliferation of dangerous misinformation threatened the world's ability to contain the novel coronavirus. Time has proven him right.

Epidemics have always spawned lies, rumors, and conspiracy theories. Still, the COVID-19 infodemic has been notable in several respects. One is the central role of social media, whose algorithms have proven to be a remarkable conduit for false information and conspiracy mongering.[2] Indeed, despite some efforts by Facebook, Twitter, YouTube, and other platforms to remove falsehoods about the pandemic, they continued to spread at alarming rates.

Also notable is the role played by prominent political leaders. In Brazil, President Jair Bolsonaro minimized COVID-19 and touted ineffective drugs.[3] In the United States, President Donald Trump reassured Americans that they had nothing to fear from

---

[1] Dep't Global Communications, *UN Tackles "Infodemic" of Misinformation and Cybercrime in COVID-19 Crisis*, UNITED NATIONS (Mar. 31, 2020), www.un.org/en/un-coronavirus-communications-team/un-tackling-%E2%80%98infodemic%E2%80%99-misinformation-and-cybercrime-covid-19.

[2] Federico Germani & Nikola Biller-Andorno, *The Anti-Vaccination Infodemic on Social Media: A Behavioral Analysis*, PLOS ONE (Mar. 3, 2021), https://journals.plos.org/plosone/article?id=10.1371/journal.pone.0247642.

[3] Gabriel Stargardter, *The Man behind Brazil's Search for Miracle COVID-19 Cures*, REUTERS (May 14, 2021), www.reuters.com/business/healthcare-pharmaceuticals/man-behind-brazils-search-miracle-covid-19-cures-2021-05-14.

COVID – even though he knew that not to be true, as he told journalist Bob Woodward.[4] Later, Trump promoted ineffective treatments such as hydroxychloroquine and cast doubt on the benefits of masking.[5] Following his lead, other Republican officeholders and conservative media celebrities spread COVID denialism, antivax misinformation, and the wonders of unproven remedies.[6] To offer just one startling example, in December 2021, Republican senator Ron Johnson of Wisconsin suggested gargling with mouthwash to cure COVID-19.[7]

Such falsehoods found fertile soil in an environment that was rife with distrust of expertise and deepening political polarization. In a July 2021 poll, almost half of respondents agreed that it was definitely or likely true that the CDC was hiding information about the negative effects of COVID-19 vaccines, and almost 25 percent mistakenly believed that the vaccines cause infertility in women.[8] In September 2021, about 35 percent of Americans who had heard of ivermectin or hydroxychloroquine as potential treatments believed they were effective against COVID-19, although they are not.[9] In another fall 2021 poll, a majority of respondents either believed or did not know if it was true that the government was exaggerating the number of deaths, and 24 percent believed or did not know if it was true that COVID vaccines contained a microchip.[10] Not surprisingly, given the torrent

---

[4] Alana Wise, *Trump Admits Playing Down Coronavirus's Severity, According to New Woodward Book*, NPR (Sept. 9, 2020), www.npr.org/2020/09/09/911109247/trump-admitted-to-playing-down-the-coronaviruss-severity-per-new-book.

[5] Daniel Victor et al., *In His Own Words, Trump on the Coronavirus and Masks*, N.Y. TIMES (Oct. 2, 2020), www.nytimes.com/2020/10/02/us/politics/donald-trump-masks.html.

[6] Claudia E. Haupt & Wendy E. Parmet, *Lethal Lies: Government Speech, Distorted Science, and the First Amendment*, 2022 U. Ill. L. Rev. 1809, 1813.

[7] Andrew Jeong, *A GOP Senator Suggested Gargling Mouthwash to Kill the Coronavirus. Doctors and Listerine Are Skeptical*, WASH. POST (Dec. 9, 2021), www.washingtonpost .com/health/2021/12/09/ron-johnson-mouthwash-covid.

[8] The Media School Report, Press Release, *Nearly Half of Survey Respondents Believe Vaccine Misinformation*, IND. UNIV. BLOOMINGTON (July 14, 2021), https://mediaschool .indiana.edu/news-events/news/item.html?n=nearly-half-of-survey-respondents-believe-vaccine-misinformation.

[9] Kathy Frankovic, *Most Republicans Who Have Heard of Ivermectin as a COVID-19 Treatment Think It May Be Effective*, YOUGOVAMERICA (Sept. 2, 2021), https://today.yougov.com/ topics/politics/articles-reports/2021/09/02/most-republicans-who-have-heard-ivermectin.

[10] LIZ HAMEL ET AL., KFF COVID-19 VACCINE MONITOR: MEDIA AND MISINFORMATION, KAISER FAM. FOUND. (Nov. 8, 2021), https://www.kff.org/coronavirus-covid-19/poll-finding/ kff-covid-19-vaccine-monitor-media-and-misinformation/.

of misinformation from Republican leaders and conservative media, Republicans were far more likely than Democrats to believe COVID-related misinformation and worry that vaccines were unsafe.[11]

Such beliefs proved deadly. As Surgeon General Vivek Murthy explained, misinformation "led people to decline COVID-19 vaccines, reject public health measures such as masking and social distancing, and use unproven treatments."[12] The problem was especially pronounced among Republicans. By October 2021, 60 percent of the unvaccinated identified as Republican,[13] and death rates from COVID-19 were far higher in counties that voted for Trump in 2020 than in those that voted for Joe Biden.[14] In late 2021, the ten "reddest" counties had death rates six times higher than the ten "bluest" counties.[15]

As the misinformation and deaths continued, it often seemed that there was little that could be done to counter the barrage of falsehoods. Officials and health professionals could have and should have improved their messaging. Even so, such efforts often seemed futile against the tsunami of misinformation.

SPEECH AND HEALTH

Sitting atop of the Bill of Rights, the First Amendment's free speech clause protects one of Americans' most cherished freedoms. Under current doctrine, most laws or governmental actions that target the content or viewpoint of speech are subject to strict scrutiny and will be

[11] *Id.*
[12] CONFRONTING HEALTH MISINFORMATION: THE U.S. SURGEON GENERAL'S ADVISORY ON BUILDING A HEALTHY INFORMATION ENVIRONMENT, U.S. SURGEON GEN. (2021), www.hhs.gov/sites/default/files/surgeon-general-misinformation-advisory.pdf.
[13] Ashley Kirzinger et al., *KFF COVID-19 Vaccine Monitor: The Increasing Importance of Partisanship in Predicting COVID-19 Vaccination Status*, KAISER FAM. FOUND. (Nov. 16, 2021), www.kff.org/coronavirus-covid-19/poll-finding/importance-of-partisanship-predicting-vaccination-status.
[14] Daniel Wood & Geoff Brumfiel, *Pro-Trump Counties Now Have Far Higher COVID Death Rates. Misinformation Is to Blame*, NPR (Dec. 5, 2021), www.npr.org/sections/health-shots/2021/12/05/1059828993/data-vaccine-misinformation-trump-counties-covid-death-rate.
[15] *Id.*

upheld only if the government can show that they are the least restrictive means for achieving a compelling state interest.[16] As we have seen in these pages, that's a very high hurdle.

Importantly, freedom of speech extends not only to truthful information but also, in many contexts, to speech that is unquestionably false. Although the Supreme Court continues to permit the government to regulate perjury, fraud, defamation, and other traditional actions in which falsity is an element, the Court has rejected the idea that governments can regulate false speech simply for being untrue.[17] In 2012, Justice Anthony Kennedy, in a plurality opinion, explained, "the remedy for speech that is false, is speech that is true."[18] This viewpoint echoes one of the most influential justifications for freedom of speech: the marketplace of ideas theory. The theory is often traced to British poet and intellectual John Milton, who in 1644 stated "Let [Truth] and falsehood grapple: who ever knew Truth put to the worse, in a free and open encounter?"[19] In constitutional law, the theory's roots lie with Justice Oliver Wendell Holmes's 1919 dissent in *Abrams v. United States*, which stated that "the best test of truth is the power of the thought to get itself accepted in the competition of the market."[20] Although the Court did not adopt that view in *Abrams*, it now cites the protection of "an uninhibited marketplace of ideas"[21] as one of the chief rationales for its robust protection of speech.

Alas, the theory depends more on faith than science. Long before the pandemic, social science research cast doubt on truth's capacity to prevail over falsehoods.[22] Well-studied cognitive mechanisms, including confirmation bias, the avoidance of cognitive dissonance, and the Dunning–Kruger effect, lead people to give more credence to information that supports their predispositions than more accurate

---

[16] Reed v. Town of Gilbert, 576 U.S. 155, 171 (2015).

[17] United States v. Alvarez, 567 U.S. 709, 722 (2012) (plurality opinion).

[18] *Id.* at 727.

[19] JOHN MILTON, AREOPAGITICA, PROJECT GUTENBERG, www.gutenberg.org/files/608/608-h/608-h.htm (last updated Feb. 6, 2013).

[20] Abrams. v. U.S., 250 U.S. 616, 630 (1919) (Holmes, J., dissenting).

[21] Virginia. v. Hicks, 539 U.S. 113, 119 (2003).

[22] Caroline Mala Corbin, *The Unconstitutionality of Government Propaganda*, 81 OHIO ST. L. J. 815, 880–81 (2020).

information that contradicts their ideas.[23] The repeated repetition of falsehoods can also take hold, as Nazi propagandist Joseph Goebbels understood only too well,[24] and as Trump's "big lie" demonstrated. Individuals are also more apt to accept information offered by those they trust and with whom they have some preexisting affinity. That tendency helps to explain why people are more likely to believe their personal physician or favorite sports hero than public health officials.

The triumph of falsehoods or misimpressions regarding health appears especially likely in our post-truth era, in which politicians lie shamelessly, skepticism abounds, faith in institutions and expertise has been shattered, and social media algorithms amplify misinformation.[25] As we saw with COVID, the rapid pace of changing information and advice during a pandemic compounds the problem. As the pandemic progressed and more information became available, expert advice changed (e.g., don't wear a mask/wear a mask; wash surfaces/don't worry about surfaces). This evolution is laudable. We *want* scientists to update their advice as they learn more about a health problem. Scientists *should* continuously reassess their advice as more information becomes available. Usually, this process occurs slowly and out of the limelight. During a public health emergency, however, it is accelerated and far more visible. This torrent of changing and sometimes conflicting information can sow confusion and distrust. Making matters worse, during the COVID-19 pandemic, experts often failed to explain clearly why their advice changed even as critics pounced on those changes. With experts' credibility undermined, people relied on the advice of their "friends," media pundits, and celebrities. That advice was frequently dangerous.

That truth need not prevail over falsehoods does not mean that freedom of speech plays no rule in truth's advancement. Robust protections for free speech make it hard for governments to censor scientific discourse or keep people, as one sheriff tried to do early in

[23] Wendy E. Parmet & Jeremy Paul, *Post-Truth Won't Set Us Free: Health Law, Patient Autonomy, and the Rise of the Infodemic*, in COVID-19 AND THE LAW: DISRUPTION, IMPACT, AND LEGACY (I. Glenn Cohen et al. eds., forthcoming 2025).

[24] Corbin, *supra* note 22, at 859.

[25] Philip M. Napoli, *What if Speech Is No Longer the Solution? First Amendment Theory Meets Fake News and the Filter Bubble*, 70 FED. COMM. L. J. 55 (2018).

the pandemic, from speaking out about an illness.[26] Indeed, during the early days of COVID, America's strong tradition of free speech – aided undoubtedly by the Supreme Court's vigorous rejection of content-based regulations – prevented political leaders from stifling private-sector scientists as the Chinese government did early in the pandemic.[27] Although Trump did try to limit what federal officials could say,[28] most scientists and lay persons in the United States were free to offer their views, advice, and predictions. Although this allowed the dissemination of misinformation, it also ensured that valuable and accurate advice could be shared with the public, even when the government was not happy with that information.

The need to protect such discourse, even at the price of allowing falsehoods, is not the only justification for protecting speech. In *Mills v. Alabama* (1966), the Court sugested another rationale, stating that "a major purpose of [the First] Amendment was to protect the free discussion of governmental affairs."[29] This position echoes scholars such as Alexander Meiklejohn[30] and Robert Post, who emphasize the connection between free speech and democratic self-governance. According to Post, the First Amendment "protects the communicative processes" through which the public debates and influences the policy choices made by elected officials.[31] Thus, freedom of speech safeguards the public's ability to debate policies and vote for politicians whom they believe will enact the policies they favor. Because many of those policies relate to health, it follows that freedom of speech helps populations use their influence to promote policies that protect their health.

Freedom of speech also supports self-governance relating to health in other, less obvious ways. It enables activists and nongovernmental

[26] *See* Cohoon v. Konrath, 563 F. Supp. 3d 881 (E.D. Wis. 2021).

[27] Annie Sparrow, *The Chinese Government's Cover-Up Killed Health Care Workers Worldwide*, FOREIGN POLICY (Mar. 18, 2021), https://foreignpolicy.com/2021/03/18/china-covid-19-killed-health-care-workers-worldwide.

[28] Jack Brewster, *CDC Director: Agency Was "Muzzled" under Trump*, FORBES (Jan. 24, 2021), www.forbes.com/sites/jackbrewster/2021/01/24/cdc-director-agency-was-muzzled-under-trump/?sh=7aed952a6fed.

[29] Mills v. Alabama, 384 U.S. 214, 218 (1966).

[30] Alexander Meiklejohn, *What Does the First Amendment Mean?*, 20 U. CHI. L. REV. 461 (1953).

[31] ROBERT POST, DEMOCRACY, EXPERTISE, AND ACADEMIC FREEDOM: A FIRST AMENDMENT JURISPRUDENCE FOR THE MODERN STATE 40–43 (2012).

organizations to spread their messages, which can, in turn, advance or undermine health. The work of HIV activists in the 1980s and 1990s provides an illuminating example. In the absence of an adequate governmental response to that pandemic, activists mobilized not only to influence the government but also to educate the public about HIV/AIDS.[32] Given the widespread homophobia and reluctance to discuss sex at the time, protections for speech were essential to such prevention efforts.

Free speech can also protect individual autonomy in ways that relate to health. As Justice Louis Brandeis wrote in *Whitney v. California* (1927), "Those who won our independence believed that the final end of the state was to make men free to develop their faculties. ... They valued liberty both as an end and as a means."[33] Thus, freedom of speech is valuable not just for its impact on truth, policy, and politics, but because of its meaning to individuals. In that sense, respect for autonomy broadly conceived requires respect for self-expression.

Freedom of speech can be especially important for autonomy relating to health. As the California Supreme Court recognized in 1972 in *Cobbs v. Grant*, people need to receive information to "chart" their own course regarding their health.[34] Assume, for example, that an individual wishes to avoid a severe case of COVID-19, but also fears that vaccines may harm their fertility (again, they do not). Respect for the individual's autonomy and fulfillment of their choices demands that they receive accurate information – that being vaccinated won't harm their fertility. That, at least, is the theory behind the doctrine of informed consent. But individuals will be unable to receive accurate information if the state either censors medically sound information[35] or compels clinicians to give patients inaccurate information, as some states have done with regard to the risks of abortion.[36] In that sense, patient autonomy demands that clinicians be free to provide patients with medically sound advice. On the other hand, precisely because patients look to their providers for medically accurate information,

[32] Max D. Siegel, *Lessons from a Plague*, 4 WM. & MARY POL'Y REV. 292, 311–12 (2013).
[33] Whitney v. California, 274 U.S. 357, 375 (1927) (Brandeis, J., concurring).
[34] Cobbs v. Grant, 502 P. 2d 1, 10 (Cal. 1972).
[35] Claudia E. Haupt, *Professional Speech*, 125 YALE L. J. 1238, 1270–72 (2016).
[36] Sonia Suter, *The First Amendment and Physician Speech in Reproductive Decision-Making*, 43 J. L. MED. & ETHICS 22, 28–30 (2015).

respect for patient autonomy also supports the regulation of professional speech to ensure that physicians give patients advice that comports with the understanding of what legal scholar Claudia E. Haupt calls the "knowledge community."[37] Both malpractice law and medical licensing have traditionally provided such regulation. During the COVID-19 pandemic, some scholars have argued that physicians'who peddled misleading information to the public writ large and not simply to their own patients should also face professional sanctions.[38]

COMMERCIAL SPEECH

Despite free speech's exalted status among the pantheon of constitutionally protected liberties, the idea that the First Amendment requires the unregulated informational environment that we faced during the pandemic is of relatively recent vintage. For most of our history, state common law doctrines (such as defamation) and police power regulations (such as product labeling laws) were thought to be compatible with the First Amendment. Indeed, the Supreme Court did not hold that the First Amendment applied to the states – and hence, limited the police power – until 1925.[39] Even then, the Court explained that a state could "punish those who abuse this freedom by utterances inimical to the public welfare, tending to corrupt public morals, incite to crime, or disturb the public peace."[40] Vigorous judicial protection for speech, including speech that could harm health, only came after the New Deal Court rejected the old police power jurisprudence and later courts embraced a more individualistic conception of civil liberties.

Since the mid-twentieth century, the Court has increased both the reach and the rigor of its free speech jurisprudence, such that government today has little leeway for regulating speech that threatens public health. To offer just a few examples, the Court has recognized a First Amendment defense to claims for intentional infliction of emotional

---

[37] Haupt, *supra* note 35, at 1286–99.

[38] Philip A. Pizzo et al., *When Physicians Engage in Practices That Threaten the Nation's Health*, 325 JAMA 723, 723–24 (2021).

[39] Gitlow v. New York, 268 U.S. 652 (1925).

[40] *Id.* at 667.

distress even if the speech causes bodily harm.[41] The Court has also ruled that in the absence of other illegal activity, states cannot proscribe hate speech,[42] despite the impact that such speech can have on the health of individuals and targeted communities.[43] In addition, as will be discussed more in Chapter 9, the Court has equated campaign donations with speech in ways that can threaten the democratic process and the government's ability to enact laws that protect health. And in 2011, in *Brown v. Entertainment Merchants Association*, the Court ruled that a state law barring the sale of violent video games to minors was unconstitutional regardless of the potential impact of such games on children's health.[44] In one interesting pandemic-related example of the expansiveness of the speech clause, a federal district court ruled that Florida's ban on vaccine mandates for cruise ships was unconstitutional as a content-based regulation of speech.[45]

The so-called commercial speech doctrine has been especially important for seeding the infodemic and Americans' vulnerability to severe disease during the COVID-19 pandemic. In the first half of the twentieth century, even as the Court granted greater protection for most forms of speech, it accepted the traditional view that the First Amendment did not apply to advertising or marketing. That stance left the federal government and the states relatively free to regulate advertising and product labeling.

In 1975, in *Bigelow v. Virginia*, the Court altered course. *Bigelow* concerned a state law barring advertisements for abortion.[46] In striking the law, the Court, in an opinion by Justice Harry Blackmun, the author of *Roe v. Wade*,[47] explained that "speech is not stripped of First Amendment protection merely because it appears in [an advertisement]."[48] Nevertheless, using language that invoked the old police power jurisprudence, Blackmun accepted that "advertising, like all

---

[41] Snyder v. Phelps, 562 U.S. 443 (2011).
[42] R.A.V. v. City of St. Paul, 505 U.S. 377 (1992).
[43] RICHARD DELGADO & JEAN STEFANCIC, UNDERSTANDING WORDS THAT WOUND 12–13 (2004).
[44] Brown. v. Ent. Merchs. Ass'n, 564 U.S. 786, 799–800 (2011).
[45] Norwegian Cruise Line Holdings, Ltd. v. Rivkees, 553 F. Supp. 3d 1143 (S.D. Fla. 2021).
[46] Bigelow v. Virginia, 421 U.S. 809 (1975).
[47] Roe v. Wade, 410 U.S. 113 (1973).
[48] 421 U.S. at 818.

public expression, may be subject to reasonable regulation that serves a legitimate public interest."[49] He also noted that the state had a "legitimate interest in maintaining the quality of medical care,"[50] but concluded that Virginia had gone too far by blocking the public's capacity to learn about out-of-state abortion services. Blackmun thus seemed to view protections for commercial speech as necessary to ensure that individuals can receive information that can help them make informed choices about their own health. Yet Blackmun was not ready to treat commercial speech like other forms of speech. He signaled that the Court would accept reasonable regulations and deferred ruling on whether states could regulate advertising for activities that, unlike abortion, they could "legitimately regulate or even prohibit."[51]

That question was raised squarely the next year in *Virginia State Board of Pharmacy v. Virginia Citizens Consumer Council,*[52] which concerned a law that regulated advertisements for pharmacies. Writing again for the Court, Blackmun continued to connect protections for commercial speech with the interests of consumers[53] (sometimes referred to as "listeners" in First Amendment discussions). Yet he saw listeners' interests as being protected not by speech regulations, which he called "highly paternalistic," but by their ability to receive unregulated information.[54] In that way, he accepted the marketplace of ideas theory. Still, he acknowledged that "commonsense differences" between commercial speech and other forms of speech counseled that the former should receive less fulsome protection than other forms of speech.[55] What that actually meant, he did not say.

In 1980, in *Central Hudson Gas and Electric Corp. v. Public Service Commission of New York,*[56] the Court attempted to clarify its approach to commercial speech by establishing a four-prong test for determining the constitutionality of commercial speech regulations.

[49] *Id.* at 826.
[50] *Id.* at 827.
[51] *Id.* at 825.
[52] Va. State Bd. of Pharmacy v. Va. Citizens Consumer Council, 425 U.S. 748 (1976).
[53] *Id.* at 763–69.
[54] *Id.* at 770.
[55] *Id.* at 771 n.24.
[56] Cent. Hudson Gas & Elec. Corp. v. Pub. Serv. Comm'n, 447 U.S. 557 (1980).

Under the test, which is often considered a form of intermediate scrutiny, a court must first ask if the speech is false or misleading. If so, it can presumably be regulated. If not, the court must ask whether the state interest in regulating the speech is substantial, whether the regulation directly advances that interest, and whether it does so in a manner that is no more extensive than was necessary to serve the state's interest.[57]

The application of the *Central Hudson* test proved challenging, with the Court upholding some speech regulations and rejecting others. Over time, however, the Court's approach has become increasingly strict.[58] This has complicated efforts to protect health. An important example is the Court's opinion in *Lorillard Tobacco Co. v. Reilly* (2001),[59] which reviewed Massachusetts's regulations of cigarette and cigar advertisements. After finding that the regulation of cigarette advertising was preempted by federal law,[60] the Court, in an opinion by Justice Sandra Day O'Connor, held that the regulation of advertising for cigars, which were not subject to any federal laws, failed the *Central Hudson* test because the state could not show that the regulation was not more burdensome than necessary to achieve the state's goal. Although O'Connor ostensibly used the *Central Hudson* test, her analysis had all the hallmarks of strict scrutiny, signaling that regulations of advertisements for dangerous products would face a rough road in the courts.

Any doubt as to the strictness of the test evaporated the next year in *Thompson v. Western States Medical Center*, which held that a federal law banning advertisements by compounding pharmacies (which were mostly unregulated at the time) was unconstitutional.[61] Once again, O'Connor, who wrote the Court's opinion, relied heavily on the fourth prong of the *Central Hudson* test, stressing that the government had to prove that the regulation was necessary to protect health. The decision also rejected "the notion that the Government has an interest in preventing the dissemination of truthful commercial

---

[57] *Id.* at 566.
[58] Wendy E. Parmet & Jason Smith, *Free Speech and Public Health: Unraveling the Commercial-Professional Speech Paradox*, 78 OHIO ST. L. J. 887, 890 (2017).
[59] Lorillard Tobacco Co. v. Reilly, 533 U.S. 525 (2001).
[60] *Id.* at 551.
[61] Thompson v. W. States Med. Ctr., 535 U.S. 357 (2002).

information in order to prevent members of the public from making bad decisions with the information."[62] In other words, the Court saw the choice as to whether to consume dangerous pharmaceuticals as a purely individual one, and viewed First Amendment protections for advertising as a way to enable individuals to receive information that might inform their own choices. Any earlier recognition that reasonable speech protections might support the public's health seemed to disappear.

The dissent by Justice Stephen Breyer, who was joined by Chief Justice William Rehnquist and Justices John Paul Stevens and Ruth Bader Ginsburg, framed the issue very differently. According to Breyer, federal law exempted compounding from most drug regulations because it filled a need for patients who had particularized contraindications for mass-produced drugs.[63] But because the drugs were not standardized, they posed unique dangers. By promoting compounding drugs to more patients, – some of whom might not need compounding – advertising threatened to encourage patients to use potentially unsafe or unsterile drugs. For this reason, Breyer explained, Congress could have reasonably concluded that the regulation of advertising protected public safety. Thus, Breyer viewed the advertising regulation as a public health measure rather than a question of individual choice.

Within a decade, Breyer's prescience became apparent. Compounding took off, with some compounding pharmacies effectively operating as unregulated, nationwide manufacturers. In 2012, more than sixty individuals died from meningitis due to contaminated compounded drugs manufactured and sold nationwide by the New England Compounding Center.[64] As Kevin Outterson explained, *Thompson* allowed the center to build a national market for its unregulated (and unsafe) products.[65]

---

[62] *Id.* at 374.

[63] *Id.* at 380 (Breyer, J., dissenting).

[64] Jess Bidgood, *Compounding Pharmacy Owner Not Guilty of Murder after 60 Meningitis Deaths*, N.Y. TIMES (Mar. 22, 2017), www.nytimes.com/2017/03/22/us/meningitis-new-england-compounding-center-barry-cadden.html.

[65] Kevin Outterson, *Perspective: Regulating Compounding Pharmacies after NECC*, 367 N. ENG. J. MED. 1969, 1971 (2012).

More broadly, the Court's decisions in *Lorillard, Thompson*, and like cases helped convince the FDA to loosen its regulation on pharmaceutical advertising, paving the way for direct-to-consumer advertising and the now ubiquitous drug ads on television and in other popular media.[66] These ads, in turn, have helped train consumers to believe – as the Court seemed to accept in *Thompson* – that they are capable of deciding (based only on an ad or other information they came across) whether a particular drug or remedy is right for them. Many Americans are also accustomed to seeing ads that offer to connect them with a physician (who is perpetually "standing by"!) who will prescribe the advertised product. Thus, while many ads remind people to speak to their doctors, they also send the message that individuals can figure out what drugs are right for them without seeking expert advice.

During the COVID-19 pandemic, such conditioning led many Americans to be credulous about the mounds of misinformation that swamped traditional and social media. Some consumers of misinformation seemed to feel that they did not need to listen to experts to decide whether they should be vaccinated or what treatments they should take if they became sick. Instead, like star quarterback Aaron Rodgers – who said he rejected vaccination based on his own research, and talked to podcast host Joe Rogan when picking a COVID treatment – many Americans felt competent to assess COVID preventions and treatments on their own.[67] Others were happy to go to websites such as AmericasFrontlineDoctors.org, which sold tote bags and T-shirts and offered (for a fee) to connect consumers with physicians who could prescribe unproven remedies such as ivermectin.[68] To consumers accustomed to the deregulated informational marketplace that the Court helped to unleash, this route probably seemed perfectly natural. Health decisions – even those like vaccination that can affect others – had come to be seen as purely personal ones that need not rely on expertise.

---

[66] *See* Julie Donohue, *A History of Drug Advertising: The Evolving Roles of Consumers and Consumer Protection*, 84 MILBANK Q. 659 (2006).

[67] *Aaron Rodgers Explains Decision to Not Get COVID-19 Vaccination in His First Comments since Positive Test*, NFL (Nov. 5, 2021), www.nfl.com/news/aaron-rodgers-explains-decision-to-not-get-covid-19-vaccination-in-first-comment.

[68] *See* AMERICA'S FRONTLINE DOCTORS, https://americasfrontlinedoctors.org (last visited May 7, 2022).

WARNING: THIS PRODUCT CAN KILL YOU

In 1943, the Supreme Court held that children could not be expelled from public school for refusing to salute the flag.[69] Justice Robert H. Jackson's opinion for the Court in *West Virginia State Board of Education v. Barnette* proclaimed that "if there is any fixed star in our constitutional constellation, it is that no official, high or petty, can prescribe what shall be orthodox in politics, nationalism, religion, or other matters of opinion or force citizens to confess by word or act their faith therein."[70] With that, the Court ruled that the First Amendment protected so-called compelled speech.

For many decades, the Court did not apply *Barnette* to commercial speech. Indeed, even as the Court increased its scrutiny of laws that banned or limited commercial speech, it remained deferential to laws that mandated commercial warnings or disclosures. The key case was *Zauderer v. Office of Disciplinary Counsel.*[71] In it, after striking several Ohio regulations restricting attorney advertising, the Court, in an opinion by Justice Byron White, upheld a provision that required lawyers who advertise their willingness to work on a contingent fee basis to disclose the fact that clients might still have to pay certain expenses. White explained that the interests at stake when the state mandates the disclosure of "purely factual and uncontroversial information" were "not of the same order" as the interests protected by *Barnette.*[72] Hence, he concluded, such regulations should be upheld as long as they are not "unjustified or unduly burdensome" and are "reasonably related to the State's interest in preventing deception of consumers."[73]

For many years, *Zauderer* was widely thought to hold that laws that mandated the inclusion of factually correct information in a commercial context were subject to the rational basis test, the loosest form of judicial review. As a result, it was far easier, legally speaking, for governments to require accurate product information and warning labels than it was to ban or limit advertisements for dangerous products.

---

[69] W.Va. State Bd. Educ. v. Barnette, 319 U.S. 624, 642 (1943).
[70] *Id.* at 642.
[71] Zauderer v. Off. of Disciplinary Couns., 471 U.S. 626 (1985).
[72] *Id.* at 651.
[73] *Id.*

This two-tiered approach comported with the Court's individualist perspective and faith in the marketplace of ideas. In the name of consumer choice, governments could not bar consumers from receiving factually correct (even if dangerous) information, but they could require that advertisers provide consumers with additional factual information relevant to their choices.

Whether such "warnings" actually protect consumers is questionable. Research suggests that consumers pay little heed to many warning labels.[74] Nevertheless, some warnings – especially those that are graphic and well-designed – can influence behavior and correct misconceptions about a product's dangers.[75] Regardless of their impact, product warnings have become a mainstay of American life and one of the favored legal tools for addressing the risks associated with unhealthy products such as cigarettes and sugary beverages. Interestingly, many of these risks, including cancer and obesity, are themselves risk factors for severe disease from COVID-19.[76] In that sense, America has relied heavily on warning labels rather than advertising or product bans to combat the misimpressions that advertisers have created over the years about products that increased Americans' susceptibility to severe outcomes from COVID-19.

Yet the government's capacity to demand warning labels is also threatened by the courts' increasingly strict interpretation of the First Amendment. In 2012, in *R.J. Reynolds Tobacco Company v. Food and Drug Administration*, the D.C. Circuit struck FDA regulations that required graphic warning labels on cigarette packages and advertisements.[77] In its opinion, the court held that *Zauderer*'s rational basis review only applied to laws that remedy deception. Then, applying the *Central Hudson* test, the court ruled that the FDA had failed to provide "a shred of evidence" that the graphic warning labels would reduce the number of Americans who smoked.[78] In reaching that conclusion,

---

[74] Claudia E. Haupt & Wendy E. Parmet, *Public Health Originalism and the First Amendment*, 78 WASH. LEE L. REV. 231, 287 (2021).

[75] *Id.* at 286.

[76] *People with Certain Medical Conditions*, CTRS. FOR DISEASE CONTROL & PREVENTION, www.cdc.gov/coronavirus/2019-ncov/need-extra-precautions/people-with-medical-conditions.html (last updated May 2, 2022).

[77] R. J. Reynolds Tobacco Co. v. FDA, 696 F. 3d 1205, 1221–22 (D.C. Cir. 2012).

[78] *Id.* at 1218–19.

the appeals court adopted the type of skeptical and unforgiving review of the agency's scientific evidence that became commonplace after Justice Amy Coney Barrett joined the Supreme Court in 2020. In addition, in a passage that foreshadowed Justice Neil Gorsuch's later questioning of whether the pandemic continued to constitute a compelling state interest,[79] the court questioned whether the FDA had a "substantial interest in discouraging consumers from purchasing a lawful product, even one that has been conclusively linked to adverse health consequences."[80]

The D.C. Circuit later overruled *R.J. Reynolds* to the extent that it limited *Zauderer* to laws designed to address deception.[81] Nevertheless, the FDA's ability to require graphic warning labels on cigarette boxes and advertisements remained hobbled. After *R.J. Reynolds* and fearing new legal challenges, the FDA delayed issuing new graphic warning requirements, even though they are common around the world,[82] the Family Smoking Prevention and Tobacco Control Act[83] requires them, and studies show that they save lives.[84] And when the FDA finally issued new regulations in 2020, a federal district judge in Texas postponed their implementation while First Amendment litigation that was delayed by the pandemic proceeded.[85]

First Amendment litigation has also stymied efforts to warn the public about the link between sugary sodas and obesity and diabetes – conditions that were also associated with high levels of hospitalization and death from COVID-19.[86] For example, in 2015, San Francisco enacted an ordinance that required advertisers of sugary beverages

---

[79] Does 1–3 v. Mills, 142 S. Ct. 17, 20–21 (2021) (Gorsuch, J., dissenting).

[80] *R. J. Reynolds*, 696 F. 3d at 1218 n.13.

[81] Am. Meat Inst. v. U.S. Dep't of Agric. 760 F. 3d 18, 20–23 (D.C. Cir. 2014).

[82] Gregory Curfman, *Graphic Cigarette Warning Labels, the First Amendment, and Public Right to Accurate Public Health Information: Graphic Cigarette Labels Back Under Legal Scrutiny*, 2 JAMA HEALTH F. 1, 1 (2021).

[83] 15 U.S.C. § 1333.

[84] Jamie Tam et al., *Estimated Prevalence of Smoking and Smoking-Attributable Mortality Associated with Graphic Health Warnings on Cigarette Packages in the US from 2022 to 2100*, 2 JAMA HEALTH F. e212852 (2021), doi:10.1001/jamahealthforum.2021.2852.

[85] *R. J. Reynolds Tobacco Company et al. v. U.S. Food & Drug Administration et al.*, No. 6:20-CV-00176 (E.D. Tex. 2020), PUBLIC HEALTH LAW CTR., www.publichealthlawcenter.org/litigation-tracker/r-j-reynolds-tobacco-company-et-al-v-us-food-drug-administration-et-al-no-620-cv (last visited May 6, 2022).

[86] *See People with Certain Medical Conditions, supra* note 76.

to warn that "drinking beverages with added sugar(s) contributes to obesity, diabetes, and tooth decay."[87] Not surprisingly, the beverage industry sued.

In its initial review of the regulation in *American Beverage Association v. City and County of San Francisco*, a panel of the US Court of Appeals for the Ninth Circuit ruled that rational basis review under *Zauderer* was not appropriate because the warning was neither uncontroversial nor factually accurate.[88] According to the court, the warning was not factually accurate because the consumption of sugary beverages does not always "contribute[] to obesity, diabetes, and tooth decay."[89] The court added that the regulation was not uncontroversial because it conveyed "disputed policy views."[90] Thus, the court seemed to suggest that rational basis review would not apply if a required warning evoked controversy. That outcome invited advertisers to create controversy just to avoid having to warn about the risks of their products.

The panel's analysis suggested that any law requiring anything but the driest and dullest (and less effective) warning labels would be subject to searching and skeptical judicial review. The following year, even as the full Ninth Circuit reviewed the panel's decision in *American Beverage*, the Supreme Court seemed to adopt and expand the panel's position, leaving governments with even fewer tools to combat misleading or incomplete commercial speech.

SANCTIONING MISINFORMATION

The decades-long battle over abortion has played an outsized role in the First Amendment's application to health-related speech. In *Bigelow*, the Court that decided that *Roe v. Wade* expanded the speech clause's reach to commercial speech in order to protect an individual's ability to learn about the availability of abortion services. Sixteen years later, a far more conservative Court rejected a First Amendment

---

[87] Am. Beverage Ass'n v. City & Cnty of San Francisco, 871 F. 3d 884, 888 (9th Cir. 2017), *aff'd en banc*, 916 F. 3d 749 (9th Cir. 2019).
[88] *Id.* at 895.
[89] *Id.* at 884.
[90] *Id.* at 896.

challenge to a regulation barring recipients of federal family planning grants, known as Title X funds, from counseling patients about or referring them to abortion services.[91] According to the Court, the government was not suppressing speech, it was simply setting the terms of the grants that it was funding.

The next year, in *Planned Parenthood v. Casey*, the Court dismissed another First Amendment challenge to a law requiring abortion providers to inform patients about abortion's impact on the fetus.[92] In their dispositive joint opinion, Justices O'Connor, Kennedy, and David Souter quickly rejected the providers' claim that the compelled speech doctrine applied, writing that the First Amendment rights of a physician in the context of a physician-patient relationship are "subject to reasonable licensing and regulation by the State."[93]

In the years that followed, many states enacted laws that required physicians to provide specific – and sometimes misleading or erroneous – information to patients before performing an abortion. For example, South Dakota compelled providers to tell patients that abortions are associated with suicide and suicidal ideation; Texas and Alaska required providers to give patients brochures suggesting a link between abortion and breast cancer.[94] Lower courts analyzed these laws in inconsistent ways that often seemed to depart from standard First Amendment doctrine, leading legal scholar Caroline Mala Corbin to argue that abortion law created a "distortion" in free speech jurisprudence.[95] Just as importantly, in defending these laws as well as other abortion restrictions, governments relied on deeply flawed scientific evidence that contradicted the overwhelming consensus of experts in the field.[96] By accepting such evidence, the courts showed that expertise had little cachet and that science could be treated as yet another combatant in the culture wars.

This erosion of reliance on expertise and the distortion of truth became especially apparent in the legal battles over crisis pregnancy

[91] Rust v. Sullivan, 500 U.S. 173, 203 (1991).
[92] Planned Parenthood of Se. Pa. v. Casey, 505 U.S. 833, 844–46 (1992).
[93] *Id.* at 884.
[94] B. Jessie Hill, *Sex, Lies, and Ultrasound*, 89 UNIV. COLO. L. REV. 421, 425–29 (2018).
[95] Caroline Mala Corbin, *Abortion Distortions*, 71 WASH. & LEE L. REV. 1175, 1176–77 (2014).
[96] *Id.* at 1180–87.

centers (CPCs), organizations that provide pregnant people with a variety of services and goods alongside antiabortion counseling. In many cases, CPCs offer pregnancy tests and sonograms and give the appearance of a health clinic, even though they do not provide unbiased counseling and are often not staffed by licensed professionals.[97] In response, and adopting the belief that more information is the antidote to falsehoods, some cities and states enacted laws requiring CPCs to make certain truthful disclosures. For example, California required licensed CPCs to notify clients that the state provides free or low-cost pregnancy services, including abortions; it also required unlicensed CPCs to tell clients that they are not licensed.

In 2018, in *National Institute of Family and Life Advocates v. Becerra* (hereinafter referred to as *NIFLA*), the Supreme Court held that those requirements violated the speech clause.[98] Writing for the Court, Justice Clarence Thomas first considered the state's claim that its regulation of licensed clinics should be subject to rational basis review under *Zauderer*. Thomas disagreed, holding that strict scrutiny was required because the mandated disclosure was not limited to "purely factual and uncontroversial information about the terms under which … services will be available," and that abortion was "anything but an 'uncontroversial'" topic.[99] Thus, like the Ninth Circuit panel in *American Beverage*, he limited *Zauderer* to cases in which the compelled speech did not touch on a controversial topic.

The state also argued that the regulation should be upheld as a form of professional speech. Thomas rejected this too, stating that the Court had not recognized professional speech as a distinct type of speech.[100] Nevertheless, he accepted that "regulations of professional conduct that incidentally burden speech" have been considered constitutional.[101] According to Thomas, informed consent laws, such as those upheld in *Planned Parenthood v. Casey*, fall within that category. California's law did not, because it did "not facilitate informed consent

---

[97] Aziza Ahmed, *Informed Decision Making and Abortion: Crisis Pregnancy Centers, Informed Consent, and the First Amendment*, 43 J. L. MED. & ETHICS 51, 51–54 (2015).

[98] Nat'l Inst. of Fam. & Life Advoc. v. Becerra, 138 S. Ct. 2361 (2018).

[99] *Id.* at 2372 (quoting *Zauderer*, 471 U.S. at 650–51).

[100] *Id.* at 2371–72.

[101] *Id.* at 2373.

to a medical procedure."[102] He added that government regulations
of professional speech could thwart the "uninhabited marketplace of
ideas in which truth will ultimately prevail."[103]

California's requirements for unlicensed centers fared no better.
One might have thought that a law requiring an unlicensed facility
to disclose that it was unlicensed would easily fall within *Zauderer*.
Certainly, the information was factual; it was also well-tailored to
remedy deception. Nevertheless, without deciding if the mandated
disclosure was the type that would merit rational basis review under
Zauderer, Thomas concluded that strict scrutiny was required because
California had failed to establish that its mandate was neither "unjustified [n]or unduly burdensome."[104] In reaching that conclusion, he
noted that "California points to nothing suggesting that pregnant
women do not already know that the covered facilities are staffed by
unlicensed medical professionals,"[105] implying that a state could only
try to remedy deception if it produced a study demonstrating that consumers were deceived. Thus, though he did not overrule *Zauderer*,
he used what was effectively a form of strict scrutiny to determine
whether strict scrutiny should apply. This approach resembles the
Court's comparability analysis in the COVID free exercise cases.[106]
In each instance, the Court applied skeptical and stringent review to
determine if strict scrutiny was actually required.

As in *Thompson*, Breyer warned in his *NIFLA* dissent about the
potential health impact of the majority's decision. Noting that "much,
perhaps most, human behavior takes place through speech," Breyer
argued that "the majority's approach at the least threatens considerable litigation over the constitutional validity of much, perhaps most,
government regulation."[107] The ubiquitous laws requiring health-
related disclosures would be particularly endangered. Perhaps in
response to this worry, Thomas offered a reassurance: "[W]e do not
question the legality of health and safety warnings long considered

---

[102] *Id.*
[103] *Id.* at 2374 (quoting McCullen v. Coakley, 573 U.S. 464, 476 (2014)).
[104] *Id.* at 2377 (quoting *Zauderer*, 471 U.S. at 651).
[105] *Id.*
[106] *See* Chapter 4.
[107] *Becerra*, 138 S. Ct. at 2380 (Breyer, J., dissenting).

permissible, or purely factual and uncontroversial disclosures about commercial products."[108] Yet by barring even factually unassailable disclosures about controversial topics and requiring governments to prove the necessity for any warnings, Thomas's opinion for the majority potentially weakened yet another public health tool.

During the pandemic, the lower courts had few opportunities to consider the application of *NIFLA* or any of the Court's other recent free speech cases to COVID-related misinformation. In large measure, this was because neither the federal government nor the states undertook significant efforts to stop the proliferation of false or misleading speech relating to COVID-19 or vaccines. The Federal Trade Commission, which has authority over false consumer advertising, initiated only a handful of enforcement actions against companies that it charged with making false product claims.[109] State medical boards also failed (with rare exceptions) to discipline physicians who disseminated misinformation.[110] To fight the infodemic, governments generally relied on countering false messages with accurate ones and the voluntary decisions of private social media companies to police their own platforms. (Importantly, under Section 230(c) of the Communications Decency Act, social media companies have protection against any potential claims relating to the speech disseminated by or posted by others on their platforms.)[111]

Still, in a few instances, state efforts to shield people from misinformation were found unconstitutional. Most interesting was California's attempt in 2021 to shield people seeking vaccinations from harassment.[112] Right to Life, a nonprofit antiabortion advocacy group, challenged the law, claiming that it prevented the organization from conducting its antiabortion advocacy next to a Planned Parenthood clinic that administered vaccines. A federal district court agreed with Right to Life, ruling that the law was subject to strict scrutiny and that

---

[108] *Id.* at 2376.

[109] *Coronavirus Responses: Enforcement Actions*, FED. TRADE COMM'N, www.ftc.gov/coronavirus/enforcement (last visited Jan. 27, 2021).

[110] Geoff Brumfiel, *A Doctor Spread COVID Misinformation and Renewed Her License with a Mouse Click*, NPR (Nov. 4, 2021), www.npr.org/sections/health-shots/2021/11/04/1051873608/a-doctor-spread-covid-misinformation-and-renewed-her-license-with-a-mouse-click.

[111] 47 U.S.C. § 230(c).

[112] Right to Life Cent. Cal. v. Bonta, 562 F. Supp. 3d 947, 951–52 (E.D. Cal. 2021).

the state was unlikely to show that it was narrowly tailored to achieving a compelling state interest.[113]

Such cases, however rare, showed that First Amendment doctrine left governments with few weapons to contain misinformation around COVID. Yet as the pandemic has shown, the marketplace of ideas does not assure the triumph of either truth or health. Many if not most Americans accept that as the price of freedom. And without question, efforts to crack down on misinformation would raise new threats. Still, it's worth recalling that freedom of speech did not always include an absolute right to spread information that threatened health, and that for the majority of American history, states retained some significant leeway to protect the public against dangerous commercial speech. A return to that status quo ante would not mark the end of freedom of speech; it would simply restore the balance that existed throughout most of American history. It would also give public health a fighting chance.

Neither the Supreme Court nor its free speech doctrine bear primary responsibility for the infodemic. They have, however, helped to usher in our post-truth, figure-it-out-yourself informational environment. During the pandemic, that state of affairs proved deadly.

---

[113] *Id.* at 960–66.

9 AN UNHEALTHY POLITY

The United States was not healthy during the COVID-19 pandemic – and not just because of the deaths and illness attributed to the novel coronavirus and the diseases that worsened during the pandemic.[1] Nor was it due solely to the many preexisting conditions that led the United States to have a lower life expectancy than peer nations prior to the pandemic.[2] The United States was also unhealthy because its democracy was in peril. The insurrection at the Capitol on January 6, 2021, and President Donald Trump's "big lie" that helped ignite it were just some of the signs of decay. Following that violence, 147 Republican members of Congress continued to contest the 2020 presidential election, voting to reject Biden electors.[3] In 2021, at least nineteen states enacted measures making it harder to vote in future elections,[4] and fourteen states passed laws to make it easier for state legislatures or partisans to overturn the popular vote.[5] By 2022, it seemed uncertain

---

[1] *See* Steven H. Woolf et al., *Excess Deaths from COVID-19 and Other Causes in the US, March 1, 2020, to January 2, 2021*, 325 JAMA 1786, 1789 (2021).

[2] AMERICA'S HEALTH RANKINGS, INTERNATIONAL COMPARISON, 2019 ANNUAL REPORT (2019), www.americashealthrankings.org/learn/reports/2019-annual-report/international-comparison (last visited June 13, 2022).

[3] Karen Yourish et al., *The 147 Republicans Who Voted to Overturn Election Results*, N.Y. TIMES (Jan. 7, 2021), www.nytimes.com/interactive/2021/01/07/us/elections/electoral-college-biden-objectors.html.

[4] BRENNAN CENTER, VOTING LAWS ROUNDUP: DECEMBER 2021 (Jan. 12, 2022), www .brennancenter.org/our-work/research-reports/voting-laws-roundup-december-2021.

[5] Matt Basilogambros, *Republican Legislators Curb Authority of County, State Election Officials*, PEW CHARITABLE TRUSTS (July 28, 2021), www.pewtrusts.org/en/research-and-analysis/blogs/stateline/2021/07/28/republican-legislators-curb-authority-of-county-state-election-officials.

whether the winner of the next presidential (or any other) election would be permitted to take office.[6]

The public seemed to sense the danger. In January 2022, according to a Quinnipiac University poll, 58 percent of Americans believed that "the nation's democracy is in danger of collapse."[7] More frighteningly, close to the first anniversary of the Capitol insurrection, a *Washington Post*–University of Maryland poll reported that one in three Americans – including 40 percent of Republicans, 41 percent of Independents, and 23 percent of Democrats – believed that political violence could be justified.[8]

Many political scientists and experts on political violence shared the public's alarm. In June 2021, more than one hundred political scientists released a statement of concern. Citing Republican-led efforts to alter election laws, they explained that "these initiatives are transforming several states into political systems that no longer meet the minimum conditions for free and fair elections. Hence, our entire democracy is now at risk."[9] Experts also pointed to the breakdown of the norms that allow democracy to flourish, as well as the increasing intolerance that political actors and activists showed to their political opponents. Barbara F. Walter, who studies civil wars, suggested that the United States might be facing a new civil war.[10] Canadian political scientist Thomas Homer-Dixon urged his country to prepare for the possibility of political instability and widespread violence in the United States.[11]

---

[6] Richard L. Hasen, *Identifying and Minimizing the Risk of Election Subversion and Stolen Elections in the Contemporary United States*, 135 HARV. L. REV. 265, 282–94 (2022).

[7] Tim Malloy & Doug Schwartz, *Political Instability Not U.S. Adversaries, Seen as Bigger Threat, Quinnipiac University National Poll Finds; Nearly 6 in 10 Think Nation's Democracy Is in Danger of Collapse*, QUINNIPIAC UNIV. POLLING INST. (2022), at 1, https://poll .qu.edu/images/polling/us/us01122022_ubjw88.pdf.

[8] Meryl Kornfield & Mariana Alfaro, *1 in 3 Americans Say Violence against Government Can Be Justified, Citing Fears of Political Schism, Pandemic*, WASH. POST (Jan. 1, 2022), www.washingtonpost.com/politics/2022/01/01/1-3-americans-say-violence-against-government-can-be-justified-citing-fears-political-schism-pandemic.

[9] *Statement of Concern: The Threats to American Democracy and the Need for National Voting and Election Administration Standards*, NEW AM. (June 1, 2021), www.newamerica.org/ political-reform/statements/statement-of-concern/.

[10] BARBARA F. WALTER, HOW CIVIL WARS START: AND HOW TO STOP THEM (2021).

[11] Thomas Homer-Dixon, *The American Polity Is Cracked, and Might Collapse. Canada Must Prepare*, GLOBE & MAIL (Dec. 31, 2021), www.theglobeandmail.com/opinion/ article-the-american-polity-is-cracked-and-might-collapse-canada-must-prepare.

Even if these dire predictions are wrong, the country may still, as American legal scholar Jack Balkin suggested, "slide into a soft authoritarianism, [with] an increasingly corrupt form of government propped up by propaganda, conspiracy theories, and cultural welfare."[12] With this, "although the outward forms of constitutional democracy will be preserved, the actual norms of democracy will continue to decay."[13] Or, perhaps, democracy will simply continue to wither and diminish, bit by bit. Either way, its retreat is dangerous, not just for our civic life but for our health.

Looking at the landscape, scholars have identified many factors to explain democracy's erosion. These include rising inequality, racial resentment in the face of demographic change, anger toward increasing secularization, the rise of social media, and heightened polarization. An increasing resort to "constitutional hardball," in which political actors forsake norms of comity and forbearance to exploit constitutional ways to accrue power, is also implicated.[14] So, too, are Supreme Court decisions.[15] The institution that supposedly stands guard to preserve the Constitution has enabled its diminishment, striking yet another blow to our long-term health.

DEMOCRACY AND HEALTH

The relationship between the health of a nation's residents and its political structure is complex. Autocratic regimes can sometimes respond more quickly and more effectively to a health crisis than democratic governments,[16] as was evidenced by China's early ability to limit COVID-19 cases and deaths, albeit at a great cost to liberty

---

[12] Jack M. Balkin, *How to Do Constitutional Theory while Your House Burns Down*, 101 B.U. L. Rev. 1723, 1731 (2021).

[13] *Id.*

[14] *See* Mark Tushnet, *Constitutional Hardball*, 37 J. Marshall L. Rev. 523, 523 (2004).

[15] Michael J. Klarman, *The Degradation of American Democracy – and the Court*, 134 Harv. L. Rev. 1, 179–223 (2020).

[16] Gokhan Karabulut et al., *Democracy and COVID-19 Outcomes*, 203 Econ. Letters 109840 (2021).

individual health and well-being.[17] Yet autocratic regimes may also cover up health problems, scapegoat vulnerable individuals, and use a crisis to consolidate power. Further, as China's increasingly harsh lockdowns in response to the omicron variant in 2022 illustrate, autocratic regimes may be unwilling or unable to listen to critics and adjust course when the situation demands it.[18]

More broadly, a pandemic's toll depends not just on a country's emergency response but on a wide range of prepandemic social and political determinants that may make its population more or less susceptible to both pathogens and misinformation, more or less trusting of science and expertise, and more or less inclined to consider the common good. It is here where autocratic regimes may fall short. And it is here, as much as with our failed emergency response, that America's weakened democracy left it vulnerable.

Numerous empirical studies report a strong positive association between democracy and population health.[19] A 2015 study that looked at data from sixty-seven countries found a "strong positive association between democratic governance and better individual health," even after adjusting for individual and country-level confounders.[20] A 2019 study that analyzed data from 173 countries between 1900 and 2012 found that democracy has "contemporary and lasting effects on population health."[21]

Researchers offer many explanations for democracy's positive association with health. One is that democratic governments may be more "responsive" to popular demands for investment in education, health care, and other social factors that promote health.[22] Because SDOH are dependent on political decisions, populations in democracies can and often do use their ability to influence policies to improve

---

[17] *See* Vivian Wang, *Why China Is the World's Last "Zero Covid" Holdout*, N.Y. TIMES (Nov. 15, 2021), www.nytimes.com/2021/10/27/world/asia/china-zero-covid-virus.html?_ ga=2.7842932.732859912.1641790242-711096141.1592804144.

[18] *See* Li Yuan, *China's "Zero Covid" Mess Proves Autocracy Hurts Everyone*, N.Y. TIMES (Apr. 13, 2022), www.nytimes.com/2022/04/13/business/china-covid-zero-shanghai.html.

[19] *E.g.* Karabulut et al., *supra* note 16

[20] Patrick M. Krueger et al., *Democracy and Self-Rated Health Across 67 Countries: A Multilevel Analysis*, 143 SOC. SCI. & MED. 137, 141 (2015).

[21] Yi-ting Wang et al., *Does Democracy Enhance Health? New Empirical Evidence 1900–2012*, 72 POL. RSCH. Q. 554, 554 (2019).

[22] Krueger et al., *supra* note 20, at 137.

their health. Sometimes that conflicts with corporate interests, due to the significant role of so-called commercial or corporate determinants of health (CDOH),[23] which are the "factors that influence health which stem from the profit motive."[24] These can encompass dangerous consumer products, such as tobacco or ultra-processed food, which contribute to chronic diseases. CDOH also include dangerous employment conditions, pollution, and many other health-harming by-products of the modern economy.

In a healthy democracy, we might expect voters to push elected officials to mitigate these dangers, even though doing so limits the "freedom" of those who profit off of them. That does not mean that voters would always or even usually demand that governments take all the steps that health advocates might desire. Health is not the only goal that humans care about. Indeed, throughout the pandemic, many Americans prioritized other interests over health. Moreover, voters are often happy to accept commercial practices that harm their health if they provide jobs or pleasure. (Think about how many people continue to smoke, knowing that it may kill them.) Still, because of health's centrality to human flourishing, voters often want their governments to protect their health. In a well-functioning democracy, elected officials will be sensitive to those concerns. That's one reason why judicial decisions prioritizing negative liberty over public health undermine self-governance.

There are other mechanisms through which democracy can affect health. For example, in an autocratic regime, officials may be chosen more for loyalty than competence, and even those who are competent may be more concerned about pleasing senior leaders than instituting effective health policies.[25] Democratic governments may be also less able to suppress information (including about their own failings) that can help individuals keep themselves and their families healthy. In addition, the type of political activism and civic engagement that

---

[23] *See* Martin McKee & David Stuckler, *Revisiting the Corporate and Commercial Determinants of Health*, 108 AM. J. PUB. HEALTH 1167, 1169 (2018).

[24] Cassandra de Lacy-Vawdon & Charles Livingstone, *Defining the Commercial Determinants of Health: A Systematic Review*, 20 BMC PUB. HEALTH 1022, 1031 (2020).

[25] Georgy Egorov & Konstantin Sonin, *Dictators and Their Viziers: Endogenizing the Loyalty-Competence Trade-Off*, 9 J. EUR. ECON. ASSOC. 903, 921 (2011).

democracies rely on and foster can augment social capital and trust, which are themselves positively associated with health.[26]

In considering the relationship between democracy and health, it is crucial to remember that a liberal democracy requires more than competitive elections. There also has to be roughly equal representation and access to the franchise, and elections need to be relatively fair and free, with the losing side willing to stand down. Freedom of press and speech, as well as respect for the rule of law and the independence of the judiciary, are also critical traits of a liberal democracy.[27]

The extent to which these characteristics exist in nations commonly thought of as democracies differ. In countries such as the United States, where large segments of the population lack equal access to the franchise and are underrepresented in the political process, political leaders may be less concerned about and less willing to safeguard the health of underrepresented groups. Instead, public policies may be disproportionately directed to the needs of those who have more political influence. This disproportionality may explain why policies often fail to protect the health and well-being of noncitizens, who cannot vote.[28] It also sheds light on the health disparities experienced by people of color who have been systematically underrepresented and devalued in the American political system. As a report by the Union of Concerned Scientists explains, "with less ability to protect themselves at the ballot box, millions of citizens, especially the socioeconomically vulnerable, are unable to change the direction of public policy in their states."[29] Worse, as political leaders neglect the health of some communities, their members may become less healthy and thereby less able to advocate for their health. The result, the report warns, is that "the electorate becomes even more distorted to favor healthier voters."[30] Believing that their own good health is due to their actions,

---

[26] ROBERT PUTNAM, BOWLING ALONE: THE COLLAPSE AND REVIVAL OF AMERICAN COMMUNITY 337–38 (2000).

[27] Aziz Huq & Tom Ginsburg, *How to Lose a Constitutional Democracy*, 65 UCLA L. REV. 78, 87 (2018).

[28] *See* Chapter 7.

[29] Michael Latner, *Our Unhealthy Democracy: How Voting Restrictions Harm Public Health – and What We Can Do about It*, UNION OF CONCERNED SCI. 1 (2019), www.ucsusa.org/resources/our-unhealthy-democracy.

[30] *Id.*

these healthier votes may in turn be supportive of policies that treat health as a matter of personal responsibility.

In the United States, this feedback loop has a distinctly racial and racist hue. From the founding of the republic until today, disenfranchisement has often been plotted along racial lines. Further, as scholar and author Heather McGee discusses, racism has long undermined Americans' capacity to perceive their interdependency and support policies that promote the common good.[31] That's why, as McGee shows, cities would rather close public pools than integrate them. It also helps to explain why so many states have refused to expand their Medicaid programs.[32] A polity that devalues the health of some, even if it maintains the nominal structures of a democracy, may endanger the health of all. That fact was all too apparent during the COVID-19 pandemic.

THE CONSTITUTIONAL ROOTS OF DEMOCRACY'S DECLINE

The Constitution that the Founders bequeathed to us did not create a liberal democracy under any definition of that term. Most critically, it protected slavery. It also allowed states to limit the franchise to white male property owners. Even after the abolition of slavery and the expansion of the franchise to women voters, Black voters, and people lacking property, the Constitution remains "hardwired" to thwart popular sovereignty.[33] The Framers feared giving the public too much power and therefore established a republic that divided power and tempered the influence of majorities. To give just a few well-known examples, the Constitution requires supermajorities in both houses of Congress in order for legislation to pass over a presidential veto. This makes it challenging for Congress to enact popular measures if

---

[31] HEATHER MCGEE, THE SUM OF US: WHAT RACISM COSTS EVERYONE AND HOW WE CAN PROSPER TOGETHER 17–40 (2021).

[32] James A. Monroe, *Partisanship, Dysfunction, and Racial Fears: The New Normal in Health Care Policy?*, 41 J. HEALTH POL., POL'Y & L. 827, 841 (2016).

[33] Jack M. Balkin & Sanford Levinson, *Democracy and Dysfunction: An Exchange*, 50 IND. L. REV. 281, 298–309 (2016).

a president disapproves. Conversely, the need to pass legislation in two houses makes it difficult for presidents to enact their own agendas when their party does not hold large majorities in each house.

The Electoral College further dilutes majority control, allowing for the election of presidents who lose the popular vote – an outcome that has occurred twice in the past twenty-five years. The Constitution also grants each state, regardless of its population, an equal number of senators. As a result, Wyoming, which has fewer than six hundred thousand people, has as much voice in the Senate as California, which has more than thirty-nine million residents.[34] Further, the steep hurdles that Article V places on amending the Constitution make it exceptionally hard for majorities to alter its less democratic elements. Less obviously but equally importantly, the Constitution tolerates (though it may not compel) a strong form of judicial review that permits an unelected judiciary to wield extraordinary power to override majoritarian wishes. The fact that, as now, some of these justices may be appointed by presidents who lost the popular vote and confirmed by senators who represent less than a majority of the nation only compounds the antimajoritarian bias.[35]

True, many of the more antimajoritarian traits of the American polity could, at least in theory, be addressed without constitutional change.[36] For example, the current version of the filibuster, which essentially allows forty-one senators (who may come from less populated states) to block most legislation, exacerbates the antimajoritarian cast of the Senate. The filibuster is not, however, constitutionally required; it's only a Senate rule that a majority can override, as it has for judicial appointments. Likewise, the disproportionate representation of rural states in the Senate could be mitigated, though not eliminated, by granting statehood to the District of Columbia and Puerto Rico. Expanding the number of representatives in the House could also permit a more proportional division of representatives among the states. Even the problem of presidents taking office after losing the

[34] *US States – Ranked by Population 2022*, WORLD POPULATION REV., https://worldpopulationreview.com/states (last visited May 9, 2022).

[35] Philip Bump, *The Minoritarian Third of the Supreme Court*, WASH. POST (Dec. 2, 2021), www.washingtonpost.com/politics/2021/12/02/minoritarian-third-supreme-court.

[36] Balkin & Levinson, *supra* note 33, at 302–5.

popular vote could potentially be overcome by an interstate compact assigning electors to the winner of the popular vote.[37]

The problem with all these workarounds, and many others that have been proposed, is that the antidemocratic provisions that they seek to redress makes their enactment highly improbable. Political minorities, after all, have little reason to cede the power they have, especially in an era of heightened political polarization. Indeed, we may have come to a point where the antidemocratic aspects of our government that are hardwired into our system have converged with winner-take-all politics to create a type of retrenchment that makes reform improbable.[38] For this, the Supreme Court bears considerable responsibility.

Recall that in 1938, the Court in *Carolene Products* offered the protection of democracy as a rationale for heightened judicial review.[39] By the twenty-first century, the Court had abandoned that position.[40] One way it has done so is by dispensing with deference to the political branches in matters relating to health and the public's well-being. This shift has left policymakers with fewer choices and less ability to compete on the basis of policies as opposed to cultural symbols. Another way the Court has abandoned the protection of democracy is by making it easier for politicians to entrench their own power even while disabling them from instituting mechanisms to protect democracy. In short, the Court has allowed politicians to play hardball while blocking their ability to engage in a softer form of politics. This handicap, so to speak, has weakened leaders' capacity or desire to compromise and develop effective solutions to the health (and other) problems that Americans face.

Critics will object that majoritarianism can also threaten democracy. Indeed, it can. Unchecked, majoritarianism can descend into a type of populism that threatens minority interests and invites authoritarianism. That's why protections for individual rights and respect for

---

[37] *Id.* at 292–93.

[38] *See* PAUL STARR, ENTRENCHMENT: WEALTH, POWER, AND THE CONSTITUTION OF DEMOCRATIC SOCIETIES xiii–xv (2019).

[39] United States v. Carolene Products Co., 304 U.S. 144, 152 n.4 (1938); *see* JOHN HART ELY, DEMOCRACY AND DISTRUST: A THEORY OF JUDICIAL REVIEW 105–16 (1980).

[40] Nicholas O. Stephanopoulos, *The Anti-Carolene Court,* 2019 SUP. CT. REV. 111, 112–17.

the rule of law are widely considered to be essential components of a democratic regime. Getting and maintaining the right balance between individual rights and popular sovereignty is the hardest challenge for constitutionalism; it probably can never be fully realized. Still, when the scales tip too far toward the entrenchment of political power and the erosion of popular sovereignty, democracy – and health – can be imperiled as surely as they can be by the disrespect of individual rights.

THE PANDEMIC ELECTION

Before we consider some of the ways in which the Court's actions have contributed to the decline in our democracy and what that means for health, it's worth exploring the Supreme Court's response to the unique challenges presented by the 2020 election. These decisions allowed the 2020 election to go forward remarkably well despite the raging pandemic. They also permitted Joe Biden, the winner of both the Electoral College and the popular vote, to take office despite Donald Trump's attempts to overturn the election. For that, the Court should get some credit: It refused to be complicit in an attempted coup. But its 2020 decisions also contained ominous warnings about how it may resolve future threats to our democracy.

In 2020, the nation's capacity to hold a safe and fair election was uncertain. The election took place amidst a resurging pandemic, before vaccines were available. Hence, in-person voting could be deadly. To stay safe, many more Americans than usual tried to vote by absentee ballot, but changes implemented by Trump's newly appointed post-master general, Louis DeJoy, raised concerns about the US Postal Service's capacity to return ballots in time to be counted.[41]

Responding to these challenges, many states eased rules that restricted absentee ballots, extended the deadline for ballots to be received, and added the option of voting via "drop boxes." But because of the partisan split in concern over the pandemic, the

---

[41] Steve Coll, *Is the Postal Service Being Manipulated to Help Trump Get Reelected?*, NEW YORKER (July 29, 2020), www.newyorker.com/news/daily-comment/is-the-postal-service-being-manipulated-to-help-trump-get-reelected.

expansion of absentee voting was widely thought to be more beneficial to Democratic voters, who took COVID more seriously, than to
Republican voters, who seemed less worried about in-person voting –
and indeed, about exposure to the virus in general.[42]

Not surprisingly, partisans ran to court. Democrats challenged
the failure of mainly red states to expand access to absentee voting;
Republicans challenged measures that made voting easier. Several of
these cases made their way to the Supreme Court's shadow docket
before Amy Coney Barrett joined the Court and it shifted course on
COVID mitigation measures.

Although the Court did not issue a signed opinion in a preelection
voting case, its decisions and the concurring and dissenting opinions
provided clues about the justices' views. First, the Court refused to
support lower federal court orders demanding the relaxation of voting
procedures.[43] This signaled that the Court seemed uninterested in proclaiming a federal right to absentee voting or other pandemic-related
modifications.[44] Concurring in one case, Justice Brett Kavanaugh
even cited Chief Justice Roberts's concurring opinion in *South Bay
United Pentecostal Church v. Newsom*, stating that the Constitution
"principally entrusts the safety and health of the people to the politically accountable officials of the State," a position he did not accept
either in *South Bay* or in the many other COVID mitigation cases that
would soon come before him.[45]

Second, although there was no majority opinion on this point, the
more conservative justices echoed the Court's claim in *Bush v. Gore* –
which decided the contested 2000 election for George W. Bush – that
Article II of the Constitution gives state legislatures plenary power
over the selection of their state's electors.[46] Offering support for what

---

[42] Mackenzie Lockhart et al., *America's Electorate Is Increasingly Polarized along Partisan
Lines about Voting by Mail during the COVID-19 Crisis*, 117 PROC. NAT'L ACAD. OF
SCIS. OF THE U.S. 24640, 24641 (2020).

[43] Democratic Nat'l Comm. v. Wis. State Legis., 141 S. Ct. 28, 30 (2020); Andino v.
Middleton, 141 S. Ct. 9 (2020).

[44] Tex. Democratic Party v. Abbott, 140 S. Ct. 2015 (2020); Merrill v. People First, 141 S.
Ct. 25 (2020); *Democratic Nat'l Comm.*, 141 S. Ct. at 28.

[45] *Andino*, 141 S. Ct. at 10 (Kavanaugh, J., concurring) (quoting S. Bay United Pentecostal
Church v. Newsom, 140 S. Ct. 1613, 1613–14 (2020) (Roberts, C. J., concurring)).

[46] Bush v. Gore, 531 U.S. 98, 104–5 (2000) (per curiam). *See also* 140 S. Ct. at 115
(Rehnquist, C. J., concurring).

is known as the independent state legislature doctrine in his concurring opinion in *Democratic National Committee v. Wisconsin State Legislature* (which was decided on the same day that Barrett took the oath of office), Justice Neil Gorsuch wrote, "The Constitution provides that state legislatures – not federal judges, not state judges, not state governors, not other state officials – bear primary responsibility for setting election rules."[47] In his concurrence in that same case, Kavanaugh added that a "state legislature's decision either to keep or to make changes to election rules to address COVID-19 ordinarily 'should not be subject to second-guessing by an unelected federal judiciary, which lacks the background, competence, and expertise to assess public health and is not accountable to the people.'"[48] Again, he showed no such concerns about the judiciary's competence in COVID mitigation cases.

In 2020, the Court's failure to require safer voting procedures and the belief of some justices that state legislatures have absolute power over presidential elections proved inconsequential. Despite the pandemic, more than 159 million Americans, voted – the most ever.[49] The election also saw an enormous rise in absentee (or mail-in) voting.[50] Moreover, although Trump tried to persuade Republican officials in several swing states to change the outcome of the vote – he even summoned Michigan legislators to the White House and infamously asked Georgia's secretary of state to "find" the votes he needed to win that state[51] – no state legislature overturned the popular vote. Several Republican attorneys general, however, did attempt a last-ditch ploy to keep Trump in office by asking the Supreme Court to intervene, in *Texas v. Pennsylvania*.[52]

---

[47] *Democratic Nat'l Comm.*, 141 S. Ct. at 29 (Gorsuch, J., concurring).
[48] *Id.* at 30–31 (Kavanaugh, J., concurring) (quoting *Andino*, 141 S. Ct. at 10 (Kavanaugh, J., concurring)).
[49] James M. Lindsay, *The 2020 Election by the Numbers*, COUNCIL ON FOREIGN RELATIONS (Dec. 15, 2020), www.cfr.org/blog/2020-election-numbers.
[50] Nathaniel Rakich & Jasmine Mithani, *What Absentee Voting Looked Like in All 50 States*, FIVETHIRTYEIGHT (Feb. 9, 2021), https://fivethirtyeight.com/features/what-absentee-voting-looked-like-in-all-50-states.
[51] Andy Sullivan & Michael Martina, *In Recorded Call, Trump Pressures Georgia Official to "Find" Votes to Overturn Election*, REUTERS (Jan. 3, 2021), www.reuters.com/article/us-usa-election-trump/in-recorded-call-trump-pressures-georgia-official-to-find-votes-to-overturn-election-idUSKBN2980MG; Ed White et al., *Trump Summons Michigan GOP Leaders for Extraordinary Meeting*, ASSOCIATED PRESS (Nov. 19, 2020), https://apnews.com/article/trump-invites-michigan-gop-white-house-6ab95edd3373ecc9607381175d6f3328.
[52] Texas v. Pennsylvania, 141 S. Ct. 1230 (2020)(mem.).

That case was extraordinary in several ways. Seventeen state attorneys general tried to invoke the Supreme Court's seldom-used original jurisdiction to throw out the election results in another state. On December 11, 2020, in a brief, unsigned opinion, the Court dismissed the case for lack of standing. The Court's order stated simply, "Texas has not demonstrated a judicially cognizable interest in the manner in which another State conducts its elections."[53] With that, the Court refused to support Trump's attempt to overturn the 2020 election.

The decision in *Texas v. Pennsylvania* didn't mean, however, that the Court was unwilling to endorse other subversions of democracy. To the contrary, it had already opened the door to them.

PROTECTING THE RIGHTS OF CAMPAIGN DONORS

Money has an outsized effect on politics and policymaking. Those who have and spend significant sums in the political process have a greater voice than ordinary citizens, undermining the equality of representation (however imperfect) that is central to the legitimacy of a democratic polity.[54] Large contributions can also distort public policies away from the interests and concerns of the public as a whole.[55] This distortion can exacerbate the adverse CDOH as corporations and wealthy individuals use their influence to thwart regulations that might mitigate the negative health effects of corporate products or policies. It can also weaken the public's trust in the political system.[56]

The Supreme Court's first major sojourn into campaign financing laws came in 1976 in *Buckley v. Valeo*.[57] The case, which was decided the year after the Supreme Court extended First Amendment protections to commercial speech,[58] concerned several provisions of the Federal Election Campaign Act of 1971 (FECA), as amended after

---

[53] *Id.*
[54] James Lindley Wilson, Democratic Equality 50–55 (2019).
[55] Larry Bartels, Unequal Democracy: The Political Economy of the New Gilded Age 3 (2d ed. 2016).
[56] Rebecca L. Brown & Andrew D. Martin, *Rhetoric and Reality: Testing the Harm of Campaign Spending*, 9 N.Y.U. L. Rev. 1066, 1076–77 (2015).
[57] Buckley v. Valeo, 424 U.S. 1 (1976).
[58] Bigelow v. Virginia, 421 U.S. 809, 821–25 (1975).

the Watergate scandal.[59] In particular, FECA limited contributions by
individuals and group to $25,000 per year total and up to $1,000 per
year to any single candidate; it also prohibited spending of more than
$1,000 per year "relative to a clearly identified candidate" and con-
tained reporting and disclosure requirements.[60]

In a lengthy per curiam opinion, the Court upheld FECA's reporting and requirements and public financing provisions. But the Court
also equated spending on campaigns with freedom of speech and
association.[61] In effect, the Court viewed laws regulating how much
money someone spends on a campaign as akin to laws limiting what
they could say.

After making that critical leap, the Court announced several standards and distinctions that have shaped the complex contours of its
campaign financing jurisprudence. First, looking to its commercial
speech cases, it purported to apply "exacting scrutiny," which appeared
to be somewhat less strict than "strict scrutiny."[62] Thus, at least initially, the Court treated restrictions on campaign spending somewhat
more favorably than viewpoint restrictions on speech. Second, the
Court distinguished direct contributions to campaigns from so-called
independent expenditures not spent in coordination with a campaign.
According to the Court, the latter did not raise the same risk of corruption or its appearance as direct expenditures and therefore warranted
more First Amendment protection.[63] Of course, in the real world, the
distinction between direct and uncoordinated expenditures may be
thin, as Justice Byron White noted in his concurring opinion.[64] The
positions that candidates take are likely influenced by their understanding of the money that large donors will spend to influence their electoral prospects, even if the expenditures aren't coordinated with their
campaigns. Likewise, the public may fear that a candidate is beholden
to a donor even when the money is spent independently of a campaign.

---

[59] Federal Election Campaign Act of 1971, Pub. L. No. 92–225, 86 Stat. 3 (1972) (amended
as by Federal Election Campaign Act Amendments of 1974, Pub. L. No. 93–443, 88
Stat. 1263 (1975)).
[60] *Buckley*, 424 U.S. at 13.
[61] *Id.* at 19.
[62] *Id.* at 16–17, 44–45, 94.
[63] *Id.* at 45.
[64] *Id.* at 262–64 (White, J., concurring).

After *Buckley*, the Court continued to utilize the exacting scrutiny standard and strike many, but not all, campaign finance laws.[65] For example, in 1978, in *First National Bank of Boston v. Bellotti*, the Court extended *Buckley*'s reasoning to corporations, striking a Massachusetts law that forbid banks and business corporations from spending money on ballot initiatives.[66] A few years later, the Court applied *Buckley* to hold that FECA's requirement that independent expenditures by non-profit corporations be financed through a separate fund or political action committee (PAC) violated the First Amendment.[67]

In 1990, in *Austin v. Michigan Chamber of Commerce*, the Court altered course.[68] By a 6–3 vote, it upheld a Michigan law that banned corporations from using their funds in support of or opposition to any candidate for statewide office. Writing for the majority, Justice Thurgood Marshall accepted that the law touched on core First Amendment speech and had to be narrowly tailored to serve a compelling state interest (he seemingly dropped the use of exacting scrutiny). He then found that the ban passed that test because it was narrowly tailored to address the risk to elections posed by corporate wealth. Marshall explained, "corporate wealth can unfairly influence elections when it is deployed in the form of independent expenditures, just as it can when it assumes the guise of political contributions."[69] Hence, he was willing to look beyond the formal distinction between independent and direct expenditures and consider the risk that corporate wealth posed to elections.

In 2002, Congress enacted the Bipartisan Campaign Reform Act (BCRA), commonly known as the McCain-Feingold Act.[70] BCRA was designed to address the loopholes in federal election laws, including the proliferation of totally unregulated "soft money," and the rise of issue ads – those that do not purport to support a candidate, but do for all intents and purposes.

The next year, in *McConnell v. Federal Election Commission*, the Court upheld several key provisions of BCRA, including limits on

---

[65] *See* Jacob Eisler, *The Deep Patterns of Campaign Finance Law*, 49 CONN. L. REV. 55 (2016).

[66] First Nat'l Bank of Bos. v. Bellotti, 435 U.S. 765 (1978).

[67] Fed. Election Comm'n v. Mass. Citizens for Life, Inc., 479 U.S. 238, 255–56 (1986).

[68] Austin v. Mich. Chamber of Comm'n, 494 U.S. 652 (1990).

[69] *Id.* at 660.

[70] Bipartisan Campaign Reform Act of 2001, Pub. L. No. 107–155, 116 Stat. 81.

contributions to political parties and a prohibition on corporate expenditures for advertising for identified candidates within thirty days of an election.[71] In so doing, the Court pointed to evidence in the congressional record connecting unregulated soft money to "manipulations of the legislative calendar, leading to Congress' failure to enact, among other things, generic drug legislation, tort reform, and tobacco legislation."[72] The Court also recognized that "the danger that officeholders will decide issues not on the merits or the desires of the constituencies, but according to the wishes of those who have made large financial contributions" is "just as troubling to a functioning democracy as classic *quid pro quo* corruption."[73] The Court thus accepted that campaign expenditures could affect both the content of public policy and the functioning of democracy.

Justice Anthony Kennedy, concurring in part and dissenting in part, saw the issues very differently. To him, the gravest risk was to the liberty of individual donors and spenders. To protect their freedom, he argued that Congress should only be able to regulate "actual or apparent *quid pro quo* arrangements."[74] The potentially deleterious impact of large expenditures on public policy and public trust was not, in his view, grounds for regulating campaign spending.[75]

In 2010, after its composition changed, the Court adopted Kennedy's views in *Citizens United v. Federal Election Commission*.[76] One of the most controversial decisions of this century, *Citizens United* considered a challenge to a section of BCRA, which had been affirmed in *McConnell*, barring corporations from spending money on communications (such as advertisements or documentaries) that identify candidates on any "broadcast, cable, or satellite communication" within thirty days of an election for federal office. In a decision written for a splintered majority, Kennedy overruled both *Austin* and *McConnell*, deeming them significant departures from First Amendment "principles." As in *McConnell*,

---

[71] McConnell v. Fed. Election Comm'n, 540 U.S. 93, 192–94 (2003).

[72] *Id.* at 150.

[73] *Id.* at 153.

[74] *Id.* at 294 (Kennedy, J., concurring in part and dissenting in part) (quoting *Buckley*, 424 U.S. at 45).

[75] *Id.* at 294.

[76] Citizens United v. Fed. Election Comm'n, 558 U.S. 310 (2010).

Kennedy emphasized the burdens that BCRA placed on a corporation's right to free speech. Equally, he read the government's interest in regulating campaign expenditures to extend only to the prevention of quid pro quo arrangements or the appearance of such arrangements.[77] "The appearance of influence or access," he explained, "will not cause the electorate to lose faith in our democracy."[78]

In an opinion concurring (as to the disclaimer and disclosure provisions) and dissenting (as to the other provisions), Justice John Paul Stevens, who was joined by Justices Ruth Bader Ginsburg, Stephen Breyer and Sonia Sotomayor, chided the majority for failing to respect its own precedent and ruling on constitutional questions that he believed the Court did not need to reach.[79] He also rejected the majority's assertion that corporations should be treated as individuals for First Amendment purposes, noting the "distinctive potential of corporations to corrupt the electoral process."[80]

Despite its notoriety, *Citizens United* did not completely obliterate the federal government's capacity to regulate campaign spending. Most importantly, Kennedy accepted BCRA's requirement that ads financed by individuals or corporations other than the candidate clearly state the name of whoever was responsible for them.[81] But the Supreme Court was not finished dismantling government's capacity to counter the influence of large donors. The next year in *Arizona Free Enterprise Club's Freedom Club PAC v. Bennett*, the Court, in an opinion by Roberts, found Arizona's attempt to even the playing field by providing "matching funds" to candidates who accept public financing unconstitutional. According to Roberts, by dulling the impact of private donations, the law violated the First Amendment's guarantee of "freedom."[82]

Three years later, in *McCutcheon v. Federal Election Commission*, the Court struck BCRA's $25,000 limit on individual contributions to all candidates.[83] In a plurality opinion, Roberts equated writing a

---

[77] *Id.* at 357.
[78] *Id.* at 360.
[79] *Id.* at 398–99 (Stevens, J., concurring in part and dissenting in part).
[80] *Id.* at 423.
[81] *Id.* at 367 (majority opinion).
[82] Ariz. Free Enter. Club's Freedom Club PAC v. Bennett, 564 U.S. 721, 750 (2011).
[83] McCutcheon v. Fed. Election Comm'n, 572 U.S. 185 (2014).

check to a campaign with voting and reiterated Kennedy's view that
the government's interest in regulating campaign spending was limited to policing quid pro quo corruption. Roberts added that "the
line between *quid pro quo* corruption and general influence may seem
vague at times, but the distinction must be respected to safeguard basic
First Amendment rights."[84] In 2022, Roberts kept to that distinction
in an opinion for a six-justice majority upholding on First Amendment
grounds Senator Ted Cruz's challenge to a BCRA provision limiting
the use of contributions collected after an election to repay a candidate's own loans to their campaign.[85]

The Court in *Citizens United* and *McCutcheon* seemed to accept
laws requiring the disclosure of campaign contributions. Indeed,
Roberts described them as powerful tools for stopping abuse.[86] Yet the
fate of these requirements is also in doubt. In June 2021, in *Americans
for Prosperity Foundation v. Bonta*, the Court ruled that a California law
requiring nonprofit organizations to disclose the names of their donors
violated the First Amendment's protections for association.[87] Although
that case did not concern campaign disclosure laws, "the Court's willingness to strike down the [California] regulation and raise the bar on
the 'exacting scrutiny' standard suggests that campaign finance regulations and other compelled disclosure regimes—even for business corporations—may be dismantled or threatened in the future."[88]

As noted above, the Court's campaign finance decisions rest on
a problematic analogy between spending money and speaking out.
Citizens United and *McCutcheon* also rely on an unconvincing distinction between quid pro quo corruption and all other forms of influence.
It is a distinction, according to legal expert Gene Nichol, that "no one,
literally no one, involved in politics believes [this] to be true."[89]

Public health researchers have criticized the Court's campaign
finance cases for their adverse impact on health. Public health scholar

[84] *Id.* at 209 (Roberts, C. J., plurality).
[85] Fed. Election Comm'n v. Cruz, 142 S. Ct. 1638 (2022).
[86] *McCutcheon*, 572 U.S. at 223–24.
[87] Americans for Prosperity Found. v. Bonta, 141 S. Ct. 2373 (2021).
[88] Elizabeth Pollman, *The Supreme Court and the Pro-Business Paradox*, 135 HARV. L. REV., 220, 224 (2021).
[89] Gene Nichol, *Citizens United and the Roberts Court's War on Democracy*, 27 GA. ST. L. REV. 1007, 1014 (2011).

William Wiist argued that *Citizens United* "expands corporate rights to disproportionately influence the electoral process and thus health policymakers."[90] Offering the history of the tobacco industry's decades-long success in thwarting regulation, Wiist added that *Citizens United* allows corporate contributions to "influence proposed or existing health policies concerning restrictions on taxation of unhealthful foods and beverages; advertising of unhealthful products such as sugar-sweetened drinks, high-fat foods, or alcohol to children or vulnerable communities; requirements for restaurant menu labeling; or issues of reproductive rights, air quality standards, global climate change, comprehensive school health education, worker health and safety, gun show background checks, and others."[91] The impact on public health, he warned, "may be catastrophic."[92]

That warning may not have been hyperbole. *Citizens United* unleashed a "flood of corporate money" into politics.[93] Much of that money went to "independent-expenditure-only" political action committees, commonly known as super PACs.[94] There has also been a "tremendous uptick in nonprofit political activism."[95] As public health expert Nicholas Freudenberg documents, some of the new money that rushed into the political arena came from corporations whose products have a substantial adverse impact on health. For example, after *Citizens United* contributions by the McDonald's Corporation's PAC jumped dramatically.[96] Perhaps not surprisingly, government efforts to regulate the food industry over the same period stalled, leaving the obesity problem – which proved so lethal during the pandemic – largely unaddressed.[97]

---

[90] William H. Wiist, Citizens United, *Public Health, and Democracy: The Supreme Court Ruling, Its Implications, and Proposed Action*, 101 AM. J. PUB. HEALTH 1172, 1172 (2011).

[91] *Id.* at 1173.

[92] *Id.* at 1172.

[93] Klarman, *supra* note 15, at 203.

[94] Douglas M. Spencer & Abby K. Wood, *Citizens United, States Divided: An Empirical Analysis of Independent Political Spending*, 89 IND. L. J. 315, 330 (2014).

[95] James Sample, *The Decade of Democracy's Demise*, 69 AM. U. L. REV. 1559, 1567 (2020).

[96] NICHOLAS FREUDENBERG, LETHAL BUT LEGAL: CORPORATIONS, CONSUMPTION, AND PROTECTING PUBLIC HEALTH 109 (2014).

[97] *People with Certain Medical Conditions*, CTRS. FOR DISEASE CONTROL & PREVENTION (last updated May 2, 2022), www.cdc.gov/coronavirus/2019-ncov/need-extra-precautions/people-with-medical-conditions.html. *See* Chapter 6.

Perhaps more important to health is the impact of large campaign contributions on the public's trust in the democratic process.[98] Post–*Citizens United*, Americans increasingly viewed their government as corrupt, an outcome that Justice Breyer had predicted in his *McCutcheon* dissent.[99] In a study of surveys of public attitudes, Rebecca L. Brown and Andrew D. Martin found that when donations increase over a certain level, citizens lose their faith in the "ability of a representative to follow the wishes of her constituents. ... Simply put, it does not take a bribe to corrode [people's] faith in the democratic process."[100] Unfortunately, the Court has left the government with few tools for reversing such cynicism or mitigating the accumulation of oligarchical power that follows when government policies focus on the interests of donors rather than citizens.[101]

THE CONCERNING EROSION OF VOTING RIGHTS

If the Court's campaign finance cases limit Congress's ability to stem the influence of large donors on our politics, its voting rights cases impede Congress's capacity to preserve the influence of Black and minority voters. In both cases, the Court has used judicial review to weaken democracy.

Through much of American history large portions of the population have been denied access to the ballot. (White) women did not receive the right to vote until the ratification of the Nineteenth Amendment in 1920. For Black Americans, the wait was far longer. Even though the Fifteenth Amendment that was ratified during Reconstruction prohibited the denial of the franchise on the basis of race, most Black Americans – especially in the South – lacked meaningful access to the ballot until the passage of the 1965 Voting Rights Act (VRA).[102] Widely perceived as one of the most important civil

[98] Rebecca L. Brown & Andrew D. Martin, *Rhetoric and Reality: Testing the Harm of Campaign Spending*, 90 N.Y.U. L. REV. 1066, 1089–90 (2015).
[99] McCutcheon v. Fed. Election Comm'n, 572 U.S.185, 238 (Breyer, J., dissenting); Brown & Martin, *supra* note 98, at 1090.
[100] Brown & Martin, *supra* note 98, at 1090.
[101] *See* STARR, *supra* note 38, at 204.
[102] Voting Rights Act, Pub. L. No. 89–119, 70 Stat. 437 (1965).

rights laws in American history, the VRA helped to unwind practices that kept Black Americans, especially in the former Confederacy, from voting. Section 2 of the VRA barred any "standard, practice, or procedure" that results "in a denial or abridgement of the right of any citizens of the United States to vote on account of race."[103] Sections 4 and 5 required that "covered jurisdictions," which originally were those that had imposed literacy or other tests, to receive "preclearance" from the Department of Justice or a federal court before instituting any changes in their voting procedures to ensure that they did not block access to voting on account of race.[104]

Initially, the Supreme Court seemed to support voting rights. In 1966, in *Harper v. Virginia Board of Elections*, it ruled that the poll tax was unconstitutional.[105] The same year, in *Katzenbach v. Morgan*, the Court affirmed the VRA's constitutionality.[106] More recently, a far more conservative Court has been far less sympathetic to voting rights. For example, in 2008, in *Crawford v. Marion County Election Board*, the Court upheld Indiana's voter identification law, which requires citizens to present photo identification as a condition of voting.[107] The following year, in an opinion by Roberts, the Court questioned the constitutionality of the VRA's preclearance provisions.[108] Although Roberts ultimately based his decision on statutory rather than constitutional grounds, he stated, "Things have changed in the South," and the "evil that § 5 is meant to address may no longer be concentrated in the jurisdictions singled out for preclearance."[109]

Four years later, in *Shelby County v. Holder*, the Court reached the constitutional issue and held Section 4 of the VRA, which set the formula for determining which jurisdictions are subject to the act's preclearance requirements, was unconstitutional.[110] Once again, Roberts wrote the Court's opinion. In it, he acknowledged that "voting

---

[103] *Id.*
[104] *Id.*
[105] Harper v. Va. Bd. of Elections, 383 U.S. 663 (1966).
[106] Katzenbach v. Morgan, 384 U.S. 641 (1966).
[107] Crawford v. Marion Cnty. Election Bd., 553 U.S. 181 (2008).
[108] Nw. Austin Mun. Util. Dist. No. 1 v. Holder, 557 U.S. 193 (2009).
[109] *Id.* at 202, 203.
[110] Shelby Cnty. v. Holder, 570 U.S. 529 (2013).

discrimination still exists," but argued that the VRA violated norms of federalism, which, as in *National Federation of Independent Businesses v. Sebelius* (2012), he claimed helps to secure liberty.[111] He added that Section 4 also violated the Constitution's requirement that all states be treated as equal sovereigns. While these deviations from constitutional principles may have been justified in 1965, Roberts wrote, they could no longer be, as Black citizens had achieved voting parity in many of the states that were subject to preclearance. He concluded by noting that Section 2 of the VRA – which bars discrimination on account of race – remained in place, and that "Congress may draft another formula based on current conditions," which would be "an initial prerequisite to a determination that exceptional conditions still exist."[112] Thus, although he did not hold that preclearance would be unconstitutional with the right formula, he wasn't promising that it would be constitutional.

The Roberts Court was not finished narrowing voting rights. In 2018, in *Husted v. A. Philip Randolph Institute*, it rejected a challenge under the 1993 National Voter Registration Act to an Ohio law – this one requiring the state to purge from the voting roles voters who had not voted in two years and had failed to respond to a preaddressed, postage-paid card asking them to verify their address.[113] Then, in *Brnovich v. Democratic National Committee* (2021), the Court turned its attention to Section 2(b) of the VRA, which *Shelby* left untouched.[114] Section 2(b) states that the VRA is violated when, "based on the totality of circumstances, it is shown that the political processes leading to nomination or election in the State or political subdivision are not equally open to participation by members of a class of citizens protected" by the act.[115] The challengers argued that Arizona laws prohibiting the counting of ballots cast in the wrong precinct and making it a crime for anyone other than a postal or elections official, voter's caretaker, family member, or household member to collect an absentee ballot disparately impacted minorities and violated Section 2(b).

---

[111] *Id.* at 536, 544–55; Nat'l Fed'n of Indep. Bus. v. Sebelius, 567 U.S. 519, 536 (2012).
[112] *Holder*, 570 U.S. at 557.
[113] Husted v. A. Philip Randolph Inst., 138 S. Ct. 1833 (2018).
[114] Brnovich v. Democratic Nat'l Comm., 141 S. Ct. 2321 (2021).
[115] Voting Rights Act § 2(b).

In an opinion by Justice Samuel Alito, the Court disagreed. Interpreting Section 2(b)'s "totality of circumstances" language, he argued that lower courts should consider five factors, including the state's strong interest in preventing voter fraud and the degree to which the law departs from practices that were standard in 1982, when the current language of Section 2(b) was added.[116] Thus, practices that were common when the act was passed – and which Congress presumably passed the VRA to address – would now receive special solicitude from the Court, even if empirical evidence showed that they significantly reduced minorities' ability to vote.

In a blistering dissent, Justice Elena Kagan, who was joined by Breyer and Sotomayor, revisited the nation's sorry history of denying minorities access to the ballot.[117] She then argued that post-*Shelby*, Section 2 was more important than ever to the "operation of our democracy," and that the majority had undermined it by imposing "a list of mostly made-up factors, at odds with Section 2 itself."[118] She concluded that "of all laws, [the VRA] deserves the sweep and power Congress gave it."[119]

The Court has also made it very difficult to challenge racial gerrymandering, sometimes known as voter dilution. In these cases, the challengers claim that a state has drawn its electoral map in such a way as to reduce the representation of a particular racial group (or groups). In *Shaw v. Reno* (1993), a case challenging the creation of a majority-minority district, the Court held that an electoral map that was "neutral on its face" as to race could nevertheless violate the Fourteenth Amendment's equal protection clause if the map could be understood as an effort "to separate voters into different districts on the basis of race."[120] However, in cases challenging maps that are less favorable to minorities, the Court has been less willing to find impermissible racial gerrymandering. For example, in *Easley v. Cromartie* (2001), the Court ruled that partisanship could be a valid defense to a charge that gerrymandering was racially motivated.[121] Given the alignment

---

[116] 141 S. Ct. at 2338–40.
[117] *Id.* at 2352–55 (Kagan, J., dissenting).
[118] *Id.* at 2361, 2362.
[119] *Id.* at 2373.
[120] Shaw v. Reno, 509 U.S. 630, 649 (1993).
[121] Easley v. Cromartie, 532 U.S. 234, 253 (2001).

between race and partisanship, this holding provides partisans with an easy way to reduce the representation of racial minorities.

The Court has also emphasized that plaintiffs who challenge racial gerrymandering bear the burden of establishing intent, and that a district's roots in a racially biased map does not establish that the map's subsequent reenactment was racially motivated.[122] In *Merrill v. Milligan* (2022), the Court, from its shadow docket, stayed a decision by a three-judge federal court blocking Alabama's congressional map, which was expected to yield only one majority-Black district – even though Black voters constitute 27 percent of the state's population.[123] The five-justice majority issued no opinion, but Kavanaugh, in a concurring opinion that Alito signed, stated that courts "ordinarily should not enjoin a state's election laws in the period close to an election."[124] He added that the questions as to whether the VRA required a second majority–minority district, and whether the equal protection clause would prohibit such a requirement, "appear to be close."[125]

In dissent, Roberts agreed that the full Court should reconsider (and possibly tighten) the requirements for voting dilution claims, but argued that a stay was inappropriate because the lower court appeared to have followed the law as it then was.[126] In another dissent, Kagan, joined by Breyer and Sotomayor, lambasted the majority for using its shadow docket to "undermine[] Section 2 and the right it provides."[127] A few weeks later, the Court expressed no concerns about judicial involvement in state voting maps when, again from the shadow docket, it threw out an election map approved by the Wisconsin Supreme Court on the grounds that it violated the equal protection clause.[128] In the majority's view, the state court mistakenly applied the VRA to justify its consideration of race in drawing a map that would increase minority representation.

---

[122] Abbott v. Perez, 138 S. Ct. 2305, 2324 (2018).

[123] Merrill v. Milligan, 142 S. Ct. 879 (2022).

[124] *Id.* at 879 (Kavanaugh, J., concurring) (citing Purcell v. Gonzalez, 549 U.S. 1 (2006) (per curiam)).

[125] *Id.* at 881.

[126] *Id.* at 882–83 (Roberts, C. J., dissenting).

[127] *Id.* at 883 (Kagan, J., dissenting) (quoting Brnovich v. Dem. Nat'l Comm., 141 S. Ct. 2321, 2351 (Kagan, J., dissenting)).

[128] Wis. Leg. v. Wis. Election Comm'n, 142 S. Ct. 1245 (2022).

The Court's inconsistent attitude toward the judiciary's role in electoral map cases is also evident from its approach to cases that challenge partisan gerrymandering. Partisans have always drawn election maps to their advantage, but thanks to technological advances and heightened partisanship,[129] the practice has now become a "fine art."[130] Legal historian Michael Klarman offers a powerful example: In 2018, Democrats won 53 percent of the popular vote in Wisconsin but only 36 percent of the seats in the state legislature.[131] More troubling, once a party gains control of a state during a redistricting year, it can redraw lines to entrench its control.

While recognizing that such extreme partisan gerrymandering is "incompatible with democratic principles," the Court has permitted it to proliferate. In *Rucho v. Common Cause* (2019), the Court, in another opinion by Roberts, held that challenges to partisan gerrymandering were not subject to judicial review.[132] According to Roberts, courts lack the capacity to develop tests for determining whether or not a political map is "fair,"[133] and judicial intervention in such cases would mark "an unprecedented expansion of judicial power."[134] Not surprisingly, Roberts did not explain why concerns about the expansion of judicial power were not salient in *Citizens United*, *Shelby*, and other cases in which the Court limited the VRA.

Taken together, the Court's voting rights cases have helped to usher in what legal scholar James Sample has called "the decade of democracy's demise."[135] Within hours of the Court's decision in *Shelby*, for example, states that had been subject to preclearance began to impose restrictions on voting that the Justice Department had previously blocked under the VRA.[136] After the 2020 election and Trump's "big lie," the march toward restricting voting rights in ways

---

[129] Christopher Esposito, *Gerrymandering and the Meandering of Our Democratic Principles: Combatting Partisan Gerrymandering after* Rucho, 30 S. CA. INTERDISC. L. J. 195, 198 (2021).

[130] Klarman *supra* note 15, at 47.

[131] *Id.*

[132] Rucho v. Common Cause, 139 S. Ct. 2484 (2019).

[133] *Id.* at 2500.

[134] *Id.* at 2507.

[135] Sample, *supra* note 95, at 1559.

[136] Klarman, *supra* note 15, at 5–6.

that have "foreseeably adverse effects on minority voters" accelerated.[137] According to the Brennan Center for Justice, at least nineteen
states passed thirty-four laws restricting access to voting in 2021.[138]
In this "new trend," legislatures have begun to take up bills "to allow
partisan actors to interfere with election processes or even reject election results entirely."[139] Given the Court's nod to the plenary power
of state legislatures over presidential elections, these legislatures have
good reason to believe that federal courts will refuse to block efforts to
throw out the popular vote, especially if it is rationalized as necessary
to protect voter integrity.

Extreme partisan gerrymandering exacerbates polarization. It
makes races less competitive in a general election, leading candidates
to cater more to primary voters than to the electorate as a whole. This
trend in turn reduces legislators' interest in working across the aisle.[140]
In addition, because general elections are less competitive, gerrymandering can lead to declines in voter turnout and a diminution of voters'
confidence in elections and government more broadly.[141]

THE THREAT TO HEALTH

The risks to democracy and health are apparent. As certain communities face more barriers to voting and reduced representation, politicians have less and less reason to consider their health, especially when
policies to safeguard health clash with the interests of donors or their
own partisan bases. This may help to explain why numerous proposed
laws that relate to health and are highly popular, such as measures
addressing the high cost of prescription drugs, are so hard to pass.[142] It
may also explain why some states have continued to resist expanding

---

[137] *Brnovich*, 141 S. Ct. at 2355 (Kagan, J., dissenting).
[138] BRENNAN CTR. FOR JUSTICE, VOTING LAWS ROUNDUP: DECEMBER 2021 (2022), www
.brennancenter.org/our-work/research-reports/voting-laws-roundup-december-2021.
[139] *Id.*
[140] Esposito, *supra* note 129, at 202–3.
[141] *Id.* at 203–4.
[142] Liz Hamel et al., *Public Opinion on Prescription Drugs and Their Prices*, KAISER FAMILY
FOUND. (Apr. 5, 2022), www.kff.org/health-costs/poll-finding/public-opinion-on-
prescription-drugs-and-their-prices.

Medicaid despite referenda votes supporting expansion.[143] The public's voice may simply no longer matter.

A similar phenomenon was evident throughout much of the pandemic. Although many Americans grew weary of COVID-related restrictions as the pandemic dragged on, a clear majority supported social distancing measures in 2020, and mask and vaccine mandates through 2021 and into 2022.[144] Yet as the virus resurged, many political leaders rejected any public health measures.[145] Several states went so far as to ban vaccine mandates – even by private employers.[146]

Why this disconnect between the public's preferences about health policies and those adopted by political leaders? One possibility is that politicians were "following the science" more closely than the public. Indeed, the protection of the public's health (and presumably its long-term interest) may sometimes require policies that majorities reject. Conceivably this might help to explain why many political leaders kept schools open in 2021 and 2022, despite substantial fears raised by many parents and teachers.[147] As time went on, the science suggested that the cost of keeping schools closed generally outweighed the costs of keeping them open. But the idea that politicians who rejected vaccine and mask mandates were simply following the science doesn't pass the laugh test. A more plausible answer is that as elections have

[143] Phil McCausland, *Missouri Governor Won't Fund Medicaid Expansion, Flouting State Constitution and Voters*, NBC NEWS (May 13, 2021), www.nbcnews.com/politics/politics-news/missouri-governor-won-t-fund-medicaid-expansion-flouting-state-constitution-n1267265.

[144] Gabriela Schulte, *Poll: Nearly 3 in 4 Support Reinstating Mask Mandates if COVID-19 Cases Rise*, HILL (Jun. 20, 2021), https://thehill.com/hilltv/what-americans-thinking/563893-poll-74-percent-support-reinstating-mask-mandates-if-their-area; *Steady Support for Vax Mandates*, MONMOUTH UNIV. POLLING INST. (Nov. 11, 2021), www.monmouth.edu/polling-institute/reports/monmouthpoll_us_111121; *Majority of Americans Support Mask Mandates for Travel, AP-NORC Poll Finds*, PBS NEWSHOUR (Apr. 20, 2022), www.pbs.org/newshour/health/majority-of-americans-support-mask-mandates-for-travel-ap-poll-finds.

[145] Trip Gabriel et al., *With Some Voters "Ready to Move On," Democrats Search for New Message on Virus*, N.Y. TIMES (Jan. 25, 2022), www.nytimes.com/2022/01/25/us/politics/coronavirus-democrats-midterm-elections.html.

[146] Maggie Davis, *The Shifting Legal Landscape of COVID-19 Vaccine Requirements*, ASS'N OF STATE & TERRITORIAL HEALTH OFFS. (Nov. 3, 2021), www.astho.org/communications/blog/shifting-legal-landscape-of-covid-19-vaccine-requirements.

[147] CTRS. FOR DISEASE CONTROL AND PREVENTION, TRANSMISSION OF SARS-CoV-2 IN K–12 SCHOOLS (2021), www.cdc.gov/coronavirus/2019-ncov/science/science-briefs/transmission_k_12_schools.html (last updated Dec. 15, 2021).

become less competitive, politicians paid less heed to the views of the public writ large and catered more to their own bases.

For its part, the Supreme Court, through its donor and voter rights cases, has helped to cement political entrenchment and the divorce between public policy and the public's views. In this sense, the Court has become, in the words of Harvard law professor Nicholas Stephanopoulos, the "anti-*Carolene* Court": It refrains from strictly reviewing laws that restrict political processes even as it aggressively strikes social and economic legislation.[148]

The result is a government that is less responsive to the public's interest and less capable of protecting those interests. This is a recipe for a loss of trust in government, as well as the withering of the social compact that the American courts recognized when they cited *salus populi*.[149] Believing that laws and policies are either ineffective or corrupt, Americans may (understandably) be inclined to conclude that all they can do is look out for themselves, thus hardening the type of hyperindividualism that became all too apparent throughout the COVID-19 pandemic. If distrust becomes great enough, then people may turn to populist and demagogic leaders who promise that they alone can solve the problems of the average (read: middle-class white) American by scapegoating minorities.

This is a playbook for authoritarianism. But even if we can avoid the worst outcomes, the Court has helped to create a nation increasingly unable to respond effectively to the myriad threats to health and well-being, including those that arise from climate change and future pandemics. If – as the current Court seems to suggest – our Constitution demands this feebleness, we should ask if it is pathogenic. Is it?

[148] Stephanopoulos, *supra* note 40, at 112–17.
[149] *See* Chapter 2.

CONCLUSION

"A Republic, if You Can Keep It"

According to Johns Hopkins University's COVID-19 tracker, on May 17, 2022, the United States reached a grim milestone: One million Americans had died from COVID-19.[1] That toll, which is far more than that experienced by any other wealthy country,[2] is greater than the sum of American lives lost in every war in the twentieth century.[3] It exceeds the number of Americans who died from the 1918 influenza pandemic.[4] And the number, which is likely an undercount, does not include the "excess deaths" – the lives lost from delayed health care or increases in stress, mental illness, and substance use. It also does not count the pain of long COVID; the grief of the more than 140,000 children who lost a caregiver due to the pandemic;[5] or the millions who lost jobs, incomes, and careers. The losses are so great that we seem to have become numb to them. As science journalist Ed Yong observed, "the sheer scale of the tragedy strains the moral

---

[1] Doug Donovan, *U.S. Officially Surpasses 1 Million COVID-19 Deaths*, JOHNS HOPKINS UNIVERSITY & MEDICINE CORONAVIRUS RES. CTR. (May 17, 2022), https://coronavirus .jhu.edu/from-our-experts/u-s-officially-surpasses-1-million-covid-19-deaths.

[2] Steven Thrasher, *There Is Nothing Normal about One Million People Dead from COVID*, SCI. AM. (Feb. 10, 2022), www.scientificamerican.com/article/there-is-nothing-normal-about-one-million-people-dead-from-covid.

[3] Aaron O'Neill, *Number of United States Military Fatalities in All Major Wars Involving the United States from 1775 to 2022*, STATISTA (Feb. 3, 2022), www.statista.com/statistics/ 1009819/total-us-military-fatalities-in-american-wars-1775-present.

[4] Helen Branswell, *Covid-19 Overtakes 1918 Spanish Flu as Deadliest Disease in American History*, STAT NEWS (Sept. 20, 2021), www.statnews.com/2021/09/20/covid-19-set-to-overtake-1918-spanish-flu-as-deadliest-disease-in-american-history.

[5] *See* Thrasher, *supra* note 2.

imagination."[6] Certainly, as this third pandemic year unfolds, it seems as though the United States has decided to move on; more and more people are acting like the pandemic is over, even if it is not.

But our lives and health are not all that have been lost. Over the course of the pandemic, our social fabric has unraveled. Consider the spike in unruly behavior on airplanes; the harassment of health officials, doctors, and nurses; the looming threats of political violence; the increasing bellicosity of the culture wars; the loss of common purpose.

All of these fissures deepened in June 2022, when the Supreme Court issued two landmark decisions that further endangered Americans' health. The first case, *New York State Rifle and Pistol Association v. Bruen,*[7] came just weeks after a spate of mass shootings across the United States, including one at a school in Uvalde, Texas, that killed nineteen children and two teachers,[8] and another at a supermarket in Buffalo, New York, which killed ten people.[9] Writing for a six-justice majority, Justice Clarence Thomas held that New York's law requiring individuals seeking a license to carry concealed firearms to show a special need for carrying a weapon violated the Second Amendment. In the second case, *Dobbs v. Jackson Women's Health Organization,*[10] Justice Samuel Alito wrote an opinion for a five-justice majority that overruled *Roe v. Wade*[11] and *Planned Parenthood v. Casey,*[12] obliterating the constitutional right to abortion.

A full discussion of these cases is beyond the scope of the present volume, but a few observations are worth noting. First, as in the COVID cases discussed throughout these pages, the Court was unconcerned about the impact of its rulings on Americans' health. In *Bruen,* the Court admonished lower courts for even considering the state's interest – in other words, for considering the lives that firearm regulations might save.

---

[6] Ed Yong, *How Did This Many Deaths Become Normal?*, ATLANTIC (Mar. 8, 2022), www .theatlantic.com/health/archive/2022/03/covid-us-death-rate/626972.

[7] N.Y.S. Rifle & Pistol Ass'n v. Bruen, 142 S. Ct. 2111 (2022).

[8] *2 Mass Shootings - 1,700 Miles Apart but Bound by Startling Similarities*, NPR, May 27, 2022, https://www.npr.org/2022/05/27/1101490738/uvalde-buffalo-mass-shooting-similarities

[9] Mihir Zaveri et al., *"All These Innocent Lives": These Were the Victims in the Buffalo Attack*, N.Y. TIMES (May 15, 2022), www.nytimes.com/2022/05/14/nyregion/victims-buffalo-shooting.html.

[10] Dobbs v. Jackson Women's Health Org., 142 S. Ct. 2228 (2022).

[11] Roe v. Wade, 410 U.S. 113 (1973).

[12] Planned Parenthood S.E. Pa. v. Casey, 505 U.S. 833 (1992).

Thomas wrote, "When the second Amendment's plain text covers an individual's conduct, the Constitution presumptively protects that conduct. The government must then justify its regulation by demonstrating that it is consistent with the Nation's historical tradition of firearm regulations."[13] In short, laws that might reduce firearm-related deaths and injuries are invalid unless the Court finds them analogous to restrictions that were in place in 1787, when firearms were far less lethal. Likewise, in *Dobbs*, Alito relied on his reading of the legal status of abortion in the Middle Ages through 1973, when *Roe* was decided, to conclude that the right to an abortion is not "deeply rooted in the nation's history," and hence should not be recognized.[14] In reaching that conclusion, Alito paid scant attention to both the short-term impact of forced birth on women's health or the long-term effects that banning abortion will have on the SDOH and thereby on public health. Indeed, the opinion did not even suggest that women might have a right to terminate a pregnancy when their own lives are at stake.

Also, as in many of the cases discussed previously, the justices seemed indifferent to the views of the health experts who weighed in on the subjects. Instead of learning from contemporary science, the Court was content to base its rulings on its take of long-ago historical practices. It also seemed eager, as in the COVID cases, to invite further litigation and contestation. For example, in *Bruen*, the Court did not simply strike New York's law, it offered a new test for Second Amendment rights that left the status of many other, long-accepted gun regulations uncertain. Likewise, in *Dobbs*, the Court rejected Chief Justice John Roberts's call for judicial restraint, opting to overrule *Roe* even though the state had not asked the Court to do so in its petition for review, and even though doing so was not essential to Court's ruling.[15] As if that was not sufficient, in his concurring opinion, Thomas suggested that other landmark privacy cases relating to birth control, sodomy, and same-sex marriage must also fall[16] – a provocation that

---

[13] *N. Y. S. Rifle & Pistol Ass'n* 142 S. Ct. at 2117.

[14] *Dobbs*, 142 S. Ct. at 2281.

[15] *Id.*, at 2310–11(Roberts, C. J., concurring).

[16] *Id.*, at 2301 (Thomas, J., concurring)(citing Griswold v. Connecticut, 381 U.S. 479 (1965); Lawrence v. Texas, 539 U.S. 558 (2003); and Obergefell v. Hodges, 576 U.S. 644 (2015)).

the majority and Justice Brett Kavanaugh sought to calm[17] but could not quell. If anything is certain after *Dobbs*, it is that uncertainty reigns, as antiabortion states attempt to impose their will on out-of-state providers[18] and litigants take up Thomas's invitation to challenge other once-settled rulings.

Bruen also displayed the same privileging of negative liberty over self-governance and the liberty offered by public health protections that was apparent in so many recent cases. According to Thomas, Second Amendment rights must take precedence over all other interests. And just as the Court viewed personal choice as the appropriate response to COVID, it saw self-defense as the primary response to the contagion of gun violence. Yet as with COVID, individual actions will have social consequences.

In one important sense, *Dobbs* was somewhat different. In contrast to *Bruen* and most of the pandemic-era cases discussed above, *Dobbs* rejected a claim of negative liberty. Indeed, in his opinion, Alito seemed to stress the virtues of self-governance, writing "It is time to heed the Constitution and return the issue of abortion to the people's elected representatives."[19] He also argued that courts "cannot 'substitute their social and economic beliefs for the judgment of legislative bodies.'"[20]

It is, however, hard to take the *Dobb* Court's commitment to self-governance in earnest, coming as it did a day after *Bruen* and following years of decisions limiting the scope of self-governance even – as in the case of abortion – when there is no explicit textual support for the liberty at issue.[21] Viewed in that light, *Dobbs*'s nod to self-governance seems little more than a self-serving justification for dismantling a right that has long been anathema to social conservatives. That the Court cares little for self-governance is further evident from the short shrift it gave to the arguments that access to safe abortions is critical to women's participation in social and political life (i.e., their capacity for

---

[17] 142 S. Ct. at 2258; *id.*, at 2309 (Kavanaugh, J., concurring).

[18] Jacob Bogage & Christopher Rowland, *Chasm Opens between States over Abortion Pills and Out-of-State Care*, WASH. POST (June 25, 2022), www.washingtonpost.com/business/2022/06/25/abortion-pills-supreme-court.

[19] *Dobbs*, 142 S. Ct. at 2243.

[20] *Id.*, at 2277 (quoting *Ferguson v. Skrupa*, 372 U.S.726, 729–30 (1963)).

[21] *See* Chapters 6 and 9.

self-governance), and that prohibitions on abortion violate a woman's right to equal protection under the law.[22] If self-governance matters to the majority, it does so only for some issues and for some people, and only in a context in which extreme gerrymandering will make it exceptionally difficult for the majority's will to prevail.[23]

In this ominous climate, can we (to paraphrase Benjamin Franklin and the quote that titles this chapter) keep our republic? Or is our Constitution, to quote Justice Robert H. Jackson, a "suicide pact"[24] that propels discord and contagion while precluding our capacity to be healthy, physically and politically? The answer to these questions is surely "no," though whether we can manage to maintain both our health and our democracy remains uncertain.

REAL LIBERTY

In 2022, many Americans were weary of public health restrictions and mandates. Increasingly, they saw COVID in individualistic terms, and many of them believed that measures to contain it violated their freedom. In the pandemic's third year, liberty at times seemed to encompass the right not only to wave your arms but to hit your neighbor's nose in doing so.[25] Yet as earlier chapters discuss, freedom has not traditionally been understood to be either that expansive or that thin. Neither our Constitution nor our laws used to be read to allow individuals to endanger the health of others. True, the Constitution guarantees certain "fundamental" rights; what they are and how zealously courts should protect them have long been and will continue to be contested, as the uproar over *Dobbs* demonstrates. But as Chapter 4 discusses, many of the rights that people have claimed against public health measures during the pandemic have never been deemed fundamental. There has never been a constitutional right not to wear a mask,

---

[22] *Dobbs*, 142 S. Ct. at 2246.
[23] Jonathan Weisman & Jazmine Ulloa, *Supreme Court Throws Abortion to an Unlevel State Playing Field*, N.Y. Times (June 25, 2022), www.nytimes.com/2022/06/25/us/politics/abortion-ruling-states.html.
[24] Terminello v. Chicago, 337 U.S. 1, 37 (1949) (Jackson, J., dissenting).
[25] *See* Chapter 2.

or to go to work while contagious. Liberty – at least legally protected liberty – has never meant the right to do anything you please regardless of the impact on others.

Nor has our legal tradition, at least until now, treated the rights we do have as nearly absolute. As Chapter 2 explains, for the Constitution's first 140 years, courts accepted that rights were inherently limited by reasonable (police power) regulations that sought to protect the public's health, safety, or morals. And in determining whether such regulations were reasonable, courts typically granted state authorities broad deference. They respected expertise. They did not insist that the Constitution requires judges to look skeptically at all public health measures.

Indeed, even after the Supreme Court during the New Deal rejected the earlier police power jurisprudence and introduced strict scrutiny for laws that touched on fundamental rights,[26] it continued to affirm a wide array of public health laws, including vaccine mandates, environmental laws, and hospital regulations. Recall, for example, that the Court did not offer First Amendment protections to advertising until the late 1970s, and it applied rational basis review to most laws mandating health warnings until 2018.[27] Remember, too, that Justice Antonin Scalia's 1990 decision in *Employment Division v. Smith*[28] held that strict scrutiny was not applicable in religious liberty cases challenging generally applicable laws that did not target religion. Until the COVID-19 pandemic, even as they recognized a constitutional right to privacy, courts consistently held that vaccine and other health laws that did not include religious exemptions did not violate the First Amendment.[29]

More generally, until Justice Amy Coney Barrett joined the Court, courts usually granted health authorities broad deference and upheld most public health measures. That does not mean that all challenges to health laws failed, nor should they have. The courts have always had a vital role to play in stopping abusive, irrational, and discriminatory public health laws. But until recently, courts were not inherently suspicious of public health measures. Nor did they consistently prioritize some types of individual liberty over the public's health. Instead, as

[26] *See* Chapter 3.
[27] Nat'l Inst. of Fam. & Life Advocs. v. Becerra, 138 S. Ct. 2361 (2018).
[28] Emp. Div. v. Smith, 494 U.S. 872 (1990).
[29] *See* Chapters 4 and 5.

Roberts modeled in 2020 in *South Bay United Pentecostal Church v. Newsom*, they granted some deference, even if it was limited.[30] That long tradition – the US constitutional tradition – suggests that the Constitution does not compel the turn that the Supreme Court took on Thanksgiving Eve 2020 with *Roman Catholic Diocese of Brooklyn v. Cuomo*.[31] The adoption of the Court's new approach was a choice enabled by the death of one justice and the confirmation of another. It was not demanded by the Constitution.

Nor does the Constitution compel the thin and one-sided conception of liberty that has generally prevailed since November 2020. As *Jacobson v. Massachusetts* (1905) illustrates, courts once understood that "real liberty," to use Justice John Marshall Harlan's term, could not be achieved simply by allowing everyone to do their own thing.[32] Rather, it exists within a social compact in which people are afforded an environment, enabled by laws that restrain other liberties, that allows them to be healthy and to pursue their own goals and dreams. Given the ubiquity of contagion, liberty in that richer sense cannot be realized without laws that help us to be healthy.

That liberty can be enhanced by laws that enable a healthier society is easiest to see when we think about the price that older Americans and those who are immunocompromised have paid during the pandemic. They could not be "free" to live their lives without disease or fear unless others also took steps to slow the contagion. When most communities ceased taking such steps, those at highest risk were left with only the freedom to face a potentially fatal illness or to remain isolated.

"Real liberty," however, requires more than laws containing contagion. Vulnerability to disease and the deprivation of freedom that it creates derives not only from biology but also from a wide range of legal, social, political, and commercial factors that shape "risk factors" and create inequities. For example, people who are poor and live in overcrowded housing or who have untreated chronic illnesses due to a lack of health insurance have faced higher risks throughout the pandemic. So, too, individuals who consumed the toxic stream of

---

[30] S. Bay United Pentecostal Church v. Newsom, 140 S. Ct. 1613 (2020)(Roberts C. J., concurring).

[31] Roman Cath. Diocese of Brooklyn v. Cuomo, 141 S. Ct. 63 (2020) (per curiam).

[32] Jacobson v. Massachusetts, 197 U.S. 11, 26 (1905).

misinformation were at greater risk of rejecting vaccines and dying from COVID-19. Although the terminology that the field of public health uses today to describe such social determinants differs from that employed in the past, the recognition that health – and hence the liberty it permits – requires collective action to address these social determinants has a long pedigree, as the sanitationist movement of the nineteenth century attests.[33]

For most of our history, the Constitution has been read to permit, though not require, such actions. And for a brief moment, in the middle of the twentieth century, as Chapter 6 discusses, the Supreme Court came close to suggesting that the Constitution actually compelled governments to provide individuals with at least some of the social goods that are essential to health. Although the Court ultimately rejected that conclusion, it did so in part because it worried about another aspect of liberty: self-governance.

As Chapter 9 notes, the original Constitution offered the opportunity for self-governance only to some people (namely, wealthy white men). But through civil war, amendments, political struggle, and, yes, judicial decisions, the liberty of self-governance was extended to a far broader swath of the population. That extension is now in jeopardy. But that jeopardy is not compelled by the language or history of the Constitution. It comes from Supreme Court decisions.

The danger to self-governance is most apparent in voting rights and campaign finance cases. But the risk extends beyond access to the ballot and equal representation to the electorate's capacity to have its government reflect its will and address its concerns. In 1938, in *United States v. Carolene Products*, the Court recognized the threat that judicial review poses to self-governance.[34] Indeed, even as it explained that heightened judicial review was appropriate for laws that infringe on fundamental rights and discriminate against discrete and insular minorities, the Court reaffirmed that most laws should receive a presumption of constitutionality.[35] That presumption is often portrayed as a departure from the judicial activism of the *Lochner* period.[36]

---

[33] *See* Chapter 2.
[34] United States v. Carolene Products Co., 304 U.S. 144, 152 (1938).
[35] *Id.* at 152–154.
[36] Lochner v. New York, 198 U.S. 45 (1905).

Yet as *Jacobson* again illustrates, even the *Lochner*-era court granted a presumption of constitutionality for laws that it saw as protecting the public's health.[37]

In contrast, today's Supreme Court seems to accord inconsistent weight to self-governance and none to public health. Although the Court, in *Dobbs* and cases such as *National Federation of Independent Business v. Department of Labor*,[38] sometimes articulates concern for political decision-making, its more common stance in recent years has been aggressively suspicious of most legislative and administrative decisions, especially when they seek to improve health, redress health inequities, or improve electoral access. Further, as Chapter 4 discusses, with the significant exception of state vaccine mandates, the Court has often seemed so eager to block state and federal health laws that it is willing to cast aside procedural norms and remake law from its shadow docket. That same eagerness extends to laws that aim to reduce corporate influence in elections or protect voting rights. That is one reason why *Dobbs* is so troubling. The Court was willing to leave the fate of reproductive health to the political branches, even while weakening those branches' capacity to protect health or reflect the majority's will.

In short, this is a Court that seems to feel neither the weight of history nor the counter-majoritarian dilemma. Nor is it a Court that is troubled by the asymmetries it has created. Instead, it is a Court that appears drunk from the taste of its own power, even as it is unconcerned about the lives that may be impacted or lost due to its decisions.

The Constitution does not demand this imbalance or the privileging of only some aspects of liberty (and only some people's liberty) over others. While judicial review is a necessary component of the rule of law and can in theory protect health by preventing the scapegoating of vulnerable populations in the name of public health,[39] the Court's eager and unforgiving stance vis-à-vis most state and federal health laws is hardly essential. Instead, as we have seen, for much of our history, courts granted significant deference and solicitude to public

[37] *Jacobson*, 197 U.S. at 31–38.
[38] Nat'l Fed'n of Indep. Bus. v. Dep't of Lab., 142 S. Ct. 661, 666 (2022).
[39] *See* Chapter 3.

health laws. They also sought to temper the magnitude of their power with "prudential virtues." They read their jurisdiction narrowly – sometimes too narrowly – to avoid entering the political fray. In addition, appellate courts usually deferred to the factual findings of lower courts (and administrative agencies). And the Supreme Court valued its own precedent and resisted issuing broad, precedent-smashing judgments, especially, but not only, from the shadow docket. All of this has changed. Today, precedent and prudential virtues lie tattered as the Supreme Court seems happy to undermine the public's health and participate in the culture wars.

Legal journalist Linda Greenhouse claims that the Supreme Court's 2020 term "broke the fourth wall."[40] By that she means that the abrupt changes in the Court's decision-making that followed Barrett's confirmation shattered the illusion of an apolitical Court. If any illusion was left after that term, Justice Samuel Alito's opinion in *Dobbs* eviscerated it.[41] That such a central component of constitutional law, one reaffirmed so many times, could be overruled so swiftly following one change in the Court's composition demonstrates beyond dispute that judges are not simply "umpires" who simply call "balls and strikes," as Roberts once put it.[42] They are political players, and powerful ones at that. So exposed, it shouldn't be surprising that the public's faith in the Court has fallen precipitously.[43]

Given the profound doctrinal shifts that started with Barrett's confirmation and *RCD*, it is tempting to say that the problems we face today are due to Senate Majority Leader Mitch McConnell's decisions to deny Merrick Garland's nomination a vote in 2016 and to rush through Barrett's nomination in 2020. McConnell's hardball tactics

[40] Linda Greenhouse, Justice on the Brink: The Death of Ruth Bader Ginsburg, the Rise of Amy Coney Barrett, and Twelve Months That Transformed the Supreme Court 232 (2021).

[41] Josh Gerstein & Alexander Ward, *Supreme Court Has Voted to Overturn Abortion Rights, Draft Opinion Shows*, Politico (May 3, 2022), www.politico.com/news/2022/05/02/supreme-court-abortion-draft-opinion-00029473.

[42] *Confirmation Hearing on the Nomination of John G. Roberts, Jr., to Be Chief Justice of the United States: Hearing before the S. Comm. on the Judiciary*, 109th Cong. 55–56 (2005) (statement of Judge John Roberts).

[43] *Public's Views of Supreme Court Turned More Negative before News of Breyer's Retirement*, Pew Rsch. Ctr. (2022), www.pewresearch.org/politics/2022/02/02/publics-views-of-supreme-court-turned-more-negative-before-news-of-breyers-retirement.

yielded Trump two additional Supreme Court nominations, allowing a president who did not win the popular vote in 2016 to push
the Court to the far right. Without those seats, the Court's decisions
regarding the pandemic – and more broadly, perhaps the course of the
pandemic itself – might have been very different.

Still, the roots of our constitutional contagion – the prioritization
of some conceptions of liberty over others in ways that endanger our
health – are far deeper. It has been almost fifty years since the Court
cabined the reach of the Fourteenth Amendment's equal protection
clause in *Washington v. Davis*,[44] and ruled that the First Amendment
protected campaign contributions[45] as well as advertising.[46] More
than thirty years have passed since the Court ruled that poor Joshua
DeShaney had no constitutional right to protection from his abusive
father.[47] One can argue about whether any one of these or many of
the other decisions discussed in the preceding chapters were correctly
decided. One point, however, is worth emphasizing: Taken together,
they crafted a constitutional law that vindicated a narrow and individualistic conception of liberty while offering less and less respect
for expertise, self-governance, or the public's health. They and the
decisions that followed lost sight of *salus populi*, while magnifying
our vulnerability to contagion and sowing our current discord. If the
Constitution has become a suicide pact, it is because of the decisions
that the courts have rendered, not the Constitution itself.

A HEALTHY REPUBLIC

How can we reclaim a constitutional law that allows us to be healthy
both physically and politically? Early in the Biden administration, there
was much talk of reforming the Supreme Court. Biden appointed a
commission comprised of many of the nation's most eminent legal
scholars to study the issue. In December 2021, the commission issued
a 288-page report that stressed the Court's importance to American

---

[44] Washington v. Davis, 426 U.S. 229 (1976).
[45] Buckley v. Valeo, 424 U.S. 1 (1976).
[46] Bigelow v. Virginia, 421 U.S. 809 (1975).
[47] DeShaney v. Winnebago Cnty. Dep't of Soc. Servs., 489 U.S. 189 (1989).

law and life and the dangers currently threatening its legitimacy.[48] As could be expected given the commission's membership, the report included a thoughtful analysis of the pros and cons of potential reforms to the Court's size, structure, and jurisdiction. Like a good law school exam, it considered both sides of each argument. Although it did not offer any recommendations regarding the Court's composition, structure, or jurisdiction, it did propose changes to the management of the shadow docket and public transmission of court arguments, as well as the adoption of an advisory code of ethics.

The lack of dramatic recommendations did not matter. By December 2021, it became clear that no proposal would reach the sixty-vote threshold required to overcome a filibuster in the Senate. This points to a deeper problem. As discussed in Chapter 9, the Court's decisions about voting rights and donors' rights have cleared the way for a deepening partisan chasm and ever-greater entrenchment. The Court's antimajoritarian rulings have worked alongside other forces to make it harder for Congress to enact the very reforms that might be helpful in taming Court decisions that further entrench power. We seem to be stuck in a vicious cycle.

With no political fix on the horizon, change, if it is to come, needs to arise from within the judiciary and the broader legal culture within which it is ensconced. More specifically, it requires that both courts and the legal establishment rediscover earlier, more complex conceptions of liberty than the one that has dominated our jurisprudence in recent years. In effect, the balance between the liberty to be left alone and the liberties of health and self-governance needs to be restored. That shift, in turn, depends on a deeper recognition of the legal, social, political, and commercial determinants of health. Judges and lawyers need to understand that in a pandemic – but not only a pandemic – the risks we face are never solely questions of individual choice.

To foster this recognition, the system that educates and informs lawyers and judges, including law schools, continuing education programs, amicus briefs, and yes, even legal scholarship, must educate the bench and bar about the social dimensions of risk. All lawyers and

---

[48] PRESIDENTIAL COMM'N ON THE SUP. CT. OF THE U.S., DRAFT FINAL REPORT (Dec. 2021), www.whitehouse.gov/wp-content/uploads/2021/12/SCOTUS-Report-Final.pdf.

judges must understand that everyone's health, including their own, depends far more than they may want to believe on the actions of others and that state of our laws influence those actions and the environments in which they occur. They must understand that no one is safe or truly free unless our social compact is whole and intact. And they must understand that for most of our history, judges – even the most conservative among them – have accepted that *salus populi* was *suprema lex*.

Equally, both lawyers and judges must promote a more humble judiciary. That does not mean that courts should neglect individual liberty. It does require them to recall that liberty has multiple dimensions; it also requires recognizing that to safeguard some of those dimensions, courts should hesitate before tossing aside precedents, rushing to judgment, and reading their jurisdiction as a wide-open invitation to rule broadly. So, too, judges should remember that they are not the experts on everything, and that the tradition of modest deference to health experts that the Supreme Court tossed aside on Thanksgiving Eve 2020 had for the most part served us well for more than two hundred years. We can restore that tradition without dramatic deviations to either doctrine or constitutional norms. Doing so will no doubt infuriate both left and right at times, but it will also restore some needed balance.

Likewise, lawyers on both the right and left sides of the political spectrum must cease turning to litigation – and especially the Supreme Court's emergency docket – to win battles they lose in the political arena. The judicialization of our politics, which both the right and left have engaged in with abandon, has become dangerous to our democracy and to our health.

While doom-scrolling, it is hard to imagine how any of this can actually happen. The fourth wall has been broken. The Court's current majority seems set on a mission of radical revision, even while the threat of political violence hovers over us as menacingly as the portent of a new COVID-19 variant. Still, as this manuscript goes to press in early summer 2022, hospitalizations and deaths remain below their peaks. Hope springs eternal that the worst of COVID is behind us, even as new variants and other threats to our health – from gun violence to the loss of reproductive health services to new emerging or reemerging infections – loom large.

Maybe, just maybe, the justices will respond to the toll on the Court's legitimacy as they did in the 1930s. Although legal scholars such as Mary Ziegler have questioned whether the most conservative justices care about their reputations and the Court's legitimacy with the public writ large, particularly given the laudation they can receive from the conservative legal movement,[49] some of the justices seem to sense the need for caution, at least on some issues. That forbearance has not been evident in cases relating to abortion rights or gun control, but just perhaps it may apply to future cases concerning this or future pandemics. The majority, after all, allowed Biden's vaccine mandate for health care workers to stand.[50] And for now, the Court seems uneager to disclaim *Jacobson* outright. Perhaps the justices will even reread Justice Harlan's opinion.

Let's hope they do so before the next variant or pandemic strikes.

---

[49] Mary Ziegler, *The Conservative Justices Don't Seem Too Worried about the Court's Legitimacy*, ATLANTIC (Feb. 16, 2022), www.theatlantic.com/ideas/archive/2022/02/conservative-justices-public-reputation/622081.

[50] Biden v. Missouri, 142 S. Ct. 647 (2022).

INDEX

Abbott, Greg, 76–77
Abbott, In re, 76–77
abortion, 76–77, 97, 126, 167–70, 177–79, 212–15, 220
Abrams v. United States, 164
Administrative Procedure Act, U.S. (1946), 157
affirmative action, 146
Affordable Care Act (ACA), 4, 12–13, 133–34. *See also* Obamacare
AIDS epidemic, 21–22
  Haitian refugees, treatment of, 153–57
  human rights and, 21–22
  immigration law during, 153
A.L.A. Schechter Poultry Corp. v. United States, 105–107
Alabama Association of Realtors v. Department of Health and Human Services, 108–109
Alito, Samuel (Justice), 24, 80, 102–103, 110–13, 212, 220
Allgeyer v. Louisiana, 40–41
American Beverage Association v. City and County of San Francisco, 177
American Plan, 53
American Rescue Plan Act (ARPA), 126–27, 147
Americans for Prosperity Foundation v. Bonta, 200
Arizona Free Enterprise Club's Freedom Club/ PAC v. Bennett, 199
asymmetry of rights, 121–22
  fundamental rights in, protection of, 132–39
  negative rights and, 129–32
  positive rights and, rejection of, 122–29
  social safety net and, 119

Austin v. Michigan Chamber of Commerce, 197
authoritarianism, 7, 185, 191–92
authority. *See* federal authority
autonomy. *See* individual autonomy
Azar, Alex, 16

Balkin, Jack, 185
Barbier v. Connolly, 54
Barr, Bill, 79
Barrett, Amy Coney (Justice), 5, 25–26, 83, 102, 110–13, 150, 216–17
Baude, William, 9
Bayley's Campground v. Mills, 78
BCRA. *See* Bipartisan Campaign Reform Act
Bell, Derrick, 142–43
Berlin, Isaiah, 27
Beshear, Andy, 23
Biden, Joe, 19–20, 103. *See also* 2020 presidential election
  COVID-19 policies and, 29, 103
  public charge rule under, 158–59
  vaccine mandates and, 103
Biden v. Missouri, 110–11
the big lie, 19–20, 165, 183, 207
Bigelow v. Virginia, 169–70
Binford v. Sununu, 75–76
Bipartisan Campaign Reform Act (BCRA) (McCain-Feingold Act), U.S. (2002), 197–200
Black Lives Matter movement, 15–16, 140–41
Blackmun, Harry (Justice), 127–28, 169–70
Blackstone, Sir William, 30–31
Blue v. Beach, 45

Bolsonaro, Jair, 161
Bradley, Joseph (Justice), 39
Bradley, Rebecca Grassl, 106–107
Brandeis, Louis (Justice), 167
Brennan, William (Justice), 128
Breyer, Stephen (Justice), 85–86, 172,
    199, 202
Brnovich v. Democratic National Committee,
    204
Brown, Rebecca L., 202
Brown v. Board of Education, 142–43
Brown v. Entertainment Merchants
    Association, 169
Buck, Carrie, 54–55
Buck v. Bell, 54–55
Buckley v. Valeo, 195–96
Burger, Warren (Chief Justice), 143
Burris, Scott, 118
Bush, George W., 193–94
Bush v. Gore, 193–94

Calvary Chapel Dayton Valley v. Sisolak, 24
campaign finance laws
    Bipartisan Campaign Reform Act,
        197–98, 202
    donors' rights under, 6, 195–202
    Federal Election Campaign Act, 195–96
Carlson, Tucker, 14
Case, Anne, 119
Castle Rock v. Gonzales, 129
CDC. *See* Centers for Disease Control and
    Prevention
CDOH. *See* commercial determinants of
    health
Centers for Disease Control and Prevention
    (CDC), 1. *See also* COVID-19
    pandemic
    eviction moratorium, 107–108
    mask mandate, 109
    scope of authority for, 107–110
Centers for Medicare and Medicaid
    Services (CMS)
    Medicaid, 12–13, 103, 126, 133–34,
        136–38, 157–59, 189
    Medicare, 13, 103, 136, 139, 155
    vaccine mandate, 103, 110–11
Central Hudson Gas and Electric Corp.
    v. Public Service Commission of
    New York, 170–71
Chadwick, Edwin, 52
Chae Chang Ping v. United States, 153

Chauvin, Derek, 15, 140, 148
Chelsea, Massachusetts, 151
Chevron doctrine, 105–106, 110
China, People's Republic of, 11, 16, 166,
    185–86
    response to COVID-19, 166
    travel ban from, 16, 68–69, 153
Chinese Exclusion Act, U.S., 153
Christakis, Nicholas A., 71
Church of Lukumi Babalu Aye v. Hialeah, 80
Cicero, 33
Citizens United v. Federal Election
    Commission, 198–202
Civil Rights Act, 99, 143
Clark, Stephen, 77
CMS. *See* Centers for Medicare and
    Medicaid Services
Collins, Francis, 98
commercial determinants of health
    (CDOH), 187, 195, 222
commercial speech, 63, 64
    consumer protections and, 174–77
    under First Amendment, 168–73
    impact on infodemic, 168–73
common law traditions, *salus populi*
    suprema lex in, 33
Commonwealth v. Alger, 35
Communications Decency Act, U.S., 181
Compagnie Francaise de Navigation a Vapeur
    v. Louisiana State Board of Health,
    41–42
compelled speech, First Amendment and,
    174
Constitution, U.S. *See also* equal protection
    clause; First Amendment; free
    exercise clause
    Article I, 12–13, 104
    Article II, 193–94
    Article V, 190
    commerce clause, 65, 109–10, 134–36,
        138–39
    due process clause, 61, 129
    Eighth Amendment, 124
    Fifteenth Amendment, 202–203
    Fourteenth Amendment
        due process clause, 61, 129
        positive rights and, 123–39
        privileges and immunities clause,
            37–39
        salus populi suprema lex and, limitations
            under, 37–39, 41–42

Index

salus populi suprema lex and, limitations of, 37–42
Second Amendment, 66, 212–14
consumer protections, commercial speech and, 174–77
contagion, 215–218. *See also* COVID-19 pandemic
control of, 52, 72
fear of, 21, 43
power to tax and spend and, 12–13, 104
response to, 29–32, 44, 214
spending clause and, 111
vaccines and, 72, 96–97
Cooley, Thomas, 42
Cooper, Hannah L. F., 68
Corbin, Caroline Mala, 178
corporate determinants of health. *See* commercial determinants of health
counter-majoritarian dilemma, 62, 219
COVID-19 pandemic, 1–6. *See also* mask mandates; social distancing laws; vaccine mandates; *specific topics*
American individualism during, 3
Biden administration and, 26, 94–95, 120, 153–54, 159
Centers for Disease Control and Prevention and, 1, 12, 17, 29, 72, 94, 107–110
delta variant, 29, 51, 93
early days of, 1
Great Barrington Declaration, 14
international responses compared to U.S. response, 120
medical misinformation about, 2, 11–12
as infodemic, 12
mortality rates during, by race and ethnicity, 140–42
mortality rates for, 211–12
Omicron variant, 29, 93, 114, 186
partisan polarization during, 11–20
personal protective equipment during, 12
political polarization and, 18–20, 163
2020 presidential election affected by, 19–20
public response to, in U.S., 3–4
racial polarization during, 14–16
Black Lives Matter movement and, 15, 140–41
structural racism and, 15
religious liberty issues during, 79–86

role of courts in, 4–5, 20–24, 75–92, 100–103, 106–15, 192–95
Trump and
downplaying of pandemic, 16–18, 161–62
political use of, 2–3
state control of pandemic under, 10–11
vaccines, availability during, 91–97
World Health Organization and, 12
Crawford v. Marion County Election Board, 203
Cruz, Ted, 200
Cuomo, Andrew, 9, 17, 86. *See also Roman Catholic Diocese of Brooklyn v. Cuomo*
during COVID-19 pandemic, public response to, 11

Dahl v. Board of Trustees of Western Michigan University, 101
Dandridge v. Williams, 125
Dawes, Daniel E., 69
Deaton, Angus, 119
Defense Production Act, 91–92
DeJoy, Louis, 192
democracy. *See also* self-governance; voting rights
decline and erosion of, 184, 185, 192
constitutional roots of, 189–92
public health and, 185–89, 208–210
voting restrictions and, 183–85
Democracy and Distrust (Ely), 62
Democratic National Committee v. Wisconsin State Legislature, 193–94
Dent v. West Virginia, 41
Department of Homeland Security (DHS), 156–58
DeSantis, Ron, 18–19, 50–51
DeShaney, Joshua, 127–29, 221
DeShaney v. Winnebago County Department of Social Services, 127–29
determinants of health. *See* commercial determinants of health; political determinants of health; social determinants of health
DHS. *See* Department of Homeland Security
District of Columbia v. Heller, 66
Dobbs v. Jackson Women's Health Organization, 212–15, 219
donors' rights, under campaign finance laws, 6, 195–202

Dred Scott v. Sandford, 37
due process clause, U.S. Constitution, 61,
    129
Duncan, Stuart Kyle, 76
Dunning–Kruger effect, 164–65

Electoral College, 20, 190, 192
electoral reform, through voting
    restrictions, 183–85
Elim Romanian Pentecostal Church v.
    Pritzker, 81
Ely, John Hart, 62
Employment Division v. Smith, 79–80, 99,
    216
Environmental Protection Agency (EPA),
    12–13
Epstein, Richard, 22
equal protection clause
    race discrimination and, 143–44
    race-conscious laws and, 145–46
    racial preferences and, 146, 160
    sex discrimination and, 63
    suspect classes and, 62–63, 144
equity. *See also* equal protection clause;
    ethnic disparities; health disparities;
    racial disparities
    in vaccine access, 93–94
Estelle v. Gamble, 124
ethnic disparities, 141–42
exemptions, from vaccine mandates. *See*
    medical exemptions; religious
    exemptions
expertise, in scientific areas, erosion of trust
    in, 97, 177–78

Fauci, Anthony, 12
FDA. *See* Food and Drug Administration
federal authority, scope of, 103–113,
    133–39
    for Centers for Disease Control and
        Prevention, 107–110
    Chevron doctrine, 105–106, 110
    intelligible principle and, 105
    major questions doctrine, 106, 109–12
    New Deal legislation and, 105–106
    non-delegation doctrine and, 109–10
    Occupational Safety and Health
        Administration and, 103–104,
        110–13
    during pandemics, 113–15
Federal Election Campaign Act, 195–96

federalism, 107–108
    Affordable Care Act and, 134
    National Federation of Independent
        Business v. Sebelius, 134–38
    negative liberty and, 134–36
    police power and, 12–13, 34–35, 64–65,
        104
    Voters Rights Act and, 203–204
Field, Stephen (Justice), 39
Fifteenth Amendment, 202
First Amendment, U.S. Constitution
    commercial speech under, 168–73
    compelled speech under, 174–77
    establishment clause, 98–99
    free exercise clause, 45–46
    religious liberty under, 9–10, 27, 60,
        83, 79–90
    for health-related speech, 177–82
    for abortion-related speech, 178–79
    public health arguments and, 22
    social distancing laws and, 71–75
    speech clause, 66
First National Bank of Boston v. Bellotti,
    197
Fischer, Greg, 23
Floyd, George, 1–41, 148. *See also* Black
    Lives Matter movement
Food and Drug Administration (FDA),
    13, 173, 175–76
Food and Drug Administration v. Brown and
    Williamson Tobacco Corp., 105–106
Fourteenth Amendment. *See also* equal
    protection clause
    due process clause, 61, 129
    police power and, 37–49
    positive rights and, 129
    privilege and immunities clause, 38–39
Fourteenth Amendment, U.S.
    Constitution
    due process clause, 61
    positive rights and, 129
    salus populi suprema lex and, limitations
        under, 37–39, 41–42
    vaccine mandates and, 98
free exercise clause, U.S. Constitution,
    45–46
    religious liberty under, 60, 79–90
    COVID-19 restrictions and, 88–89,
        98–103, 216
    strict scrutiny applied under, 84, 88, 90
    vaccine mandates and, 98–103

freedom of speech, 58. *See also* commercial
    speech; First Amendment
under First Amendment, 163–68
individual autonomy and, 167
marketplace of ideas, 164, 170, 175, 180,
    182
scope of, 163–68
self-governance and, 166–67
Freudenberg, Nicholas, 201
Fullilove, Mindy, 68
Fulton v. City of Philadelphia, 81, 88–90,
    100
fundamental rights. *See also* free exercise
    clause; freedom of speech;
    Second Amendment; individual
    fundamental rights
in antebellum courts, 36
in asymmetry of rights, 132–39

Garland, Merrick, 25, 220
Gateway City Church v. Newsom, 87
gender disparities, application of public
    health laws, 53
involuntary sterilization of women,
    54–55
Ghebreyesus, Tedros Adhanom, 161
Gibbons v. Ogden, 34
Ginsburg, Ruth Bader (Justice), 25, 83,
    172, 199
Global Health Security Index, 120
Goebbels, Joseph, 165
Goolsbee, Austan, 74
Gorsuch, Neil (Justice), 24, 82, 84–85,
    87, 102–103, 111–13, 157,
    176, 194
Gostin, Lawrence O., 72
Graham v. Richardson, 154
Great Barrington Declaration, 14
Greene, Marjorie Taylor, 50
Greenhouse, Linda, 220
Grier, Robert Cooper (Justice), 32
Gunther, Gerald, 64

Harlan, John Marshall (Justice), 40, 46–48,
    104–105
Harlan, John Marshall, II (Justice), 125
Harlow v. Fitzgerald, 149
Harper v. Virginia Board of Elections, 203
Harrington, John, 69
Haupt, Claudia E., 167–68
Hazen v. Strong, 122

health, right to, 67–70
during HIV/AIDS epidemic, 68–69
in U.S. Constitution, 7, 126–27
health disparities, 159–60
health of the people is the highest law. *See*
    salus populi suprema lex
Holmes, Oliver Wendell (Justice), 49,
    54–55, 131, 164
Homer-Dixon, Thomas, 184
Husted v. A. Philip Randolph Institute,
    204

Immigration and Nationality Act, U.S.
    (1952), 156
immigration law
AIDS/HIV and, 153
Chinese Exclusion Act, 153
health impacts of, 151–59
Immigration and Nationality Act, 156
Personal Responsibility and Work
    Opportunity Reconciliation Act,
    154–56
public charge rule and
    under Biden, 158–59
    under Trump, 152, 156–58
Public Health Service Act and, 153–54
under Trump
    Department of Homeland Security
        and, 156–58
    Muslim ban, 154
    public charge rule, 152, 156–58
immigration status, as social determinant of
    health, 152
individual autonomy, 55, 66, 135. *See also*
    negative liberty
free speech protections of, 167
individual fundamental rights, 27–28.
    See also First Amendment; free
    exercise clause; negative liberty;
    Second Amendment; speech clause
individualism, American, 3
infodemic, 12
the big lie, 19–20, 164–65, 183
commercial speech during, 168–73
Communications Decency Act, 181
Dunning-Kruger effect, 164–65
knowledge community and, 167–68
misinformation during, 161–63
sanctioning of, 177–82
intelligible principle, 105
intermediate scrutiny, 63

International Covenant on Economic,
    Social, and Cultural Rights, 123
involuntary sterilization, of women, 54–55
isolation, quarantines and, 30–31, 71–72

Jackson, Robert H. (Justice), 174
Jacobson, Henning, 45–46
Jacobson v. Massachusetts, vi, 21–22, 42–49,
    99–100, 217
Jane Does 1-6 v. Mills, 101–102
January 6th insurrection, 20, 183
Jenner, Edward, 42–49
Jew Ho v. Williamson, 68
Jim Crow, 33, 54, 130, 142
    support by courts for, 33, 51,
        142–43
Johnson, Ron, 161–62
judicial deference
    by Supreme Court, 20–24

Kagan, Elena (Justice), 22, 85–86
Katzenbach v. Morgan, 203
Kavanaugh, Brett (Justice), 23–24, 82–85,
    102, 193
Kemp, Brian, 18
Kennedy, Anthony (Justice), 164, 178, 198
Kissinger, John C., 75–76
Klarman, Michael, 207
knowledge community, 167–68
Korematsu v. United States, 62–63

libertarianism, critique of public health
    laws, 28
liberty. *See also* religious liberty
    negative, 27–28
        federalism and, 134–36
    positive, 49, 57, 60, 67, 132
        self-governance and, 58
    "real," 46–47, 49, 51, 67, 70, 122,
        215–21
Lindsey v. Normet, 125
Locke, John, 27
Lombardo, Paul, 55
Lorillard Tobacco Co. v. Reilly, 171, 173

Maher v. Roe, 126
major questions doctrine, 106, 109–112
Makhlouf, Medha D., 159
Manaugh, Geoff, 67
mandates. *See* mask mandates; vaccine
    mandates

Mann, Jonathan, 21–22
marketplace of ideas, 164, 170, 175, 180,
    182. *See also* First Amendment;
    freedom of speech
Marshall, John (Chief Justice), 33–34
Marshall, Thurgood (Justice), 127
Martin, Andrew W., 202
Marysville Baptist Church v. Beshear, 23
mask mandates, 71
    asymmetry of rights and, 116–17
    children with disabilities and, 116–17
    public debate over, 91
Masters, Ryan K., 141
Mathews v. Diaz, 154–56
McCain-Feingold Act. *See* Bipartisan
    Campaign Reform Act
McCann, Michael, 70
McConnell, Mitch, 25, 220–21
McConnell v. Federal Election Commission,
    197–98
McCutcheon v. Federal Election Commission,
    199–200
McGee, Heather, 189
Medicaid, 12–13, 103, 126, 133–34,
    136–38, 155–56, 189, 208–209
medical exemptions, from vaccine
    mandates, 97, 102–103
Medicare, 13, 103, 137–38
Memorial Hospital v. Maricopa County,
    123–25
Merrill v. Milligan, 206
Messonnier, Nancy, 1, 17
Mill, John Stuart, 27–28, 91
Miller, Samuel (Justice), 38–39
Millhiser, Ian, 150
Mills v. Alabama, 166
Milton, John, 164
misinformation. *See also* infodemic
    the big lie, 19–20, 164–65
    during COVID-19 pandemic, 2–3,
        11–12
        as infodemic, 12
    during infodemic, 161–63
    sanctioning of misinformation,
        177–82
Mizelle, Kathryn Kimball, 109
Model State Emergency Health Powers Act
    (MSEHPA), 72
Mugler v. Kansas, 40
Munn v. Illinois, 40
Murthy, Vivek, 163

*National Federation of Independent Business
  v. Department of Labor*, 219
*National Federation of Independent Business
  v. Sebelius*, 134, 134–38
*National Institute of Family and Life
  Advocates v. Becerra*, 179–81
negative liberty, 27–28
  federalism and, 134–36
negative rights, 55, 58–66. *See also* free
    exercise clause
  asymmetry of rights and, 129–32
  freedom of speech, 58
  health and, 67–70
    during early HIV/AIDS responses, 68–69
  in U.S. Constitution, 7
  judicial protections of, 122–23
  political determinants of health and, 69
  religious liberty and, 60, 79–90, 98–103
  restrictions on, 68
New Deal. *See also* Roosevelt, Franklin D.
  police power jurisprudence and, 56
  scope of federal authority and, 105–106
New Deal Court
  New Deal settlement and, 60
  police power jurisprudence and, 56–58
  positive liberty and, embrace of, 57
  self-governance and, 58
  United States v. Carolene Products, 61–63
*New York State Rifle and Pistol Association
  v. Bruen*, 212–14
Newsom, Gavin, 81–82, 87
Nichol, Gene, 200
Nixon, Richard, 143
non-delegation doctrine, 105, 109–110
Novak, William, 32
novel coronavirus. *See* COVID-19 pandemic
Nuzzo, Jennifer, 154

Obama, Barack, 25
Obamacare, 12–13. *See also* Affordable
    Care Act
Occupational Safety and Health
    Administration (OSHA), 103–104,
    110–13
O'Connor, Sandra Day, 171–72, 178
Oliveira Santos, Pedro Felipe de, 132
Operation Warp Speed, 91–92
originalism, 6, 59
OSHA. *See* Occupational Safety and
    Health Administration
Outterson, Kevin, 137, 172

Palm, Andrea, 106
"the pandemic." *See* COVID-19
    pandemic
pandemics. *See also* COVID-19 pandemic
  scope of federal authority during, 113–15
*Parents Involved in Community Schools v.
  Seattle School District No. 1*, 146
Parker, Leroy, 42
partisan polarization
  during COVID-19 pandemic, 11–20
  through gerrymandering of voting
      districts, 208
patients' rights revolution, 66
Patrick, Dan, 14
Peckham, Rufus W. (Justice), 48–49
Pence, Mike, 1–2
personal belief exemptions, from vaccine
    mandates, 97
personal protective equipment (PPE), 12
Personal Responsibility and Work
    Opportunity Reconciliation Act
    (PRWORA), 155
Planned Parenthood v. Casey, 178
Plessy v. Ferguson, 54, 142–43
polarization. *See* partisan polarization;
    political polarization; racial
    polarization
police power
  jurisprudence and, rejection of, 55–58
    during Great Depression, 56
    New Deal Court and, 56–58
  misuse of, 51–55
    structural racism and, 51
  salus populi and, 51–58
political determinants of health, 69, 186
political polarization, 10–20. *See also*
    partisan polarization
  during COVID-19 pandemic, 18–20,
      163
  2020 presidential election affected by,
      19–20
positive liberty, 49, 57, 60, 67, 132
  self-governance and, 58
positive rights, 70
  Four Freedoms and, 122
  Fourteenth Amendment and, 123–30
  rejection of, in asymmetry of rights,
      125–31
Posner, Richard, 127
Powell, Lewis F. (Justice), 125–26, 143
PPE. *See* personal protective equipment

PREP Act. *See* Public Readiness and
  Emergency Preparedness Act
Presidential Commission on the Supreme
  Court of the U.S., 221–22
Privy Council, 30–31
Project Bioshield Act, U.S. (2003), 91–92
PRWORA. *See* Personal Responsibility and
  Work Opportunity Reconciliation Act
public charge rule
  under Biden, 158–59
  under Trump, 152, 156–58
public health
  democracy and, 185–89, 208–10
  public trust in, 198
public health laws. *See also* commercial
    determinants of health; police
    power; political determinants of
    health; quarantines; *salus populi;*
    social determinants of health; social
    distancing laws
  discriminatory applications of, 52–55
  American Plan, 53
  gender disparities in, 53
  involuntary sterilization of women,
    54–55
  treatment of Asian-Americans,
    44, 68
  *Tuskegee Study of Untreated Syphilis in
    the Negro Male,* 53, 142
  Model State Emergency Health Powers
    Act, 72
  salus populi suprema lex and, 30–33
  goals and meaning of, 31–33
  historical development of, 30–33
  Privy Council and, 30–31
  quarantines and, 30
  Supreme Court decisions on, 20–24
Public Health Service Act, 107, 109,
  153–54
Public Readiness and Emergency
  Preparedness (PREP) Act, 91
public trust
  in public health, 95, 198
  in science, 97

qualified immunity
  historical application of, 149–50
  police violence and, 148–50
  reformed judicial approach to, 150
quarantines
  CDC quarantine regulations, 72

historical etymology of, 30
  isolation and, 30–31
  limits of, 67–68
  police power and, 34, 42
  social distancing laws compared to, 71–72
  use during COVID-19, 11, 67–68, 73, 78
quarantinists, 31–32

racial discrimination
  in public health laws, 52–55
  as social determinant of health, 52, 118
  *Tuskegee Study of Untreated Syphilis in the
    Negro Male,* 53, 142
racial disparities. *See also* ethnic disparities
  efforts to redress, 146–48
  in mortality rates, during COVID-19
    pandemic, 140–42
  in public health laws, 52–55
racial polarization, during COVID-19
    pandemic, 14–16
  Black Lives Matter movement and,
    15–16, 140–41
  structural racism and, 15
racism, structural. *See also* immigration law
  during COVID-19 pandemic, 15
  through misuse of police power, 51
  as social determinant of health, 52, 118
rational basis test, 63
RCD. *See Roman Catholic Diocese of
    Brooklyn v. Cuomo*
"real" liberty, 49, 51, 67, 70, 122, 215–21
Reconstruction, 130, 142–43, 149, 202–203
Rehnquist, William (Chief Justice),
    127–28, 143, 172
religious exemptions, from vaccine
    mandates, 45–46, 98–103
Religious Freedom Restoration Act
    (RFRA), U.S., 99
religious liberty, 60, 79–90
  strict scrutiny applied to, 84, 88, 90
  vaccine mandates and, 98–103
RFRA. *See* Religious Freedom Restoration
    Act
rights. *See also* asymmetry of rights;
    fundamental rights; negative
    rights; positive rights; voting rights;
    individual fundamental rights
  to health, 67–70
    during early HIV/AIDS responses,
    68–69
  in U.S. Constitution, 7, 126–27

International Covenant on Economic, Social, and Cultural Rights, 123
Universal Declaration of Human Rights, 123
Rives-Villegas v. Cortesluna, 150
R.J. Reynolds Tobacco Company v. Food and Drug Administration, 175–77
Roberts, John (Chief Justice), 23–24, 82, 137–38, 146–47, 193, 199–200, 213, 216–17, 220
on constitutional law, 220
Roberts, Owen (Justice), 56
Rodgers, Aaron, 173
Roe v. Wade, 169–70, 177–78
Rogan, Joe, 173
Roman Catholic Diocese of Brooklyn v. Cuomo (RCD), 9–10, 27, 83, 132, 216–17
Roosevelt, Franklin D., 56, 122
New Deal Court and
court-packing plan and, 56
Four Freedoms and, 122
New Deal settlement in, 60
police power jurisprudence and, 56–58
self-governance and, 58
Ross, Michael A., 39
Rubin, Edward, 129
Ruger, Jennifer, 69
Rutledge, In re, 77

salus populi, 4–6, 33–36, 46, 48, 64–65, 75, 210, 221
as common good, 7
police power and, 51–58
social distancing laws and, 75
salus populi suprema lex (health of the people is the highest law), 4–5, 222–23
in common law traditions, 33
constitutional limitations of, 37–42
under Fourteenth Amendment, 37–39, 41–42
libertarian critique of, 28
public health laws and, 30–33
goals and purposes of, 31–33
quarantines and, 30
quarantinists and, 31–32
sanitarians and, 31–32
vaccine mandates and, legal challenges to, 43
Sample, James, 207

San Antonio Independent School District v. Rodriguez, 125–26
Sandhu, Jasmine, 159
sanitarians, 31–32
Scalia, Antonin (Justice), 25, 80, 129, 135, 216
scope of authority. *See* federal authority; major questions doctrine; non-delegation doctrine
scrutiny. *See* intermediate scrutiny; rational basis test; strict scrutiny; tiers of scrutiny
SDOH. *See* social determinants of health
Second Amendment, U.S. Constitution, 66, 212–14
Sekalala, Sharifah, 69
self-governance, 58, 61, 65, 70, 114, 131, 189, 213–21
freedom of speech and, 58, 166
positive liberty and, 58
shadow docket, of Supreme Court, 23–24, 82, 84–90, 102, 108, 110, 150, 157, 193, 206, 219–22
Shapiro v. Thompson, 123
Shattuck, Lemuel, 52
Shaw, Lemuel (Justice), 35–36
Shaw v. Reno, 205–206
Shelby Country v. Holder, 203–204
Sherbert v. Verner, 99
Sic utere tuo, ut alienum non laedas, 35, 36
Slaughter-House cases, 38–39, 40–41, 54
slavery
Constitution and, 189
courts and, 33, 51, 142
social determinants of health (SDOH), 52
immigration status and, 152
structural racism as, 118
social distancing laws, 71, 73–75
historical use of, 71–72
under Model State Emergency Health Powers Act, 72
salus populi and, 75
social safety net, 119
social vulnerabilities, 120–21
Sotomayor, Sonia (Justice), 85–86, 157, 199
Souter, David (Justice), 178
South Bay United Pentecostal Church v. Newsom, 23–24, 81, 87, 193, 216–17
South Bay United Pentecostal Church v. Newsom, (South Bay II), 87

speech clause, 66. *See also* First Amendment
Stephanopoulos, Nicholas, 210
Stevens, John Paul (Justice), 172, 199
Stewart, Potter (Justice), 125
Stewart, William H., 59
Stinson, Philip Matthew, 148–49
Stone, Harlan F. (Justice), 61–62
Stormans, Inc v. Wiesman, 80
strict scrutiny, 63–64, 84, 88, 90
structural racism
    COVID-19 pandemic, and, 19–20,
        93–94
    through misuse of police power, 51
    as social determinant of health, 118,
        141–42
Supplemental Nutrition Assistance
        Program (SNAP), 155
Supreme Court, U.S. *See also* individual
        fundamental rights; *specific cases and
        decisions; specific topics*
    COVID-19 pandemic and, 4–5, 20–24
    early cases during, 75–79
    judicial appointments to, under Trump,
        25–26
    mission of, 142–48
    future reforms for, 221–24
    New Deal Court
        New Deal settlement and, 60
        police power jurisprudence and, 56–58
        positive liberty and, embrace of, 57, 58
        self-governance and, 58
    public health protection decisions, 20–24
    First Amendment claims and, 22
    shadow docket and, 9, 24, 63–64, 88,
        125–26, 154, 157, 193, 206, 222
suspect classes
    equal protection and, 63
suspension principle, 75–76

Tandon v. Newsom, 87–89, 100–101, 132
Taylor v. Plymouth, 36
Texas v. Pennsylvania, 194
Thomas, Clarence (Justice), 23–24, 26, 80,
        102–103, 110–13, 157, 179
    Second Amendment cases, 212–15
Thompson v. Western States Medical Center,
        171–73
tiers of scrutiny
    intermediate scrutiny, 63
    rational basis test, 63
    strict scrutiny, 63–64, 84, 88, 90

Trump, Donald. *See also* 2020 presidential
        election
    the big lie and, 19–20, 164–65, 183
    during COVID-19 pandemic
        downplaying of pandemic, 16–18,
            161–62
        political use of, 2–3
        state control of pandemic response,
            10–11
    immigration law under
        Department of Homeland Security
            and, 156–58
        Muslim ban, 154
        public charge rule, 152, 156–58
    Supreme Court appointments under,
        25–26
*Tuskegee Study of Untreated Syphilis in the
        Negro Male*, 53, 142
2020 presidential election
    the big lie, 19–20, 164–65, 183
    COVID-19 pandemic as influence on,
        19–20, 192–95
Twilley, Nicola, 67

Union Pacific Railway Co. v. Botsford, 44
United States (U.S.). *See* Constitution;
        COVID-19 pandemic; Supreme
        Court
United States v. Carolene Products, 61–63,
        191, 218–19
    social distancing laws and, 73
Universal Declaration of Human Rights, 123
U.S. Navy Seals 1-26 v. Biden, 101
*Utility Air Regulatory Group v.
        Environmental Protection Agency*,
        105–106

vaccine mandates
    Biden and, 103
    CMS and, 103, 110–11
    end of, 50–51
    federal authority and, 103
    Fourteenth Amendment and, 43–48, 98
    under free exercise clause, 45–46
    goals and purposes of, 42, 96–97
    medical exemptions from, 97, 101–102
    Occupational Safety and Health
        Administration and, 103–104
    opposition to, 45–46, 97
    personal belief exemptions from, 97
    public debate over, 91–92

rationale for, 42, 96
religious exemptions from, 98–103
religious liberty and, 98–103
for school entry, 43–45, 50–51
vaccines. *See also* vaccine mandates
availability in low-income countries,
92–93
boosters, 94–95, 120
contagion and, as strategy against, 71–72
COVID-19 vaccines
development of, 59, 93
Operation Warp Speed and, 91–92
equity of access issues, 93–94
individual fundamental rights and, 29
misinformation and, 94–96
shortages in, 92–97
Vandine, In re, 35
*Virginia State Board of Pharmacy v. Virginia
Citizens Consumer Council,* 170
Vladeck, Stephen, 75–76
Voters Rights Act (VRA), U.S., 202–208
voting restrictions, 183–85
voting rights
case law for, 202–208
erosion of public trust in, 202–208
partisan gerrymandering and, 207–208
racial gerrymandering and, 205–206
VRA. *See* Voters Rights Act

Walensky, Rochelle, 29, 94–95
Walker, Justin, 23

Warren, Earl (Chief Justice), 143
Washington, George, 100–101
Washington v. Davis, 143–46
*West Virginia State Board of Education v.
Barnette,* 174
White, Byron (Justice), 174
White, Edward Douglass, Jr. (Justice),
41–42
White, Ryan, 69
White v. Pauly, 149
Whitney v. California, 167
WHO. *See* World Health Organization
Wiist, William, 200–201
Wiley, Lindsay F., 71
Williamson v. Lee Optical, 61, 63
Witt, John Fabian, 31–32, 36
women
gender disparities in public health laws,
53
involuntary sterilization of, 54–55
Wong Wai v. Williamson, 68
Woodward, Bob, 16, 162
World Health Organization (WHO), 12
Worthington, Robert H., 42

Yick Wo v. Hopkins, 54
Yong, Ed, 211–12

Zauderer v. Office of Disciplinary Counsel,
174–77, 179–80
Ziegler, Mary, 224

Printed in the United States
by Baker & Taylor Publisher Services